THE STORY OF THE GREAT WAR

This edition published 2025
by Living Book Press
Copyright © Living Book Press, 2025

ISBN: 978-1-76153-869-8 (hardcover)
          978-1-76153-874-2 (softcover)

First published in 1919.

This edition is based on the 1919 printing by The MacMillan Company.

A catalogue record for this book is available from the National Library of Australia

THE STORY OF THE GREAT WAR

by

Roland G. Usher

Westward Ho — 1620
Eastward Ho — 1917

CONTENTS

PREFACE

The justification for this book must be found in a remark once made to me by an Oxford professor. I had made a seminar report and had "demonstrated" that nothing adequate could possibly be known about the subject until elaborate research had been prosecuted. "Yes, yes," said the professor. "Very good, but what are we going to think in the meantime? Just tell us something brief and probable." That is exactly what I have tried to do in this book.

It would be idle to pretend that an adequate history of the war can be written so soon after the event or within such brief compass as this volume. But it is equally idle to suppose that we who have lived and fought the war can afford to wait before we think something about it until the historians can complete any portion of the monographs upon which any truly scientific notion of the war must rest. Surely, it is scant comfort to us to know that our grandchildren may understand the war. We need to know something about it now, for our opinion of its origin and course will be significant elements in every relevant decision we reach on statecraft and reconstruction. Nor am I at all prepared to admit that the generation who fought the war is entirely in error as to why and for what it was fought. Over the details of battles and diplomacy future students may wrangle to their hearts' content, but the spiritual truth about the reasons for the conflict, and the spiritual forces which won it, I feel sure we correctly apprehend now. One of the most essential facts to make clear, I feel, is this very spiritual purpose with which we fought the war. Any future impartiality — so called — or present (assumed) idealism which leaves out of the story such spiritual elements will falsify it, however numerous the details they correct.

It was tragic that the men and women who fought the war were too busy to study it. The greatest peril of the new era is that they will still be too busy with reconstruction to devote even casual attention to the great event itself, in the light of which alone can the decisions be made by which the new era is to be shaped. People are weary of working and weary of reading. Yet there was never a time when effort was more necessary nor when a little would have such significant results upon national and international events.

I hope that this volume may serve the purpose for some at least of those who have neither the time nor the inclination to read more detailed accounts, and who are not among those hypercritical gentry who will reject all present attempts as unscientific and necessarily unsuccessful. I have tried to make text, maps, and illustrations tell their lesson at a glance, to make that glance reveal something important and interpretative, to pack into these few pages the gist of the view about the war which has cost me much time and effort and which would be the core of any account I might write, however lengthy and technical. To say so much so briefly meant inevitably the possibility that some portion might not be clear and that other parts might be misunderstood. The narrative had to be reduced rigidly and much material often included in brief texts had to be left out in order that the interpretative material might find place. There was danger that the latter might fail to carry conviction without a greater area of facts about events and people. Such a decision meant in particular the complete subordination of the process by which I achieved my conclusions and the omission of the whole panoply of qualifications so dear to the professional historian. But I felt the gain more than commensurate.

I shall not be disturbed if reviewers and correspondents point out that Mr. This and General That differ from me. I am already aware that the witnesses are as numerous as the sands on the seashore and the divergencies in their accounts are like unto the leaves on the trees. A great deal of water must run under the bridge before these controversies can be authoritatively settled.

I have devoted almost as much research and thought to the selection and preparation of the illustrations and maps as to the text itself. They represent a comprehensive survey of French, Italian, and German as well as of British and American illustrated periodicals and official photographs. They will, I hope, repay study. They tell much that the reader will want to know, which I felt could be better told in this way than by direct description. So far as I know, this book is the first to contain any number of illustrations from German sources. I have particularly attempted to show how the various nations sought to rouse patriotism and stimulate endeavor by graphic methods. Many of the illustrations are therefore in themselves historical material, and show better than mere description can the spiritual attitude toward the war of the various combatants.

WASHINGTON UNIVERSITY, ST. LOUIS

June, 1919.

BOOK I

THE CAUSES OF THE WAR

THE OUTBREAK

Not in the limp and bleeding body of an Austrian Archduke, lay the cause of the great world war. That assassination, the work of an obscure rascal in a practically unknown city of southeastern Austria, was the formal excuse for the demands made by Austria upon Serbia which were the technical reasons for the war's outbreak. It was the work of men, the Austrians said, who meant to destroy Austria-Hungary; the work of men in Serbian and Russian pay; the result of a secret conspiracy against Austrian unity.

A scene connected with the assassination occurred in Berlin. There, in a splendid room, was a magnificent table, covered with damask, glittering with cut glass, spread with a profusion of flowers and expensive food. Around it sat officers of the German army, clad in their finest uniforms. At the head of the table, none other than the Crown Prince himself. He rose in his chair and said, "Gentlemen, I toast—To the Day." They leaped to their feet, and drained their glasses and cheered again and again. To what day? He meant to the day when war should be declared between Germany and England.

Another scene took place in Paris in the official residence of the President of the French Republic. The President himself stood, quite simply clad, and addressed the German Ambassador, also plainly-clad. There was here no pomp and ceremony. Few words passed, but they referred to the fate of nations. The President said very quietly: "You are arming. We know it." The Ambassador started to protest. The President raised his hand for silence. "We shall not be caught napping a second time," he said very quietly. He bowed to the Ambassador, signifying that the interview was at an end.

A man shot in southern Austria; a toast to a war between Germany and England; Germany arming against France; what connection was there between them?

One further scene took place in this chain of events, again in Berlin, again in a splendid room. The Kaiser stood, himself in full military dress, and received the greatest generals, admirals, and statesmen of Germany. He asked them solemnly if they could assure him that Russia was preparing her army for war. They told him it was true: Germany must arm immediately in self-defense. After some hesitation he signed with a gold pen the order for the mobilization of the German army. He knew and they knew that that order would produce a general European war. They all chose to precipitate it.

And where did the war begin? In Belgium, thirteen hundred miles from Serbia, a thousand miles from the Russian frontier! That tiny nation, connected neither with Austria, nor Russia, nor France, was responsible for none of their deeds. And yet in August, 1914, the first overt act of the war was its invasion by the German army—a mighty host of gray-green troops, the sun glancing from their bayonets. On they came—company after company, regiment after regiment, hundreds of thousands of them, a line apparently without end, hours passing a given point, days marching through any single city; always marching, marching to the shrill music of the fifes, the rattle of the drums, the tramp, tramp of iron-shod boots on the pavements. On they came,—Bavarians in dark blue, Saxons in light blue, Austrians in beautiful silver and gray, Prussians in gray-green.

Why should there be Germans in Belgium because an Austrian Archduke had been murdered, because Russia had mobilized her army? The reason given by the Austrians for the outbreak of the war was a fiction. It did not begin because the Archduke was killed nor because the Russians prepared their army for war. It was not begun by Germany and Austria in self-defense. Months before the murder of the Archduke the war had been decided upon. We know it from official documents and from the testimony of the men who knew. The decision was reached in April or May, 1914, if not earlier. The first preparations came in May and June. The murder of the Archduke on June 28 was employed as the best excuse they could find for beginning the war in the way most favorable for them. The Germans began an unprovoked war. Its causes lay deep in German and European history and life.

The Causes of the War

The true fundamental cause of the war was a belief in German national superiority. They were better; therefore they deserved more; being better, they ought easily to be able to get more, even if it were necessary to get it with the sword. They believed that they understood better than any other nation how to live, how to govern, how to manufacture, how to write music, paint pictures, clean streets, or grow potatoes. The word Kultur covered everything. The whole process of life was clearer to them than to others, they thought, and hence they were able to organize the community better, and to make more progress in industry, agriculture, the fine arts, in government itself. As the Kaiser declared, "The German people will be the granite block on which the good God will build and complete his work of culture in the world." Another important German said, "The German race—there can be no doubt of it—because of its nature and character, was designed by Providence to solve the great problem of directing the affairs of the whole world, of civilizing the savage and barbarous countries and of populating those which are still uninhabited."

Upon Germany, then, depended the fate of civilization itself! Without Germany civilization was lost. As Treitschke, one of their great historians, said, "The greatness and good of the world is to be found in the predominance there of German Kultur." Must not Germany then be a nation of people, powerful enough to defend this Kultur upon which the whole future of the world depended, strong enough to spread it to the nations that did not already have it? "Germany should civilize and Germanize the world, and the German language will become the world language."

The Germans must also develop their idea of civilization. "The German race is called by God to bring the earth under its control." To make their civilization permanent, they must make Germany powerful. "We intend to become a world power that will overtop other world powers so greatly that Germany will be the only real world power." Germany must be made the most powerful, the most wealthy, the largest, and the most important country in the world.

But it was very clear to the Germans long ago that Germany was not the most powerful country in the world, nor as rich as others, nor indeed as well situated as others to become either rich or powerful. She was not able to control the world; she was not strong enough to control even her own destinies. The thought galled them inexpressibly. They could not longer endure it. Germany must have her Place in the Sun; she must become a power on the sea; she must have colonies; she must have everything that any other nation had; she must have more than other nations had.

All this, certainly, other nations would not yield without force; so much the Germans knew. But if they must have it, if God meant them to have it, they should therefore get it as best they could and as soon as possible. They must conquer in war the nations who refused to recognize what Germany must have. The Crown Prince wrote, "It is only by relying on our good German sword that we can hope to conquer that Place in the Sun which rightly belongs to us and which no one will yield to us voluntarily."

And what now was Germany's position, about which they complained so bitterly? Europe is a small continent compared with America, Africa, or Asia, but in it live more large nations of people than in any of the other continents except Asia. Germany herself had some seventy millions, Austria nearly sixty, Great Britain forty-five, France forty, Russia one hundred and eighty millions. If we leave out Russia, we find these other big nations

AN ILLUSTRATION OF THE GERMAN WAR
HORSE IN "OUR HOLY WAR," 1914.
An excellent example of the pictorial attempt
to rouse the german people.

all crowded into an area nothing like as large as the United States
and with about three times as many people. The land in Europe,
therefore, was all occupied; there were already too many people to
live there prosperously and happily. But Germany was growing very
fast in numbers, and, if she was to promote Kultur as the Germans
planned, the population must increase at a still faster rate. She
must grow also in wealth; her people must make more to sell, so

that they might have more with which to buy. But Germany could not continue to grow larger without making her people poorer.

One of two things must happen. The surplus people might leave Germany and go elsewhere to live, just as many Germans had already come to the United States. They would then cease to live in Germany and would therefore cease to be a part of the true nation, however much they might still feel that they were Germans. This was not thinkable. The alternative was that all Germans must stay in the Fatherland, which must be made a place where all living Germans and all that would be born for an indefinite number of years could live in prosperity and happiness. This could be arranged only by an astounding development of manufacturing, of commerce, and of colonies.

But Germany did not have herself any supply of the most important raw materials. Clothes cannot be made without wool or cotton, and the Germans had no supply of either. Most kinds of machinery could not be made without copper and various metals of which the Germans had only a very small supply or none at all. Electricity plays a very important part in modern life and requires a great deal of rubber; the Germans had none. Gasoline for auto-mobiles; kerosene for lamps and stoves; and all sorts of petroleum products are imperative to prosperity and comfort. But Germany had no wells of oil. Without those and a good many other things, profitable manufacturing and prosperous living could not be continued.

And the Germans still lacked customers to whom they should sell the new goods they were to make. If they were to make more and more goods every succeeding year, they must sell more and more each year, and they could not sell any such increase in Germany. Customers they found in France, England, the United States, South America, Asia. But how could they be sure they would continue to buy? Raw materials they found at long distances from Germany. Cotton, copper, and oil came from the United States, rubber from

South America, wool from Australia. How could they be sure the supply would continue to arrive?

To reach both raw materials and customers, the Germans must cross the ocean. Ships must take their exports out and ships must bring imports back. Yet neither Germany nor Austria was placed on the ocean itself. The greater part of the German sea coast was on the Baltic Sea, which had a very narrow entrance controlled by Denmark. While there were many rivers in Germany, only one flowed into the North Sea, or what the Germans call the German Ocean, and Germany had only one good harbor, Hamburg. The river Rhine was a very great German river, but it was controlled by Holland. The German railroad system, which connected German trade with the rest of Europe, really centered in Belgium. All German trade, therefore, found itself a long way from its ultimate market.

Other nations were in a position to prevent the Germans from using the sea and thus could stop the stream of raw materials into Germany and of manufactured goods out. Those German ships which must go through the Baltic might meet opposition from Russia. All German ships must go through the English Channel, controlled by England on one side and by the French, Belgian, and Dutch coasts on the other side. The Germans had no coast on the Channel and no harbor there.

When the German ships got into the open ocean, they found it controlled by the British navy. Being the largest fleet, it controlled as well all water highways which German ships must take going to America, South America, and Asia. If they wished to go through the Mediterranean, they found it in the hands of the British and the French, and the Suez Canal, through which ships going to India and China passed into the Red Sea, was held by Great Britain. If they sailed around Africa, they found the Cape of Good Hope controlled by the British. If they went to the Gulf of Mexico, they found the Panama Canal owned by the United States. No water routes which the Germans must use to reach the necessary raw materials or their own customers were within German control.

But were the Germans unable to get raw materials in these countries or to sell to customers in England or in America, in India or in South America? Did any German ships ever fail to get through the English Channel or to reach a port across the Atlantic because of opposition from the British, the French, or the Americans? The Germans never claimed that any such case had occurred. German ships sailed where they pleased; Germans had customers in every country in the world, and they had never sold so many goods as in the ten years before the war. They were doing proportionately more business in fact than any other nation.

Where then was the trouble? What were they complaining about? They said that the nations who did control the sea and its approaches *might* close it and *might* refuse to let German ships go through. The British *might* close the Suez Canal, or the United States *might* refuse the Germans the use of the Panama Canal. The British *might* close the English Channel, and the Germans would not be able to go around the British Isles because there were so many rocks and storms that a ship was almost certain to be wrecked. Their customers in these nations might also refuse to buy German goods, not because they did not want the goods but because they wished to hurt Germany. The fact that Germany was great, that other nations were jealous of her civilization and did not wish to be taught by Germany how they ought to live, would cause them to injure Germany by refusing to sell to her raw materials or to buy of her manufactured goods or by closing the seas. The Germans must therefore create a situation which would make it impossible for any nation or any number of nations to prevent Germany from getting as many raw materials as she wanted or from selling as many goods as she could make. Germany must not depend upon the good will of other nations nor conduct a trade which others had it in their power to stop.

The difficulty was that in Europe Germany had enemies. There were many people, the Germans felt, who hated them. They were surrounded by enemies. There was France on the west, and Russia on the east. South of Austria-Hungary was Italy. Beyond the Channel were the British Isles. See, implored the Germans, we lie between two enemies. On one side is France, whom we defeated in the war of 1870 and from whom we took Alsace-Lorraine, for which the French have ever since longed to revenge themselves on us. Then on the other side is Russia, millions of people occupying a huge country, with vast resources. How can we cope with both France and Russia?

We have, they complained, no frontiers to defend us, no mountains to stand between us and the Russians and the French, no deep rivers which they cannot cross. Germany lacks a defensive frontier. The only protection we have is the German army, and if we should be attacked on both sides at once, we probably could not defend ourselves at all.

The Germans therefore took extended measures to deal with this peril which they believed menaced them in Europe. They made an alliance with Austria and Italy that was to provide them with help in case either France or Russia should attack them, for then Italy would attack France and Austria would attack Russia.[1] Of course they also agreed that if Russia attacked Austria or France attacked Italy, they would help in their turn. But they were more concerned about themselves than they were about others. They built a great fleet of merchant ships so that goods going to Germany might not wait on the shore somewhere for transportation because the British refused to carry them in their ships. They then

---

1   This was the Triple Alliance, Germany, Austria-Hungary, and Italy, first made in 1883 and ruptured by Italy at the outbreak of the war in August, 1914, pursuant of reservations made by the Italians at the outset. It was followed by the Dual Alliance of France and Russia in 1892; by the Anglo-French Entente of 1904; and by the Triple Entente of France, Great Britain, and Russia of 1907. An alliance is a written engagement; an entente is an informal understanding, the vital portions of which are commonly verbal; the terms of an alliance are precise, those of an entente vague; the alliance binds the nations under certain conditions, the entente is subject to further agreement before it is operative. Neither term, Triple Alliance or Triple Entente, was used during the war period, for the former at once became something less and the latter something more.

THE TRIPLE ENTENTE AND TRIPLE ALLIANCE IN 1914.

built a great navy literally to frighten the British and prevent them from closing the English Channel, the Mediterranean Sea, or the various ocean roads which the German ships followed.

They then concluded that a country to be great must have colonies. They had established long ago a few in Africa and some in the Pacific, but had failed to make money out of them, or to find them valuable customers. They must create a great colony which would provide not merely customers but also raw materials and which would not be open to attack from the sea. The British fleet was so large and so capable that the Germans were afraid they might never be able to defeat it. Hence they must locate their colony in some place which they could reach by land and which the British could not reach by sea.

They selected Mesopotamia. There had been some of the greatest empires of history; there some of the wealthiest of peoples had lived; there should rise a New Germany. They thought that they might raise cotton, grow wool, and perhaps cultivate rubber. Petroleum existed there and copper they would find in the mountains. There too was room for millions of Germans to settle and create a community which would produce for sale in Germany what Germans wished to buy and which would buy from Germany what the latter made and wished to sell.

And it was out of the reach of the British fleet. The Germans themselves would reach it by means of the Bagdad Railroad. This would run from Berlin to Vienna, down through the mountains to Constantinople, and then through Asia Minor to Bagdad. It would provide them with transportation. But they must not forget to protect it. Bagdad was a long distance from Berlin and the railroad passed through many countries which the Germans did not control. The British fleet, too, might land troops in Syria, a very short distance from the railroad and Bagdad and Berlin and the German army would be too far away to help. A new state must be created to protect the railroad and the new colony, a federated state created out of many states. Austria would be an all-important part; Turkey too must become an ally of Germany and a part of the new state, for the Turks owned the territory in which Mesopotamia was situated and most of the territory through which the railroad ran after leaving Germany and Austria. But there were two states between Austria and Turkey, Bulgaria, with whose king the Germans and Austrians easily made an alliance, and Serbia. But Serbia declined their offers. Pleading, urging, threatening failed. To control the section of the railroad that ran through Serbia, Austria must seize Serbia itself. They must have Serbia. They must control Belgrade and the crossing of the Danube. So Serbians feared and hated Austria; so men could believe in 1914 that a Serbian would kill the Austrian Archduke.

These alliances and conquests once complete, a great empire would have been created, strong enough to be independent of Europe and of the rest of the world, strong enough perhaps to dominate the rest of the world without having to conquer it. For the Germans truthfully said that they would prefer not to be compelled to conquer the world in order to Germanize it. This great empire would also be able, they thought, to destroy the British Empire. A land attack on the Suez Canal would deprive the British of their connection by sea with India and Australia, and compel them to go around Africa. Meanwhile, the Germans themselves would proceed by land along the Persian Gulf, reach India first, and conquer it. They even thought that they might afterwards conquer the whole of Asia. This is the true Pan-Germanism. It began with an attempt to keep German those who left Germany and went to live in other countries like the United States; hence the name, All-Germans, meaning that all Germans in all parts of the world should stay together and cooperate with one another. But the plan grew from that quite simple idea into this vast scheme of world conquest and dominion.

The Lesson of Prussian History

It is quite as significant to see why the Germans felt that they could change the balance of power in the world as it is to appreciate the extent and meaning of the scheme itself. They meant in effect to deprive other nations, without their consent, of territory, of influence in the world, of the practical right to decide the conditions of life in their own countries. No conqueror of antiquity had ever attempted to accomplish so much. Not even the great Napoleon in more modern times sketched out such an ambitious plan. But the Germans were convinced that it was feasible and the fact which convinced them was nothing less than the history of Prussia.

There is no more dramatic story in the world's annals. A tiny state, surrounded by powerful and hostile neighbors, somehow survived them all, absorbed several of them, and succeeded in dominating northern Europe. The rapid rise of Prussia convinced the Germans that they might accomplish anything. Consequently Germany challenged the world itself in 1914 and held out for more than four years before she was beaten. The first troops who went to Belgium wrote with chalk on the doors of the railroad carriages, "William II, Emperor of the World." There was the true German touch.

We have only to go back in imagination to a time when America was not yet discovered to see in northern Germany the tiny state of Brandenburg, so small and unimportant that it was conferred by the Holy Roman Emperor upon a certain prince of Hohenzollern.

This was in the thirteenth century and for four centuries the growth of this state was very gradual. Then, about the time when a good many English people came to New England and there began to be something resembling civilization here, the Great Elector (1640–1688) became the ruler of Brandenburg. A remarkable man with insight and executive ability, he analyzed the position of his state and its problems and defined Prussian policy for his successors. It was a small state, and because there was no more land, only a few people could live on it compared with the population of the neighboring hostile states. The soil was poor in quality, and as agriculture was then the main occupation of European countries the people themselves were poor. This small area of poor land was in the middle of a plain, no mountains surrounded it, no deep rivers protected it from invasion. Sweden and Poland on the north and east, Saxony and Austria on the south, France in the west were large, hostile, and aggressive.

To defend such a state, the Great Elector concluded every man must become a soldier and that the whole life of the country must be organized around the army. The entire physical force of the little state might conceivably defend it; its entire economic strength might sustain its army; nothing less could possibly suffice. The population was small and its resources relatively so inadequate that nothing but the most complete utilization of both could provide it with security.

The only real solution of the country's future was growth—not in wisdom but in size. For even at that relatively remote period the beginning of Prussian national conceit was apparent. There must be more land, so that there might be more people, and more people so that there might be more soldiers in the army. More land meant more food for more soldiers and so it must go on. More land, more men, more food, more soldiers. The better and stronger the army, the more land could be captured, and, as the physical strength of the state increased, its chances of growing still larger

GERMAN COLUMN PASSING THROUGH BELGIAN TOWN.

would be correspondingly better. It must fight for existence. It could only survive if it conquered its neighbors.

The land to be conquered was necessarily that occupied by friends and rivals of Brandenburg; waste land there was none. To all of the surrounding states the Elector was bound by treaties, agreements, promises, avowed or implicit. The country could grow only at the expense of others, only in defiance of the rights of others, and, it might be, only by breaking explicit treaties and promises. To accept such a principle as the binding character of treaties was to accept the limitations of Prussia's position and to renounce all plans for growth and security. This to Prussian kings has been unthinkable. The safety of the state was greater than the obligation of any written agreement. It was unfortunate but unavoidable.

The other principle which the Great Elector laid down as the result of the experience of his predecessors was the necessity of offensive campaigns by his army. He must never wait to be attacked. A successful defense in the absence of geographical frontiers could only be conducted on foreign territory. To allow the enemy to begin the war was to be defeated before the war began. Even, therefore, in a purely defensive war, his armies must take the offensive if possible.

The Great Elector had the ability and the opportunity to apply these principles. He organized his estates, built up a competent army, systematized taxation and administration, and increased more than considerably the area of his state. His successors continued to tread the path he had mapped out for them. In 1701, the title King of Prussia was assumed. They had been kings in Prussia for a century and more but only Electors in Germany and they wished now to have the title of King in Germany. Brandenburg is not Prussia, for Prussia proper is located far to the east along the Baltic, nor are the people of present Prussia the Prussians in a historical sense.

Then came to the throne in 1740 Frederick the Great, who

reigned until the year before the adoption of the Constitution of the United States. The Great Elector had left Prussia in three pieces—one around Berlin, Prussia itself, some distance to the east with Poland in between, and far off in the west along the Rhine, two or three tiny bits of territory. The object of his successors was simple in the extreme: to tie those pieces together by getting the land in between. Frederick the Great tied Prussia and Brandenburg together and added to the south the very large and rich district of Silesia. The Napoleonic wars worked havoc with Prussia but in the end at the Treaty of Vienna Prussia was strengthened and given territory on the south from Saxony and in the west from Holland and smaller German states.

After a period of slow and quiet growth and apparent humility, there came to power Bismarck, one of the ablest of all German statesmen. He undertook to unite all Germany around Prussia, and if necessary was ready to conquer Germany in order to compel it to act in concert with Prussia. Scarcely anything in history ever seemed to the people who lived through it more like a tale of the Arabian nights, like the rubbing of some lamp or the turning of some ring, than the growth in a moment of a great state and the creation of the German empire.

When Bismarck came to power, Prussia was reputed the weakest of the European powers, the least able, the least dangerous, the least well organized. Disraeli declared it ripe for partition. She had been humiliated by Austria repeatedly and it used to be said that it was idle to ask questions about Prussian policy in Berlin; one must go to Paris or Vienna for information. Apparently Prussia was hated and distrusted by the other German states; she lacked access to the Atlantic; her industrial development was rudimentary, and the poverty of the people great.

Within ten years, the situation had been revolutionized. Austria had been excluded from Germany by a rapid and successful campaign, and compelled to recognize the reorganization of Germany by Prussia in Prussian fashion. For a thousand years, Austria had been the most important German state. In 1850 it had seemed as if she might remain the most important for at least a century, and in 1866 she was excluded from Germany by force. At that same time the northern German states, who refused to come to terms with Prussia by agreement, were practically conquered and compelled to join the North German Confederation. Prussia took possession of Kiel, Hamburg, and the mouth of the Elbe, and laid the foundation of future naval power and commercial development. In 1870 war was accepted with what was supposed to be the most powerful and formidable nation in Europe, an overwhelming victory was won, and an enormous money indemnity was extorted. The offensive strategic position in Europe—Alsace-Lorraine—was taken from France and annexed to Germany, and the German Empire, uniting all German states under one extremely powerful and autocratic government, was created. In 1861 Prussia was hardly considered a great power. In 1871, the German Empire was clearly the arbiter of the destiny of Europe and likely to remain so, men thought, for half a century. There was the miracle which astounded the world, which thrilled the German people and gave them, for the first time in a century, supreme confidence in their strength and capacity. Then began the talk of German destiny to rule the world, of German supremacy, of superman, of the superiority of Kultur over all other ideas of civilization.

Then followed a miracle almost greater. The lamp was rubbed a second time, and lo! the German state, already powerful and feared, became wealthy. Ever since the Thirty Years' War, Germany as a whole had been poor, collectively and individually, and now came wealth. The railroads, the new machinery, now introduced into Germany systematically, compulsory education, all directed and developed by Bismarck, pushed Germany ahead in economic growth at a pace which was literally marvelous. The goods produced doubled and trebled in volume and value, and doubled again. The yield of farms doubled and doubled again. German ships weighed down the ocean. Presently, the German navy became formidable.

German commerce, once scarcely known outside of Europe itself, now reached to the very confines of the globe. Had not the despised stone become the head of the corner? Had not the downtrodden become the favored of God? Did not such achievements demonstrate to the naked eye and the dullest brain the latent force in the German people? The extraordinary potency of their political and individual formula? 'What was left to be done? Was there anything left that could be done worthy of such a people who had achieved within the lifetime of a single generation such a political, diplomatic, economic transformation?'

The result consecrated the method. The army had made possible the war with Austria and German unity; it had made possible the war with France and the domination of Europe. The two had fathered the economic development and made possible national wealth. The Empire was an autocratic militaristic government which did in truth cramp and fetter the individual, which led rather than followed. But had it not led to a purpose, had it not achieved that end dearest to German hearts?

Bismarck had at first been opposed by the all but unanimous opinion of the Prussian people; he had pushed forward his plans despite them; he had worked in secret but his achievements had been public and the end had been glorious. The people became accustomed to the idea that they would not understand all that transpired, that they might never know at any time what the state planned to accomplish. They came to feel that it was not wise to ask to know; better far to accept the guidance of the men who had achieved so much, better to obey without question. They shuddered to think of what might have happened during the sixties as a result of the acceptance by Bismarck of the opinions they had then held.

This attitude of the German people toward the German government made easy the planning of Pan-Germanism, guaranteed its acceptance by the people in advance without examination of its merits. The result of the previous generations' success made it a foregone conclusion that the German people would believe what was told them from Berlin; would accept the version of European politics which the state provided.

England, they were told in the schools, in magazines, in newspapers, and novels, was a hateful, hostile enemy doing its best to strangle Germany. France was better but faithless, always ready to undertake a war of revenge to recover Alsace-Lorraine. Russia was dangerous because of her size, but to be despised for her stupidity and incompetence. The real text was the greatness of Germany, the mission of Kultur, contempt for the rest of mankind, and the contention that the other nations of Europe were leagued together to destroy the results of Bismarck's success, to conquer Germany, cramp her, make her poor and humble once more.

Indeed, Germany had accomplished so much which was clearly contrary to the rights of others that the Germans became suspicious of all their neighbors. In every international event they saw subtle schemes to undo their greatness, but most of all they visited their hatred and suspicion upon England. She, most of all, they felt would gain by their downfall and by the ending of their era of prosperity. Soon after the war broke out a common method of greeting in Germany was the phrase "God punish England." And a chant of hate was written which was sung and recited with extraordinary demonstrations of approval at public meetings and theaters.

> French and Russian, they matter not,
> A blow for a blow and a shot for a shot;
> We love them not, we hate them not,
> We hold the Weichsel and Vosges-gate,
> We have but one and only hate,
> We love as one, we hate as one,
> We have one foe and one alone.
>
> He is known to you all, he is known to you all,
> He crouches behind the dark gray flood,
> Full of envy, of rage, of craft, of gall,
> Cut off by waves that are thicker than blood.
> Come let us stand at the Judgment place,
> An oath to swear to, face to face,
> An oath of bronze no wind can shake,
> An oath for our sons and their sons to take.

HATE: GERMAN ILLUSTRATION FOR THE SONG OF
HATE, PUBLISHED IN "OUR HOLY WAR," IN 1914.

Come, hear the word, repeat the word,
Throughout the Fatherland make it heard,
We will never forego our hate,
We have all but a single hate,
We love as one, we hate as one,
We have one foe and one alone—
          ENGLAND!

In the Captain's Mess, in banquet-hall,
Sat feasting the officers, one and all,
Like a saber-blow, like the swing of a sail,
One seized his glass held high to hail;
Sharp-snapped like the stroke of a rudder's play,
Spoke three words only: "To the Day!"

Whose glass this fate?
They had all but a single hate.
Who was thus known?
They had one foe and one alone —
          ENGLAND!

Take you the folk of the Earth in pay,
With bars of gold your ramparts lay,
Bedeck the ocean with bow on bow,
Ye reckon well, but not well enough now.
French and Russian they matter not,
A blow for a blow, a shot for a shot,
We fight the battle with bronze and steel,
And the time that is coming Peace will seal.
You will we hate with a lasting hate,
We will never forego our hate,
Hate by water and hate by land,
Hate of the head and hate of the hand,
Hate of the hammer and hate of the crown,
Hate of seventy millions, choking down.
We love as one, we hate as one,
We have one foe and one alone
          ENGLAND!

THE GERMAN PREPARATIONS FOR WAR

When the Germans had planned an aggressive war against France and Russia with the eventual object of crushing England, they knew at the outset that they must make such complete preparations that they would be sure to win. To fail would be the greatest catastrophe in German history. They simply must not fail. They must therefore calculate upon meeting the worst possible circumstances; they must prepare for every possible contingency; they must be as ready as their enemies were unready. They must begin the war at the moment most advantageous to them and most disadvantageous to their enemies. And they must strike the first blow.

The guarantee of victory was to be the superiority of German organization for war and must be the product of foresight and long years of preparation. All Germans must be made into soldiers, and all soldiers must be equipped with everything that could be thought of. They must be thoroughly trained in all the things that it might become essential for them to do. An army could not be made in a hurry, the Germans claimed, and it would therefore take a generation to get ready. That very fact would make them sure to win, because if their enemies must take as long a time to prepare, they would be crushed before their preparation had been begun.

They trained their men to stand the fatigue of long, forced

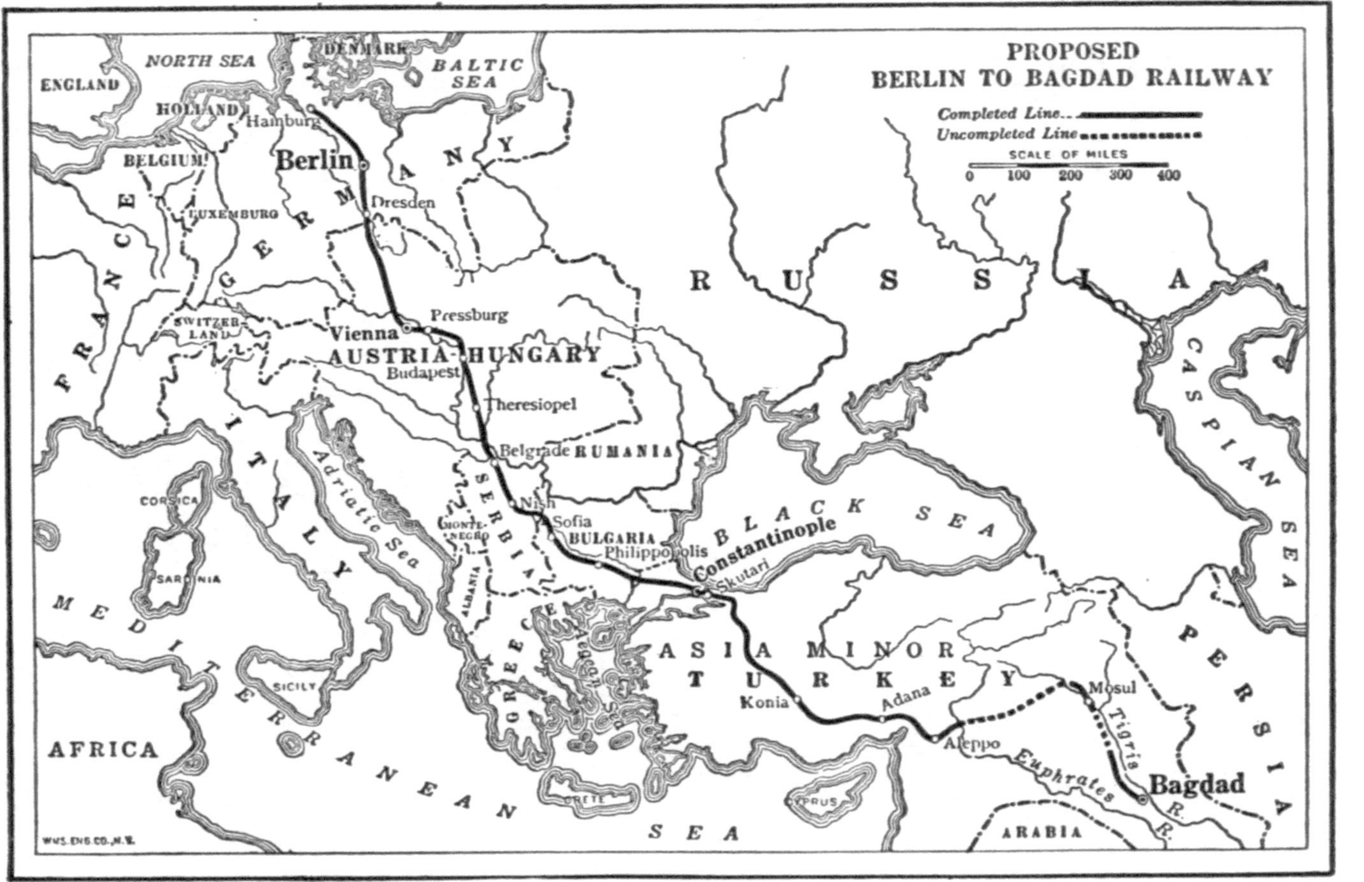

PROPOSED
BERLIN TO BAGDAD RAILWAY
Completed Line
Uncompleted Line
SCALE OF MILES
0 100 200 300 400
ENGLAND
NORTH SEA
DENMARK
BALTIC SEA
HOLLAND
Hamburg
BELGIUM
Berlin
GERMANY
Dresden
LUXEMBURG
FRANCE
SWITZER-LAND
Pressburg
Vienna
AUSTRIA-HUNGARY
Budapest
Theresiopel
Belgrade
RUMANIA
RUSSIA
ITALY
CORSICA
SARDINIA
Adriatic Sea
SERBIA
MONTE-NEGRO
ALBANIA
Nish
Sofia
BULGARIA
Philippopolis
Constantinople
Skutari
BLACK SEA
GREECE
Aegean Sea
CRETE
CYPRUS
ASIA MINOR
TURKEY
Konia
Adana
Aleppo
Euphrates
Mosul
Tigris R.
PERSIA
CASPIAN SEA
Bagdad
ARABIA
MEDITERRANEAN SEA
AFRICA
SICILY
WMS. ENG. CO., N.Y.

marches, for they knew that only men who had gone through extreme fatigue many times would ever be able to execute the sort of a movement on Paris with which they intended to begin the war. Artillery and infantry practiced marksmanship without ceasing, and the cost was enormous, but they did not propose to have the army learn how to shoot after the war began. Every pleasure automobile and taxi-cab made in Germany had the holes ready bored in its chassis for the changes necessary to transform it into a military auto; its new equipment had been prepared; and its owner and chauffeur had at all times instructions exactly where to take it the moment a certain order was issued.

There would be no time to waste when this aggressive war was launched. For every gun put into army use, a duplicate was made and put in the reserve; for every rifle were made so many thousands of extra rounds of ammunition; for every soldier so many extra uniforms and pairs of shoes. Germany must be ready to begin the war with a rush, but she must not count on ending it at the outset. She must be as well prepared with the material means of continuing it indefinitely as with those for beginning it instantaneously.

Knowing in advance that they were to fight a war with France and with Russia, the High Command decided in advance which officers should lead the troops and then sent men like Hindenburg to study the geography of Poland and men like Von Kluck to study the geography of France. These men could not of course travel as military officers, but the French noticed great numbers of German tourists walking through the country, large numbers of German artists making sketches of the French country, Germans with cameras taking pictures of hills, trees, and rivers. We know what they were doing. Some of them were generals planning their campaigns. Others were artillery officers making the calculations which should tell them exactly how to hit certain objects with their great guns when the time came. Others were infantry officers who were going to lead their troops across that country.

Quite as important as the complete preparation of the German army would be exhaustive knowledge about the armies of possible enemies. In Berlin they should know more about the French army than was known in Paris, more about the English army than was known in London, more about the Russians than the Tsar's own generals knew. They proposed to learn exactly who the officers of these various armies were, what had been their training, their probable ability. They knew how many more might be enlisted. They not only made lists of the factories making war materials, but also of the factories that might be transformed at the outbreak of the war for that purpose, and the volume of output which they could probably turn out in any given period.

Then skilled workmen would be needed. How many were already skilled in France, England, or Russia in making war materials; how many might become skilled; how long would it take to train them? They must thus find out in advance just how great a force the German army would be likely to meet in the first week of the war, what in the first month, and what in every succeeding month or year. They could then compute the exact size of a German army needed to insure victory. Victory would not be a matter of chance; it would be a mathematical calculation, and, if only the work were well done, it ought to be infallible.

They would then provide at the elbow of every British, French, and Russian general an invisible soldier of the German Empire. In the Councils of the French Premier and of the British Ministry there should be an invisible Councillor of the German nation. These were spies, men who were not known to be in German pay, selected with the utmost care so that they might send on to Berlin regularly the plans of Germany's enemies. Thus the German leaders would always know what was going on elsewhere, whom they must meet, what was being done to offset their plans. If possible, the spies should steal important military and naval secrets. If a great battleship was being built by the British, they must find out just what its construction would be and if possible get the plans.

Should the French invent something, some spy must be detailed to steal the secret.

The cleverness of these spies and the elaborate system which they devised was extraordinary. In order to prevent them from betraying each other, each man knew only the man above him and the man below him in the chain. If one man, therefore, was caught, or sold what he knew, he could not tell much. The men at the top were known to so few and the few were so very carefully chosen that betrayal was not possible. There were German spies, therefore, to be found in the greatest houses in France and England, in the confidential councils of the state, in the army, in the navy, and in business houses. Fashionable men and women were paid to pick up conversation in London and Paris drawing rooms.

The methods of reporting were extremely complicated. Most of the German spies operated as business agents and would write a letter to some German firm ordering a certain number of steam engines or so many dozen dishes. A hundred dinner plates might mean that one hundred guns were being made in a certain place. An extremely clever letter was constructed by drawing a straight line from one corner of the paper to the other, making a cross. On each one of the lines was written a word and in the middle was written a fifth word. The five together made the message. Then around those five an innocent letter was written dealing with something else. Invisible ink was also used to write between the lines of letters.

One clever spy, who had stolen a long report about French preparations during the war, was puzzled to know how to get that report back to Germany. She knew she would be searched, that every scrap of paper she had would be taken away from her, tested, and probably destroyed, and every object she had would be examined in the most thorough way. One thing only was safe. She was posing as a Swiss citizen returning home, and the French government had given her a passport to let her through the lines. The passport they would have to leave with her. She therefore copied the document she had stolen in invisible ink between the lines of her own passport. But the French were as clever as she. They put the passport into a bath of chemical to find out whether she had done precisely that trick, and the lady finished the war in prison.

It became indeed so difficult for the German spies to conceal what they were doing that they began to write upon the back of the spy in invisible ink messages too long to be learned. The Allied searchers could then take every scrap of his clothing off, burn all his papers, and the message would still go through. But they soon began to give suspected people baths of chemical, which brought out the invisible ink. So that failed, too.

The Germans thought nothing of going to the trouble of planting a man and his family in a place where they wanted a spy, of creating a business for him and having him live there for ten or fifteen years without spying on any one or reporting anything. This was frequently done in the United States and more commonly in France. By that time they calculated that any possible suspicions the police might have about him would have been thoroughly dispelled by the simple fact that he had done absolutely nothing. Then he would begin his series of reports to Berlin.

They also realized that if he were to have visits from particular individuals at stated intervals, or if he saw certain strangers from time to time it might attract attention, and they therefore provided that the reports should not be sent by mail, and never to any one individual. On a certain day the spy would go down to the railroad station and take a train for some other place, indicated in advance. He would there get off his train. Presently another train would come in from some other place and a man would get off of it, never the same man, never coming from the same place. Sometimes the man who was making the report would drop a newspaper, walk away, and the other man would pick it up. Sometimes he would secretly hand him a letter. Again he would merely shake hands with him and exchange a few words anybody could overhear but which contained the secret message. Thanks to these spies, to the cleverness of this system, the Germans did get an immense amount of information about the nations with which they went to war, which did make it easy for them to prepare, and which did make it difficult for the French, the Belgians, the English, the Russians, yes, and the Americans, too, to resist the German attack. There seems to be no doubt that there were as many German spies in America as there were in France.

The Germans now applied to their own people and to their own resources the same methods they had applied to their enemies and catalogued every man, woman, and child in Germany, found out what they could do to help the war, and taught them how to do it. They listed all the horses, cows, and pigs in Germany; every acre of land and what could be raised upon it; all the mines from which metals could be gotten for making guns. If they knew something was going to be needed when the war broke out, they created a factory to make it, appointed men to work in it, collected the raw materials it would need.

All this was imperative. If they went to war with Great Britain—and they must prepare for that emergency, however much they might hope she might not join in the war—the British fleet would probably blockade Germany and prevent her from getting supplies of all sorts from the outside world. Germany must therefore be ready to produce all the food, all the guns, clothes, shoes, and everything else that the army or the people at home might need during the war. They must be ready to keep up the war indefinitely.

They thought it would not be a long war, but if they planned to fight a short war and made preparations for that only and then something went wrong, and the war lasted a little longer than they had planned, they would lose it simply because of that error in calculation. There must not be any error. There must be food to eat as well as guns to shoot with. There must be enough horses to draw the plow or machinery to do the plowing in their stead, as there must be enough horses to draw the cannon. They must have cattle and chickens because they must have milk and eggs.

To be sure, they did not imagine that the British fleet could blockade Germany effectively. They expected to smuggle in a great deal of material through Holland, Denmark, and Sweden, and for a long time they did. But the British and the French protested to the Dutch and the Danes about this smuggling, and compelled investigation. The steamers, sailing from Holland up the Rhine into Germany, had the space between walls of the state-rooms filled with rubber, copper, and medicines. The cushions on the window seats were filled with raw cotton, and the life preservers had had the cork taken out of them and had been filled up with rubber. The life boats on the ship all had compartments which were meant to make them float even if they upset. The flooring had been taken up and the compartments had been filled up with things valuable to Germany. Down in the hold even what looked to be great piles of coal, were really great piles of copper with a little coal on top, just enough to get the ship to Germany.

The Germans also calculated that much of importance could be done toward winning the war by their spies in England, France, Russia, and the United States. They did corrupt a number of high officials in Russia. The Minister of War himself at one time was in German pay and saw to it that the food was sent where it did not belong, that the guns went to one division and the ammunition to another, that the left shoes went to one place and the right to another, so that it was not possible in some cases to fight the campaign for lack of material. Officers were also bought who directed the Russian artillery so that it killed Russians instead of Germans. Regiments were sent out to attack the German lines, no aid was sent to them, and they were all killed.

In France and in Great Britain considerable attempts were made to blow up factories and to create strikes so that the British and French should not be able to prepare. In America, in particular, where many contracts were made as soon as the war broke out to make munitions for the British and French, German agents created strikes or spoiled the shells and rifles. Ammunition was made just too large to fit the guns or the shell was arranged so as not to explode or so as to explode too soon. Agents in the Red Cross workrooms put poison and powdered glass into bandages, and others in the factories where food was canned put poison into the cans just before they were sealed. All this was planned before the war broke out and made the authorities in Berlin very sure that they were going to win.

This forty years of preparation and the character of the preparations is the best proof that the Germans meant to begin an aggressive war. Their claim that they were really defending themselves breaks down when we see that their own preparations were based upon the idea that the French, the Russians, and the British could not conceivably meet them. That shows very clearly that they did not really believe that the French or the Russians could have attacked them in 1914 with any chance of success. They fully expected in 1914 that they would win the war so soon that neither the British nor the Russians would ever be able to get ready, and that even the French might never be able fully to mobilize their army.

This length of German preparation will again show why the war lasted so long, why the Germans were apparently winning the war for the first three years, why it seemed even in 1918 as if they might still win it. Time was needed for the British, French, and Americans to make up that handicap of forty years of preparation. We could not get ready in a hurry. The Germans were right; modern armies cannot be made in a moment. Only time can create big guns, officers, competent troops.

But the Germans were wrong in one thing. They could not be beaten except by a competent army which was prepared; but the Allies had such an army—the French army. The Germans could be beaten only by excellent artillery; but the Allies had such artillery—the famous French 75's. Generals again, the Germans were quite correct in believing, could not be trained except through long years of effort. But the French realized long ago, as the British and the Americans did not, what the Germans meant to do, and French generals and staff officers were ready to fight when the war began. Otherwise the German calculations would have been infallible. They would have won the war before any of their enemies could have been ready to fight it. But the French army was capable enough, devoted enough, brave enough to hold the Germans in check while the British and the Americans got ready to come to their assistance. The story of the war, therefore, was that of staving off defeat from month to month and from year to year while this tremendous handicap in preparation could be overcome.

WHY THE WAR BEGAN IN 1914

The Germans began the war in 1914 not because they were attacked in that year but because they thought that their enemies were so peculiarly unprepared and so singularly unable to fight at all in that year that it was the most favorable moment for an aggressive war in fifteen years. Such a good chance might never return. If they waited they might lose it. The nations they intended to attack were beginning to realize the extent and meaning of the German preparations and might make some of their own which would prevent the Germans from winning a prompt and crushing victory.

There had been in the years just preceding 1914, several crises during which the Germans had felt out the attitude of the French and the British, and they had concluded that both of those nations were afraid to fight. They did not think they would dare to accept the issue of war. Here again is clear proof that the Germans began an aggressive war. They had really come to believe that, short of being actually invaded, neither the British nor the French would dare to begin a war. There had been an occasion in 1908, when Austria had annexed Bosnia and Herzegovina without the consent of the Powers, when they thought it quite possible that a general war might result from that act.

The Germans and Austrians exulted when the French and British did not compel, them to fight. In the next five years there were several other chances for the French and British to have begun a war if they had wanted to. Were they not so much afraid of Germany that they would always yield rather than accept the issue of war? The Germans therefore proposed to ask them to make one after another the vast concessions that they had in mind, each time asking as much as they thought they could without compelling the British and French to fight.

AUSTRIA-HUNGARY AND THE BALKANS.

The German spies reported in 1914 that there had never been a time when the French, British, and Russian armies had been as little ready to fight. The British army was then very small and attempts to increase it had repeatedly failed. Its equipment, the Germans thought, was very poor and attempts to make it better had been defeated. The majority of the Russian army was not equipped at all. It lacked shoes, clothing, and even rifles. There were no factories in Russia in 1914 adequate to maintain it in the field, though the state was proposing to build some very large factories.

The French had the best of the three armies, but charges were made in the French Chamber in July, 1914, that the French army was not ready for war. One of the senators, Humboldt, who is now believed to have been a German agent, charged the Minister of War with incompetence. The forts were old; the guns were antiquated; the troops without shoes. There was not enough ammunition and what there was was old. The Minister was compelled to admit there was much truth in what he said. The Germans concluded that not merely was the French army not ready, but that the French nation would have no confidence in it because of these revelations made at the very moment when the war was about to begin.

That Great Britain would join the war the Germans thought unlikely, but they believed that a much more important fact was true. They did not think Great Britain could join the war in August, 1914. There was a great quarrel going on in Ireland. It seemed possible that civil war might break out over the issue of Home Rule. A bill had been passed by the British Parliament concerning the government of Ireland, and a certain section of people in the north of Ireland, living in Ulster, had declared their intention to fight if the act was put into operation. They procured rifles and ammunition, organized a government, and practically defied England. There was grave doubt whether the British army would attempt to coerce them.

Then there was a quarrel between Canada and South Africa and the Hindus which made the Germans think that the British Empire would not join England, if England joined France against Germany. In Paris at this time a trial was going on of the wife of a former Premier of France, Madame Caillaux, for the murder of a newspaper editor. All sorts of scandals were brought to light about important men in French life, until it looked as if there was in all France scarcely an honest or a patriotic statesman. So the Germans thought, at any rate. The Russians had not yet recovered, they calculated in Berlin, from the war with Japan in 1905, and would be very slow to enter any new war. As for the United States, from which of course Great Britain and France might get considerable assistance, it looked at that time as if the United States would go to war with Mexico.

There could not therefore have been a moment, certainly there had not been for many years a time, when the enemies of Germany seemed weaker and in greater trouble than they were in July and August, 1914. The Germans and Austrians therefore made up their minds to pick a quarrel with Serbia over the murder of the Archduke. They would present demands which they thought the Serbians would be absolutely certain to refuse. They would then claim that war was necessary. They fully expected the Russians to come to the aid of the Serbians and they knew that the French had signed a treaty with Russia which compelled them to come to the aid of the Russians. This would begin the war in just the way they wanted it begun, at just the moment they wanted it begun, and with the kind of issue they could present to their own people and claim that the war was begun in self-defense. We know definitely now that the Germans had planned the war as early as April or May, 1914, and began it really in a frenzy of fear toward the end of July lest some compromise or yielding on the part of the French or the Russians should postpone it.

There cannot be any doubt that they wanted the war. Some of them were even honest enough to confess it, although the majority insisted that the war had been forced upon them by their foes. But one of the best-known German writers, Maximilian Harden, wrote as follows about the beginning of the war. "Not as weak blunderers have we undertaken the fearful risk of this war. We wanted it. Because we had to wish it and could wish it. May the Teuton devil throttle those whiners whose pleas for excuses make us ludicrous in these hours of lofty experience!... Germany strikes!... We are waging this war not in order to punish those who have sinned, not in order to free enslaved peoples.... We wage it from the lofty point of view and with the conviction that Germany, as a result of her achievements, and in proportion to them, is justified in asking, and must obtain, wider room on earth for development and for working out the possibilities that are in her... Now strikes the hour for Germany's rising power!"

And with what object then did the Allies enter the contest? With what purpose did they fight for four years against the tremendous preparations of Germany? President Wilson stated on August 27, 1917, the aims of the Allies: "The object of this war is to deliver the free peoples of the world from the menace and the actual power of a vast military establishment controlled by an irresponsible government, which having secretly planned to dominate the world, proceeded to carry the plan out without regard either to the sacred obligations of treaty or the long-established practices and long-cherished principles of international action and honor; which chose its own time for the war; delivered its blow fiercely and suddenly; stopped at no barrier either of law or mercy; swept the whole continent within the tide of blood —not the blood of soldiers only, but the blood of innocent women and children also, and of the helpless poor.... This power is not the German people. It is the ruthless master of the German people.... It is our business to see to it that the history of the rest of the world is no longer left to its handling." The Allies therefore accepted the gage thrown down by Germany with high resolve, and eventually the United States joined them. They determined to stake their all to protect democracy and civilization as they existed in the world; to preserve French, British, and American society, threatened by the Germans with extinction.

BOOK II

THE WAR IN 1914

The Campaign on Paris

The key to the German plan of campaign was the decision to begin an aggressive war, directed by a nation fully prepared against enemies not prepared to fight at all. It was again an aggressive war begun by a power located between France on one side and Russia on the other, without natural boundaries, like mountains or deep rivers, to assist her in defense. But the Germans had a tremendous advantage in strategic position. On the west they held Alsace-Lorraine, which contained the military defenses of France: they were already at the outbreak of the war inside the French defenses. To the north of Alsace-Lorraine lay Luxembourg and Belgium. In Belgium was Liege, another vital portion of the military frontier between France and Germany. If it was not in German possession, neither did France own it. Both had been rendered neutral by the Treaty of 1839 and France was precluded from using either to attack Germany. In any case the Germans were certain to reach them first. They could therefore begin an aggressive war against France with absolute confidence that the advantage was in their favor.

On the east, in Poland, the situation was extremely favorable to Germany. Poland is flanked on both sides by Prussia and Galicia. It is as if the Russian army stuck its head into the lion's mouth. If the lion can close his jaws, he will bite off the Russian's head. The lion, on the other hand, has to beware. If the Russian can force his jaws further apart, he will break them. If he can get his head in far enough between them, he will crawl down the lion's throat and strangle him. But on the whole the advantage lay with Germany. The Russians must attack in Prussia on the north and in Galicia on the south, before they could move in force from Warsaw on Berlin. This meant that the German position was extremely strong on the defensive.

The Germans also planned the war on the assumption that the inside position was one of great strength for an army beginning an aggressive war, just as they had concluded for centuries that it was a position of weakness for an army fighting on the defensive. They and the Austrians were ringed around by their enemies, but they might strike at them from any part of the circle they wished without giving their enemies as good a chance to strike back. The Germans could campaign on either front at will; they could shift the same army rapidly from France to Poland and back again. The French and Russians could not help each other. Tremendous preparations were made so that the German railroads should be adequate to ship any number of thousands of men back and forth across Germany at maximum speed. The combined French and Russian armies were immense; far greater than the German and Austrian armies; but the Germans felt that if they took the initiative at the beginning of the war they would control the situation, could fight on one frontier at a time only, and on either frontier they chose.

They determined to attack France, and the reason was simple. The French army would be ready long before the Russian and was of admirable quality, which the Germans never underrated. They supposed it would take the French at least ten days to put their full strength into the field. They knew that the utmost speed of Russian mobilization could not make possible a campaign for six weeks. The distances in Russia which the troops must travel to the frontier were great, the distances supplies must be sent were greater, and the railroads were few. Obviously the Germans had six weeks in which to attack France without danger of real interference from the Russians. They could therefore afford to throw

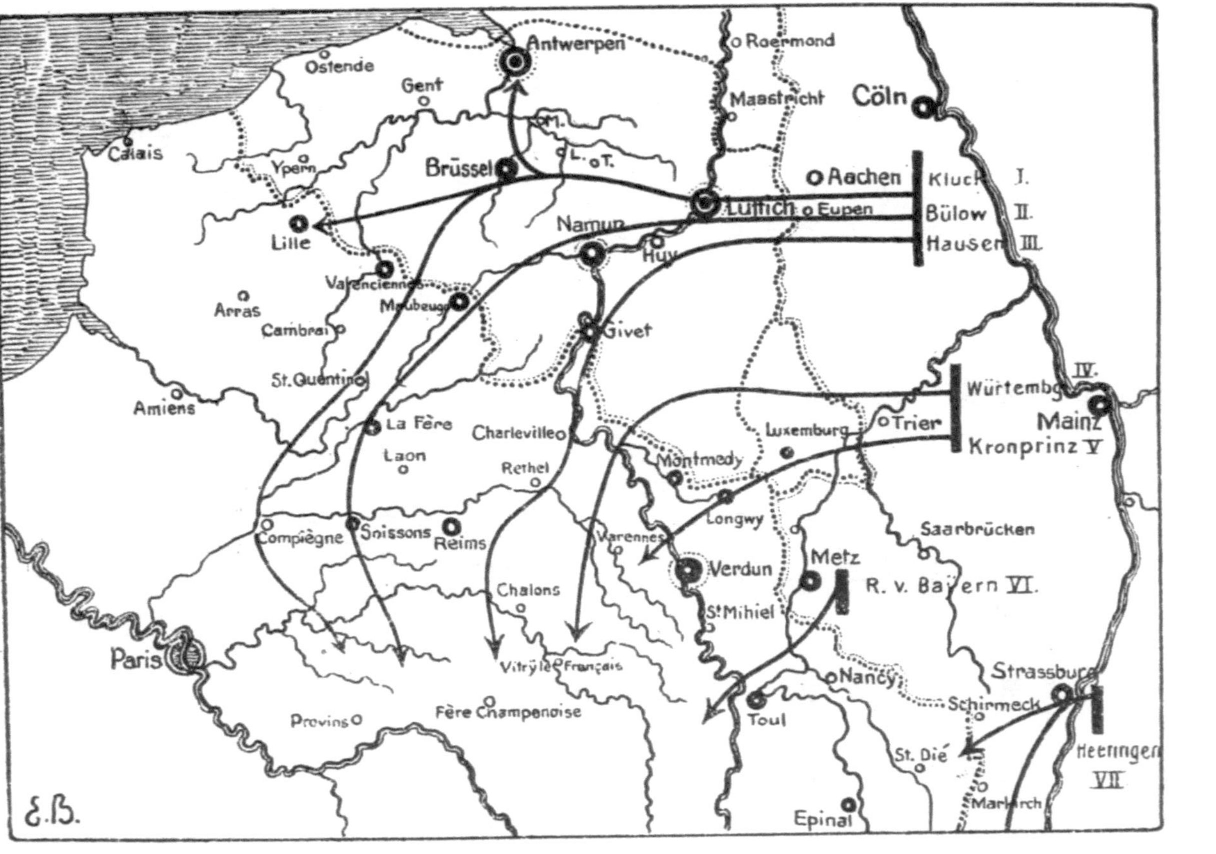

GERMAN MAP OF INVASION OF FRANCE FROM "UNSER HEILIGER KRIEG."

the great bulk of their army upon the French and would thus so outnumber them that they fully expected to destroy the French before the Russians were able to move. They would then return victorious and end the Russian menace for all time.

But how should they get at France? There were three roads on Paris. Two led through Alsace-Lorraine, and had been fortified with great care and skill by the French. While the Germans knew that their great guns would destroy any fort then existing in Europe, they also knew that such a campaign meant time, and time was the essential element in the assault. Speed was the important thing; if they could only get at France quickly enough they might be able to disperse the French army before it had assembled.

The third road crossed the Rhine at Cologne, passed into Belgium at Liege, joined the road coming north from Alsace-Lorraine and passed on through Belgium into France by a great, broad, natural gateway without mountains or rivers to obstruct an army's march. It was admirably equipped with railroads for the army's use, and, because of the treaty of neutrality, was entirely unfortified by France. If the German army was to move in a hurry, it must march, and must march where the marching was good, where the roads were easiest, and the best time could be made. Belgium was too small to resist effectively, and, once through Belgium, all roads to Paris were open. The invasion of Belgium was the only plan to consider from a military point of view.

The Germans worked on a time schedule, determined by the average speed of men actually detailed in time of peace to walk from the German frontier to Paris. In four days the army should be through Belgium; in six more it should reach Paris. That was not more rapid marching than the Germans had repeatedly done. If they could carry out such a schedule, they would infallibly be upon Paris before the French army could mobilize. It was also to be remembered—a very important and striking fact—that by some misadventure they might not destroy the French army in the first fortnight and might be compelled to fight longer. It was important to compel the French to continue the war at a maximum disadvantage.

The Germans knew the French were not ready to fight and that the continuation of the war would require an immense volume of supplies which would have to be manufactured. Moreover, this very area, which the Germans would overrun at the outset, was the industrial section of France. Here were the most important factories. Here were great coal and iron mines upon which French industry relied and upon which the French army would have to depend. Assuming the invasion's failure the Germans would still force the French to conduct the war in a way so difficult for them that, without very prompt and considerable assistance, they might not be able to continue it at all.

All this determined the diplomatic arrangements at the beginning of the war as well as the first military movements. The war must be sprung as a surprise and time must not be wasted in negotiations. Once the intentions of Germany and Austria became clear to their enemies, not an hour should be lost. The whole campaign would fail if they allowed the diplomats to write and talk

GERMAN COURTESY—1914.

about causes and purposes. Both Germany and Austria therefore fairly tumbled over each other at the end of July, 1914, to get the war actually begun. They seem to have been terrified lest in some way it should be averted, lest the favorable moment should pass without the beginning of the campaign. All attempts to postpone it, to explain the issues, or to compromise them, were therefore rejected as fast as they were made. Austria declared war on Serbia four days after the first note. Three days later the German ultimatum was delivered to France and Russia, and four days after that the German armies were in Belgium. Twelve days sufficed for all the preliminary moves of the greatest war in history.

Austria declared war on Serbia on July 28; Russia began mobilization on the Hungarian frontier on the following day; on July 30 Austria began the bombardment of Belgrade and general mobilization was ordered in Russia. Germany accordingly presented ultimatums both to Russia and to France on the last day of July and declared war on Russia on August 1, Italy promptly declaring her neutrality. August 2 saw German armies in Luxembourg and the German demand to march unopposed through Belgium. August 3 brought the Belgian refusal and the German declaration of war on France. The next morning, August 4, found the German armies in Belgium and that night at midnight Great Britain declared war on Germany.

How now should the attack be met? What could the Allies do, unprepared as they were, to meet the thrust which the Germans had calculated would be irresistible? They saw that the German campaign was based on two factors: first—on time; second—on crushing the French army. When the Germans asked the Belgians to allow them to march unimpeded through their territory, the latter knew that if they agreed to that request, Paris would be lost and the independence of Belgium would become a thing of the past. Only France and England could in the end save Belgium from annexation; but neither France nor England could possibly save Belgium from invasion at that moment.

Yet only Belgium could save Paris from capture, protect the French army from immediate defeat, thus eventually save the cause of the Allies, and by this first blow win in the end its own independence. Unless the Belgians wished to become the slaves of the Germans, they must resist. It would be the struggle of a small boy against a large and desperate man. The Belgians must fight for time, they must delay the Germans as long as possible. They would in the process be defeated, slaughtered, crushed, maimed; that much they knew. The real extent of what the Germans would do to Belgium was little suspected.

If the Belgians succeeded in delaying the Germans long enough for the French to mobilize, the latter must then keep out of the Germans' way. There is still some confusion of opinion as to the original French plan of campaign, and there is reason to believe that they hoped to strike successfully from their prepared positions in Lorraine at the German left and thus compel the evacuation of France and Belgium. However that may be, the defeat of the first preliminary assaults in Alsace, the steady rush of the Germans through Belgium, showed the futility of such strategy, and caused Joffre to adopt the plan which eventually won the first and greatest Allied victory. He must at all costs not be beaten. That, he saw, must be the key to his defensive campaign.

He must draw the Germans further and further into France and further and further away from Germany. He must compel them to march as far as possible, as fast as possible, to transport their supplies as long distances as possible, and thus maneuver them into an unfavorable position. On no account must he stand still to be crushed; that alone could give the German campaign a chance of success without giving France the same chance to defeat it. Joffre therefore ordered the armies to retreat and to continue retreating. Meanwhile, the Allied plans provided that the British were to rush over such troops as they had ready, however few they might be. Every man, every rifle, every horse might be enough to check the Germans and prevent an immediate German victory. Meanwhile something might happen.

Last and not least, inasmuch as the German calculations assumed that the bulk of the army could be sent to France because the Russians could not move, the latter should invade Prussia at once. Even if the troops walked barefoot with nothing but clubs in their hands, the army must move. It would not be prepared to attack with success but the Allies knew that the Germans would not be prepared to meet an assault in Poland. They would have to send troops from France to stop it and in that way the Russians would save Paris.

And so at Liege, the Belgians held the forts desperately against wave after wave of German attacks and resisted the great advance step by step until resistance was no longer possible. For three days the Germans were checked entirely,—three precious days! Then the Belgian army was stamped flat on the ground and over its body tramped the great columns of troops marching to Brussels and Paris. But the Germans were not four days but sixteen days going through Belgium. Sixteen days and Paris was saved! The British and French armies had had time to get to the Belgian frontier, not in full strength, but in enough force to show the astonished Germans an amount of resistance they thought absolutely improbable.

Then began one of the marvelous retreats of history. The Allied troops, French, Belgian, and British, fought gallantly and retreated superbly, but, without reinforcements, they grew more and more weary and footsore, less and less able to fight. No army was harder pressed than General French's gallant little British force around Mons.

They fought in the morning, they fought at noon, they fought at night. The officers kicked the men awake, fell asleep themselves, and were kicked awake in turn. There were men dragging and carrying their officers, horses falling dead in their tracks, and men harnessing themselves to the guns in order to save them. Motor transports moved toward the rear driven often by men sound asleep. "For forty-eight hours no food, no drink, under a hot sun, choking with dust, and marching, marching, marching, until even the pursuing Germans gave it up, and at Vitry-le-Francois the Allies fell in their tracks and slept for three hours, men, horses, and guns—while the exhausted pursuers slept behind them." Thus the British retreated from Mons after one of the most gallant and obstinate actions in history. It played almost as important a part in delaying the German advance as the resistance of the Belgians at Liege.

Behind the armies the roads were full of French fugitives fleeing from the war. Pitiful and terrible sight! Here a whole family trudging along on foot, carrying in their hands a few little articles from their homes, and driving the cow before them. There a woman had piled what little she could save on a wheelbarrow and had perched the baby on top. Here two little children were tugging at their mother's skirts while she directed a little cart drawn by the dogs used in Belgium and northern France for drawing light burdens. There children who had lost their fathers and mothers sat crying by the wayside until some of the fugitives noticed them and carried them on. Other more fortunate families with horses and carts or with automobiles were pushing on to Paris more rapidly. The roads and villages in all directions were full to bursting with a people compelled at a few hours' notice to flee for their lives. It was such a spectacle as men had thought would never again be seen in history.

In those first days it was difficult not to believe that all was lost, that the Germans had calculated too well to be beaten. How could nations, however powerful, but without time to prepare, resist such a foe? Something like despair spread throughout France and England. Then suddenly there came a change. The British and French troops were no longer afraid. They retreated still, but their hearts were light, for they had come to feel that God and His angels in the truest sense were fighting with them. Men told wonderful stories of what they had seen. At one time there was

EARLY BIRDS IN PARIS IN WAR TIME.

a great gap in the Allied line. There were no troops to fill it and meet the advancing Germans. Suddenly in that gap there stood English archers with bows and arrows, knights in armor, figures which seemed to the Germans absolutely real, but which the Allied soldiers believed to be the ghosts of the bold warriors of Agincourt, the men of the Hundred Years' War come back to save France and England.

Others at other points of the line told of seeing Germans and more Germans, in solid columns, pouring over the top of the hills. Suddenly between them and the advancing foe came a flash of brilliant light and then right before them rode "a tall man with yellow hair and golden armor on a white horse." It was St. George, the patron saint of England, come to rally the troops, come to show them that the powers of peace were with them and that the Germans were the powers of evil! The French troops also declared they saw at the moment when all seemed most desperate that same blinding flash of light. When it disappeared, there before them in the field, clad in full armor, riding a white horse was Joan of Arc, brandishing her sword high in air and shouting, "Forward!" The troops answered with a rallying shout, and, dashing forward behind her, threw back the Germans. Did St. George, Joan of Arc, and the dead of the Middle Ages actually appear? No one can say, but thousands believe that they saw them.

And so, day after day, the British and the French retreated and retreated and finally in the first week of September, the people of Paris heard one after the other the distant boom of the explosions blowing up the bridges on the Marne. Still another Allied division had crossed the river. The Germans were just behind. By September 5, the Germans had also passed the Marne and were within a few miles of Paris. Indeed orders had been issued to many German divisions to wear full dress instead of their field uniforms, so as to be ready for the formal entry into the French capital. Many of the officers had already in their pockets the orders directing them in what houses their troops were to be quartered the first night in Paris. But the Germans were never to enter Paris except as prisoners. They had been not ten days but a full month getting within sight of the city. The great scheme had failed. The French army was not crushed. The French army had mobilized. The French were ready to fight, and the British had joined them. The war, far from being won by the Germans, was indeed at that moment on the point of being lost.

From the Marne to Antwerp

The strategy of Joffre had then permitted the Germans to proceed as far as Paris. He had retreated in order to draw them into France, to compel them to extend their lines. Thus he made it as difficult as possible for them to maintain the attack and rendered its weight less every mile they proceeded away from Germany. It was just as if an open door, with the hinge at Verdun and the end of the door out on the Belgian frontier, had gradually shut as the Germans pushed, and finally closed tight on Paris. There was then a strong French line from Verdun to Paris, which General Joffre proposed to hold. As the Germans got further from their bases of supplies and reinforcements, they became fatigued with the rapid marching and fighting. They had no troops to put into the battle except those who had marched the whole distance. The French were continually receiving the aid of fresh troops of their own, which had seen no fighting, and, therefore, every mile the Germans advanced in France they became weaker and the French became stronger. They became more and more fatigued, while the French armies as a whole really remained fresh.

But General Joffre was counting in particular upon the great Russian attacks in East Prussia and Galicia. The Tsar had promised that his army should move west at all costs. That meant that German troops would have to be drawn from France to defend Prussia. The Russians launched a great cavalry attack the first week of August, which was extremely successful. It was indeed one of the most daring raids in history, but it could not maintain its ground and it was not until August 18 that a movement in force took place. This too was astonishingly successful. It swept the German forces out of East Prussia in a hurry and compelled the Kaiser to send for General Hindenburg, who had spent his life studying that territory, and to give him command of troops drawn from the army in France.

In two tremendous battles, Tannenberg, from August 26 to September 1, five whole days, and the Masurian Lakes, lasting from September 6 to 10, five more days, he defeated the first and second Russian armies, crushed, and then destroyed them. In the meantime, however, the third Russian army had made tremendous gains in Galicia, had captured Lemberg, and had already rendered perilous Hindenburg's position in the north. The victories elated the German people, but they weakened the German army in France to such an extent that Joffre was able to begin the battle of the Marne on September 6 with many more men than the Germans had to meet him, placed in a much better position, and in far superior condition.

What Joffre proposed to do, despite the tremendous scale on which the battle was fought, was particularly simple. He proposed

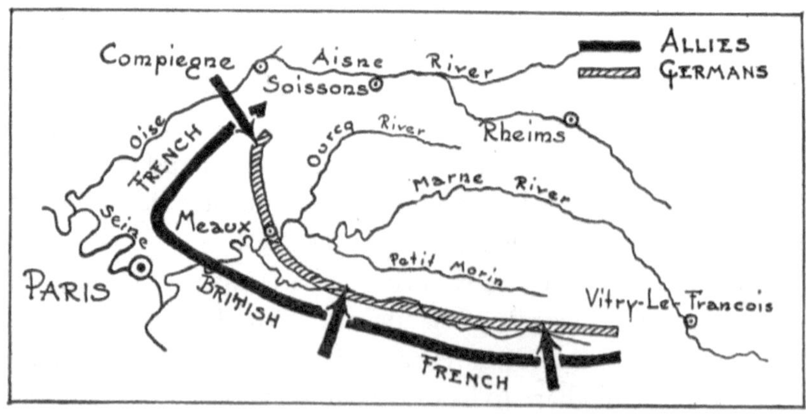

THE BATTLE OF MARNE
FROM A SKETCH BY THE AUTHOR.

to turn the German right flank and by driving it back compel the whole German line to retreat. He would thus relieve Paris from danger and continue the war on a field much more favorable to the French. The Germans had felt so sure of the superiority of their army and of the success of the drive on Paris that they had left a great area of unoccupied territory between their right wing and the coast. Their right wing was therefore unsupported and could be attacked anywhere along the line from Paris to Brussels. If the French could get in behind it, they would break the German formation. Only an army continually successful could maintain such a position. Of this overconfidence Joffre took advantage.

He now enveloped the German right wing with French and British troops, so that the Germans were between the blades of a pair of scissors. The French then attacked, and moved towards each other, thus closing the scissors, and the Germans barely got out from between in time to avoid being cut in two. Their right wing having been compelled to run, the German center was left unprotected, with the now victorious French and English on its flank and in danger of getting in behind it and attacking it in the rear. The German center, therefore, also had to retreat, and the rest of the German line, in order to avoid a similar fate, had to go back with it. They retreated many miles and intrenched themselves on the hills north of the river Aisne, which runs about parallel to the river Marne. The German army at the beginning of the battle was well south of the Marne and at its end was well north of the Aisne. Their loss in territory, therefore, was great.

One of the most picturesque and dramatic movements of the war was the daring charge of General Gallieni's army in Paris to the battle field of the Ourcq. As Von Kluck had continued his pressure upon the French left, he turned early in September southeast to separate Joffre from Paris and make the investment of the city a certainty. Gallieni saw the enemy escaping him and possibly overwhelming Joffre for want of the aid of the hundreds of thousands of men gathered in Paris for the expected siege. "If

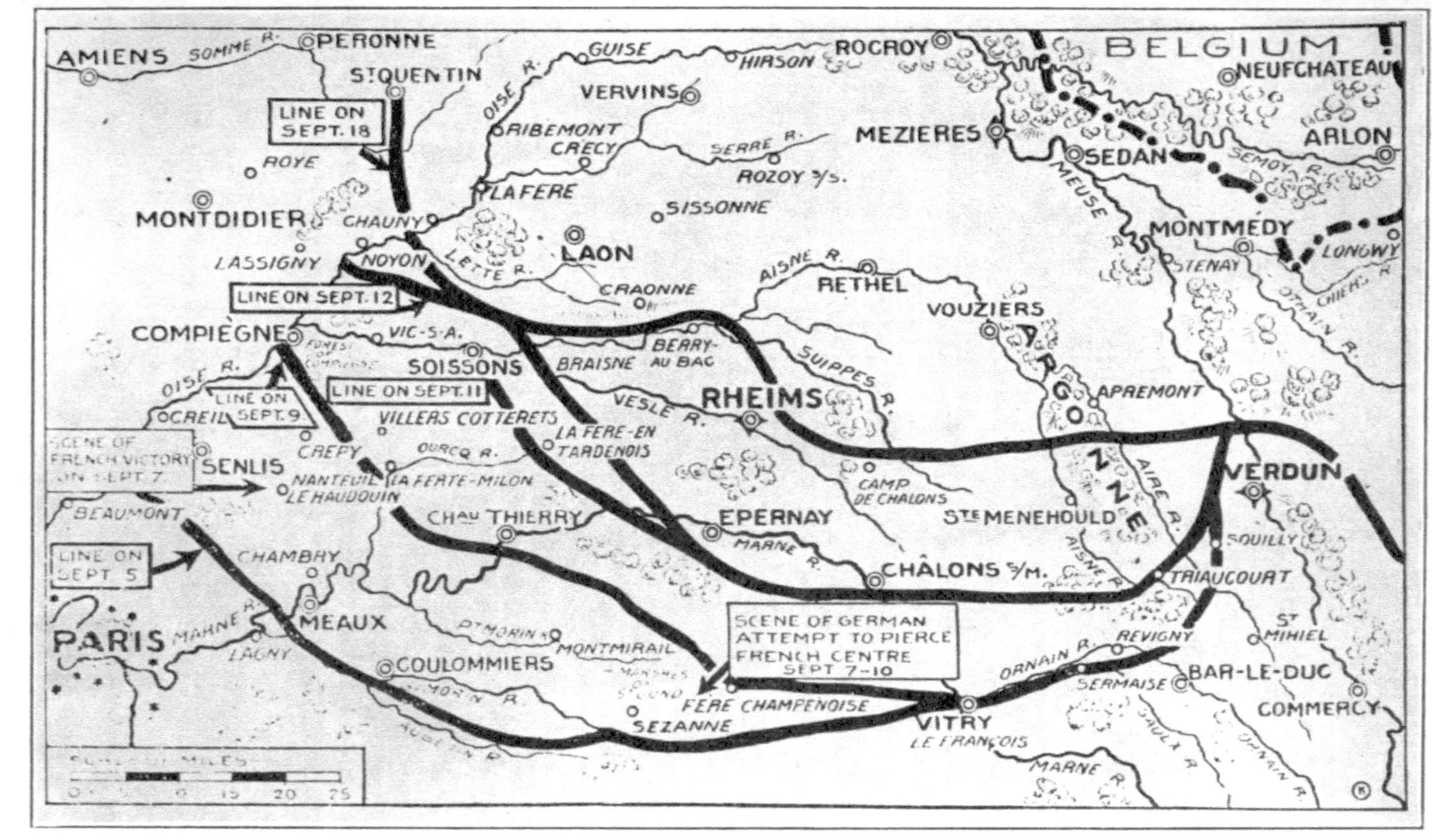

SUCCESSIVE STAGES OF THE GERMAN RETREAT DURING THE BATTLE OF MARNE.

they do not come to us," he said, "we will go to them with all the force we can muster." He gathered all the taxicabs, automobiles, and motor omnibuses in Paris, thousands of them, loaded his army upon them and started for the battle front at fifty miles an hour, leaving Paris unguarded. Suddenly Von Kluck found a great army assailing his right along the Ourcq, where a couple of hours before there had been not a French soldier. Thus began the great victory of the Marne.

At another most critical moment of the battle, General Foch, in the center of the French line, was being assailed by tremendous forces, and received from Joffre the order to retreat. He believed he

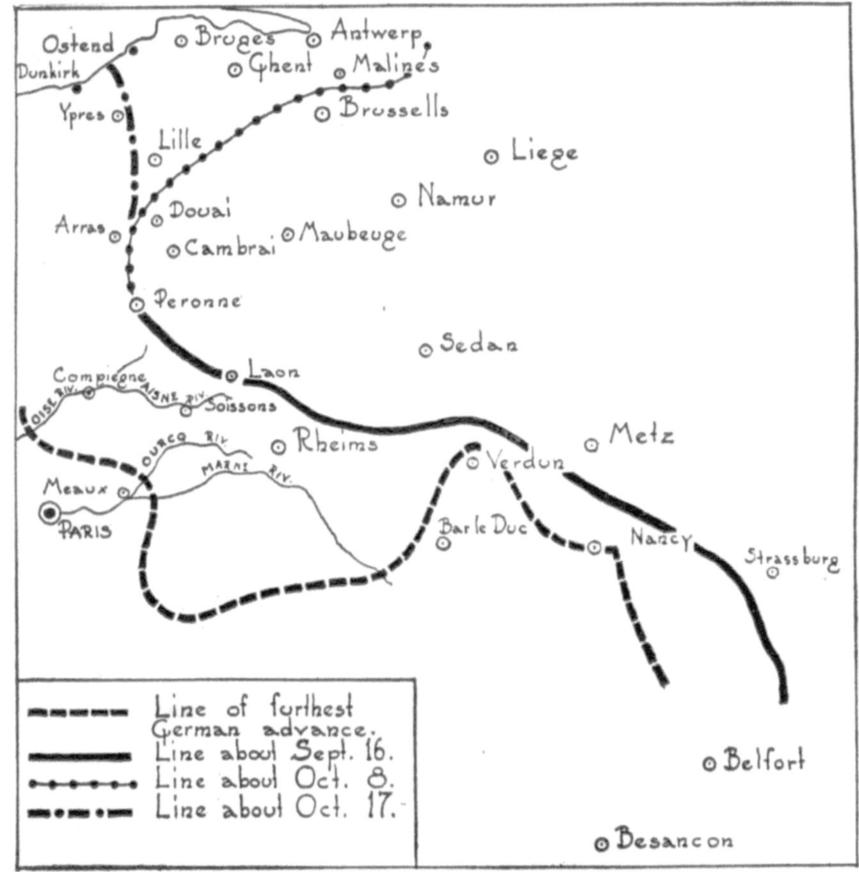

THE SHIFT IN THE BATTLE LINE FROM
SEPTEMBER 6 TO OCTOBER 17.

detected a weakening of the assault, saw a rift in the German line due to some error or misunderstood order, and instead of retreating ordered an attack. He pushed his army between two German armies, flanked them both, and the rout of the German center was complete. This was the turning point of the battle of the Marne and the decisive moment of the first years of the war. However great the credit due to Joffre, history will give the real credit for the victory to the judgment, initiative, and courage of Foch.

The Germans, however, were by no means safe. Their right wing was still a long distance from Brussels; and their reinforcements might still be flanked exactly as during the battle of the Marne. This General Joffre attempted. The Germans, in order to meet his movement, kept on extending their line toward Brussels. So day by day the chase went on to see whether the Germans could occupy certain territory before the French could get around their right wing. They succeeded, but had to extend the trench line all the way from the Aisne into Belgium. In order to have a secure base from which to protect the northern end of it, they proceeded to besiege Antwerp. They could not leave a strong fort like that in the possession of the Belgians, for the English navy might land a great army there and attack the German rear.

The fall of Antwerp was one of the surprises of the war. It had been fortified by talented engineers, and, while not considered the greatest fortress in Europe, was supposed to be able to resist for a considerable length of time any assault likely to be delivered. Only a prolonged siege could capture it, the Belgians had thought. But Antwerp fell, not in weeks, but in days (one might almost say in hours), after the first serious German assault. Here, for the first time, the Germans used one of their surprises—the 420 centimeter gun, the largest gun in the world, throwing an enormous shell filled with high explosives. One single shell was sufficient in most cases to destroy one of the Antwerp forts. Some were blown wide open; some were turned upside down. It was clear at once that every fort in Europe was worthless.

The final scenes at Antwerp were dramatic in the extreme. Great shells set fire to the city. The boom of the enormous cannon, the bursting of shells, the rain of explosives were continuous. Vast plumes of dense black smoke rose from great oil tanks burning along the river. And in the red glare of the burning city, under this great black pall, hundreds of thousands of people fled in boats down the river or on foot along its banks, carrying what little they could in their hands, but otherwise homeless, penniless, starving.

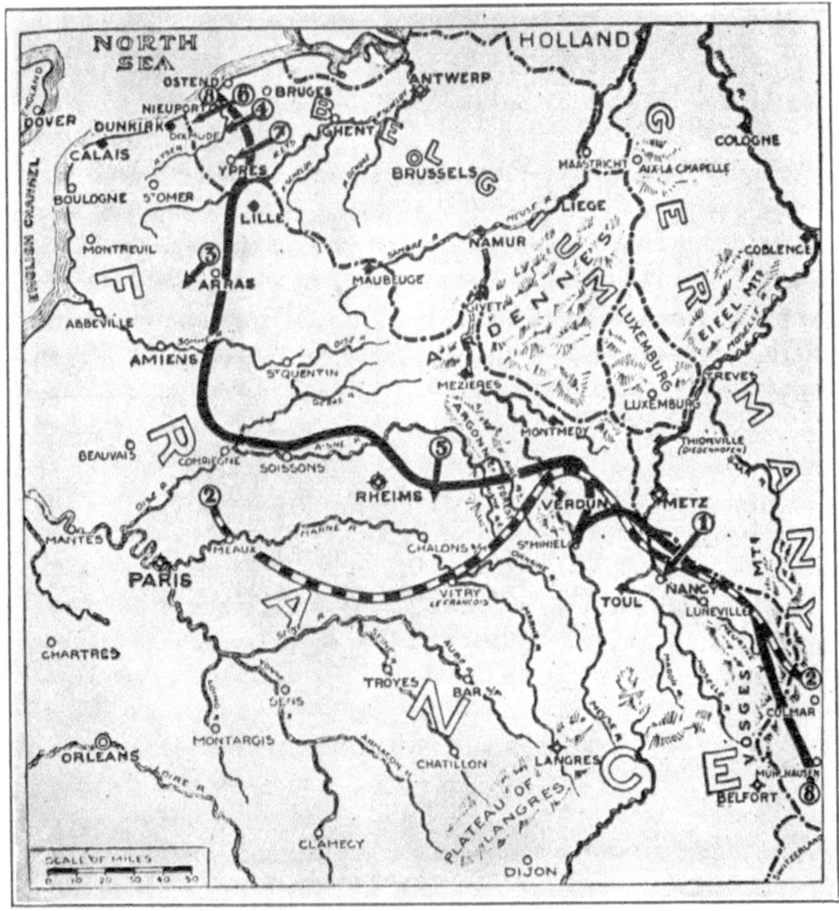

THE NUMBERED ARROWS SHOW THE SUCCESSIVE GERMAN ASSAULTS FROM OCTOBER, 1914, TO FEBRUARY, 1915. THE SOLID LINE IS THE LINE OF BATTLE IN FEBRUARY, 1915.

The Germans could not rest content with a line bent back from Paris to Antwerp and delivered in October and November their first great drive along the coast on Calais. They were eager now to do what they should have done before, occupy western France, shorten the trench line by many scores of miles, and deprive the British of the Channel ports as harbors in which to land their army and the great stream of men and equipment which must maintain it. All but a tiny little strip of Belgium fell into their hands but they did not reach Calais. The Channel ports were safe; the communications of the British army were safe; the submarines would not be able to assail Allied shipping from bases on the Channel itself.

The war now settled down in the west to a deadlock, and, with small changes, the trench line remained substantially the same until 1918. It will therefore be clear that the battle of the Marne did not win the war, for the war went on four years. But the battle was the turning point of the war, not so much because of the territory won from the Germans, but because of its moral effect upon the French and British nations. Everywhere the correspondents went after the battle they found the French quiet, silent, confident, talking about the "good news," *les bonnes nouvelles*. The legend of the power of the German army had been destroyed. It had seemed for six weeks as if the Germans could not be beaten; that they must infallibly win the war. But the moment the Germans had been beaten, the French and British became confident that, however long the war might last, they would in the end win it.

Why the British Empire Entered the War

The Germans had miscalculated; the war had not been won in the first dash on Paris. They had foreseen miraculously well every possible physical factor; their greatest errors had been psychological, and throughout the war the same factor continued to upset their calculations. They had believed that the Belgians would yield in very terror and offer no resistance. They had supposed that the French would not fight because their army was not adequately prepared. They could not conceive that the Russian army would march bravely forth to certain death. But greatest of all was the German failure to analyze the Anglo-Saxon temperament, both in England, in the British colonies, and in the United States. The British were slothful, lazy, venal, cowardly. Such was the German conclusion before the war; such was the version of the British which German newspapers and comic weeklies presented throughout the war.

The failure of the English people and of the British colonies to take the place assigned them in the German formula was almost as deadly a blow to Pan-Germanism as the battle of the Marne. Home Rule was forgotten. Men ready to spring at each other's throats a few days before remembered only that they were all British and that the Germans were in Belgium. The honor of the nation admitted of but one course; immediate assistance to Belgium and France, the prosecution of the war with every man and every penny till the German menace had been destroyed. Money, trade, business jealousies played no part in the popular decision. It would cost money, not save it; it would destroy business, not create it; it would disorganize trade throughout the world in ways that might continue to cost British profits for a generation to come. War was not profitable; war was not desirable; but honor compelled men to choose many alternatives, both perilous and disagreeable, as preferable to life with dishonor.

But it was none the less known to British statesmen, if not to the people, that the war was really directed by the Germans at Great Britain herself, that its true object was to destroy England, once France was beaten. To allow France and Belgium to fight Britain's battle was cowardly and unworthy of a great people. It was also inexpedient in the extreme. If they should be beaten, England would then be forced to fight alone. Unless the British therefore proposed to surrender to the Germans, they must begin the war at the beginning or they might never begin it at all.

Nor was there any doubt from the outset in Great Britain that the German system intended the destruction of liberty and civilization as the British understood them. Militarism and autocracy the British had abhorred for a thousand years. The German claim that all nations in the world must be forced to live in accordance with German Kultur, the British could never accept. Secret diplomacy, too, of the German type, the dishonoring of treaties and the declaration of the German Chancellor that the Belgian treaty of neutrality had been nothing but a scrap of paper was also contrary to everything for which Great Britain stood. There could be no temporizing with Germany or with German Kultur; there could be no compromise. The British notion of civilization was diametrically contrary to the German and one or the other must perish.

One of Germany's most cherished beliefs had been the idea that the British Empire would fall apart the moment war was declared. They could see no reason for the support of the mother country by her colonies and were convinced that the latter would

THE BATTLE OF THE MARNE

SKETCH BY THE FAMOUS ALSATIAN CARTOONIST, HANSI, FOR *PARIS L'ILLUSTRATION*.

prefer to stand aside. But the colonies on the contrary responded magnificently. They all declared war immediately and promised their utmost support in men, in ships, and in supplies. Enlistments proceeded with extraordinary rapidity in Canada, in Australia, in South Africa. From no port of the world indeed did a larger proportion of men enter the service nor did any troops acquit themselves with greater gallantry than did the Canadians at Ypres, Vimy Ridge, and at Lens, or the Australians and New Zealanders at Gallipoli.

In South Africa a revolt had been planned by the Germans with full expectation that the Boers would take the control of South Africa out of British hands. The German colonies on either side of the British South African colonies would furnish points of attack and bases of supply. An internal revolt should aid them and in a few days or at most weeks the entire south of Africa should be in German hands. To their amazement, the Boers, whom the British had defeated in the Boer War, proved loyal to Great Britain, a result of the statesmanlike work of the British after the earlier war had been won. The Boers themselves put down the revolt and in addition captured all the German colonies in South Africa.

In India, too, a tremendous conspiracy had been planned by the Germans and for a time the danger was extreme, but the British were soon satisfied that the number of people implicated was not considerable and that India was loyal. They were right. Hindu troops went to France with great enthusiasm, where they acquitted themselves with great bravery. The white British troops were withdrawn for service in France and the guardianship of India itself intrusted to Hindus. Yet throughout the war every conspiracy launched by the Germans failed. India remained not merely loyal but aided the prosecution of the war in every way possible.

One of the reasons why the Germans began the war was the belief that the British Empire was so weak and disloyal that it could not resist assault. One of the reasons why the Germans were defeated in the war was the loyalty and strength of the British

Empire. The Germans were sure that the war would create a new Empire surpassing in extent and power any of the old Empires. They were right; the war has created a new British Empire, stronger, more unified than ever before, a real state whose importance in times to come will be incalculable.

How the Germans Made War

When the long gray-green column of German troops approached Brussels, with bands playing and flags flying, they entered the city with the famous goose-step, as if on parade. Their object was to impress the Belgians with the discipline and strength of the German army. But as they proceeded down the gay streets in the beautiful sunshine, the Belgians saw, strapped to the stirrups of two cavalry men, two Belgian officers, their arms bound behind them, their hands handcuffed and chained, dragged hither and thither as the horses jumped and stamped. It was in this way that the conquerors of old, in Egypt, in Greece, and in Rome, in the days when there were *really* barbarians, used to lead their captives in triumphal procession. Here was Belgium, in chains, dragged at the stirrup of her conqueror!

On the street-curbing in the main square of Brussels stood a lame hawker with a tray of flowers which it was his custom to sell to the passers-by. In his eagerness to make sales on this day, when there were so many in the streets, he stepped from the curb into the street and offered a flower to an officer riding by on horseback. Without changing a muscle in his face, the officer spurred his horse and rode over him, pitching the poor lame man into the gutter and scattering his flowers over the street. "Let no Belgian so much as lift his hand towards a German soldier!" was the lesson which the Germans meant the Belgian nation to learn.

Another incident showing how the Germans made war occurred

in the triumphal entry of the long column into Antwerp. On they came, toiling infantry, clattering cavalry, rumbling artillery, regiments, divisions, one after another for hours at a time; and, in the rear of more than one division, came a great carriage, stolen from some Belgian, drawn by splendid horses, and filled, not with officers, nor yet with guns, but with bottles of champagne and violins! The Germans were conquerors,—and should they not feast? They were victors,—should they not drink and be merry? The Belgians should know that they were to celebrate the conquest of Belgium.

Let us follow the German army in its march upon Paris. They came to the little village of Aershot; they found thirty Belgian soldiers there; they led them out of the town and, without trial or investigation, shot them. Those who were not killed outright were kicked to death or brained with the butts of the soldiers' rifles. In the public square, while the Germans were completing their arrangements for the occupation of the town, a shot was heard. Immediately the Germans fell into a panic and began to shoot at random into the various houses. Then, by order of the officers, all the people who could be found were brought out of the houses into the streets; every third person in the line was taken out, marched beyond the village, and shot. The remainder were compelled to dig a ditch to bury the bodies. One hundred and fifty were killed; nearly four hundred houses were burned. The Germans marched out, eventually, over pavements spattered with blood and littered with broken wine bottles.

Here is a description of an action against the French, written by a German officer: "By leaps and bounds we got across the clearing. They were here, there, and everywhere, hidden in the thicket. Now it is down with the enemy! and we will give them no quarter.... We knock down or bayonet the wounded, for we know that those scoundrels fire at our backs when we have gone by. There was a Frenchman there stretched out, full length, face down, pretending to be dead. A kick from a strong fusilier soon taught him that we were there. Turning round he asked for quarter, but we answered:

'Is that the way your tools work, you—,' and he was nailed to the ground. Close to me I heard odd, cracking sounds. They were blows from a gun on the bald head of a Frenchman which a private of the 154th was dealing out vigorously; he was wisely using a French gun so as not to break his own. Tender-hearted souls are so kind to the French wounded that they finish them with a bullet, but others give them as many thrusts and blows as they can."

The Germans came to the wonderful city of Louvain. Beautiful old wooden houses lined its streets, in its great square stood a wonderful construction, the Town Hall, built by the magic of deft hands in the Middle Ages. There was a University, famed for the beauty of its buildings, for the learning of its professors, the splendor of its library. The Germans entered and took possession. Not long after, in some way,—the Belgians say by the carelessness of some German soldier,—a gun was discharged. At once the cry arose, "The Belgians are shooting, they are firing on Germans"; and, as usual in such cases, the German troops in the city fell into a terrible panic. Machine guns were placed so as to rake the streets, and every one who ventured out of the houses was shot down.

It was evening, and presently a red glare and a great volume of smoke showed that the Germans had fired the town. Doors were broken in with the butts of rifles, the people dragged into the street, and shot. One old man captured by a German was being conducted as prisoner and could not run fast enough to suit his captor. Prodded on with the sharp bayonet, presently he stumbled and fell; without hesitating, the soldier ran his bayonet through the body and hurried on, leaving him lying in a pool of blood. In some cases, the people were thrust back by the German soldiers into their own burning houses, from which they were seeking to escape.

Presently, their first panic of fear over, the soldiers began to loot the homes, hunting everywhere for wine, and becoming, of course, extremely drunk. They decked themselves in women's clothes, in curtains torn from the windows, in table-covers snatched from parlor tables. When some band of these drunken men would approach

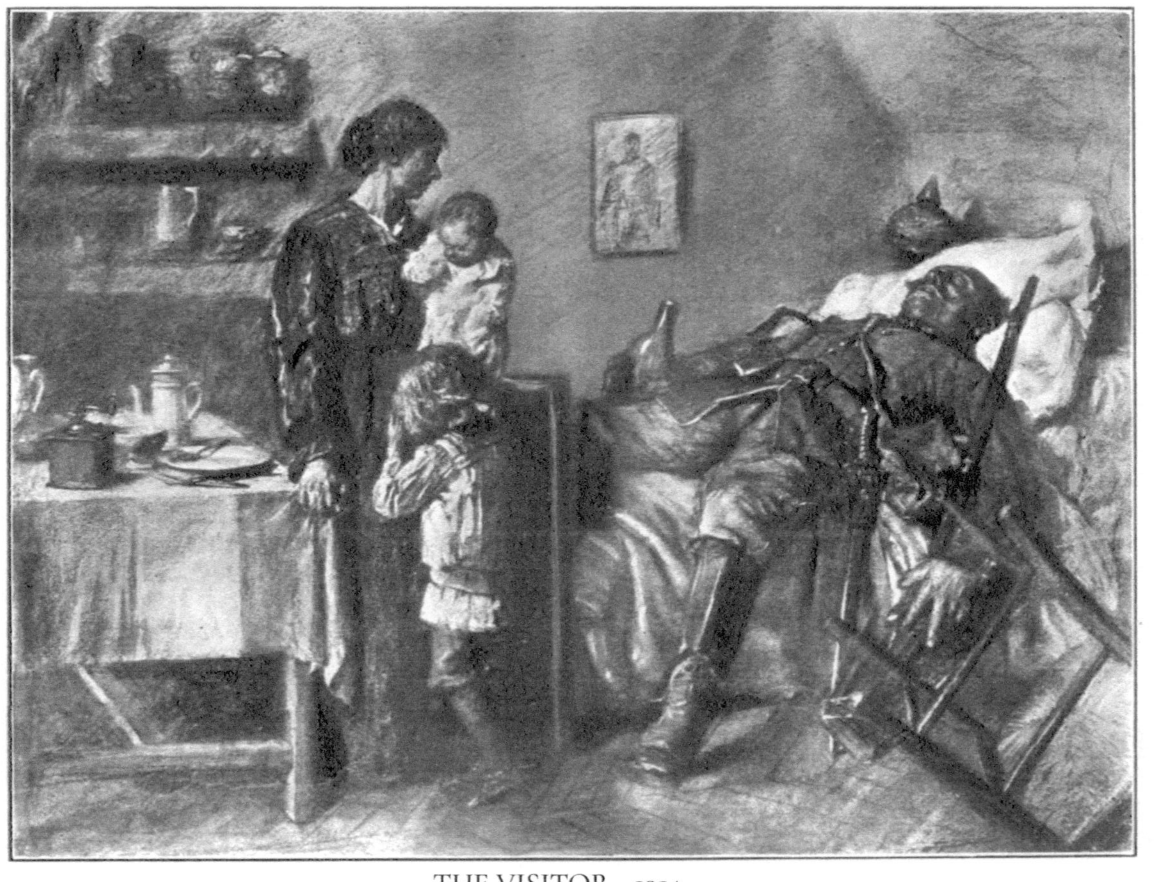

THE VISITOR—1914.

the house of some wealthy Belgian, which had not yet been sacked, one would call out, "There was firing from here," and they would all then burst out into tremendous guffaws of drunken laughter. The officers stood on the street corners, roared with laughter at this splendid joke, and calmly watched the men tear the house to pieces and pitch the property of the Belgians into the street.

In many cases, the Belgians with whom the Germans were offended were packed on cattle trucks or open flat-cars as close as they could stand and shipped into Germany. They were given no food and no water, had no chance to sleep, and, if they made the slightest complaint, were likely to be shot or bayoneted. As they passed through German towns, the train would be drawn up in the railroad station to allow the German women and children the pleasing spectacle of the Belgians who had resisted the Germans and who had been consequently punished for it. The women reviled them, called them bad names, cursed them, and very often spat in their faces. One Belgian priest, a remarkably holy man, was repeatedly slapped and buffeted.

The German officers were quartered during the nights in the finest houses of the Belgians, and later of the French, dining in the evening in the most splendid rooms of these houses, many of which were historic buildings occupied in the past by princes and even by kings. Their furniture was a priceless relic of past civilization, and the ornaments and tableware were heirlooms. Almost invariably after the dinner was over, the German officers became drunk, broke all the mirrors and windows by throwing bottles around; stamped the seats out of the chairs, cut the curtains to ribbons with their swords, and broke the crockery on the table. That the owner should have no doubt that it was done intentionally, the pile of fragments was neatly collected at each man's place; the lighted end of his cigar was allowed to burn holes through the table-cloth into the mahogany beneath, and the officer's visiting card was placed on top of the broken china.

This was "The Day" which the Germans had so often toasted.

This was their method of celebrating its arrival. The greatest gener-als—and even the Crown Prince himself were not above this sort of practice, and each commonly sent off every morning to Germany a great wagonload of pictures, statuary, and china which they coveted and therefore did not allow the officers to smash. Again, that there might be no doubt as to the purpose of this vandalism, the general wrote his name on the wall on the spot which the picture had covered.

It is not difficult to understand the looting of the homes of the wealthy, filled with precious heirlooms, but it is hard to see why the German troops should have looted so many of the little school-houses in Belgium and France. What pleasure did they receive from smashing the wooden desks at which children of six and eight had been sitting, of breaking the flower pots in the windows, tearing the blackboards from the wall, pouring ink over the books, and scattering the chalk on the floor and tramping on it? That was no mere purposeless raging, nor a readiness and desire to destroy. They meant to leave nothing behind that would be useful.

There were thousands of such incidents; hundreds of towns burned to the ground; thousands of people slain in cold blood or tortured to death. Hundreds of women killed without reason; hundreds of little children destroyed for, so far as we can see, the offense of getting in the way of some German soldier. Did you ever see a dog killing a kitten? It was so that the German army dealt with Belgium and northern France.

There was, in France, a great city in which stood one of the most wonderful of the great cathedrals, built during the Middle Ages with a skill which men no longer possess. The Cathedral at Rheims was one of the most remarkable of its kind. It had been the scene of the coronation of many French kings. There Joan of Arc knelt before her king whom she had at last crowned. There his successors had been anointed. Hardly a detail of the great building but was admitted by architects to be extraordinary. It was one of the greatest legacies of the past.

After the trench line had been established, the great Cathedral stood in sight of the German lines and within range of their guns. They declared that they saw French artillery officers, with their glasses, on the towers of the Cathedral, using it as a station from which to direct the fire of the French guns. To the Germans, this justified the destruction of the great building by shell fire. There were no French officers on the Cathedral. The greatest care was exercised by the French because they were particularly anxious not to give the Germans any excuse for injuring it. Certainly, after the first two or three bombardments, even the Germans must have known that the French were not using it, and yet shell after shell was thrown into the great building, until it was set on fire, the magnificent wooden roof burned, the windows destroyed, statues demolished, much of the delicate stonework thrown to the ground, and nothing more than a mere skeleton left to show the frightfulness of German methods.

On the first day of the bombardment of the city, when it was not yet clear that the Germans would fire on the Cathedral, the French carried into the building a great number of wounded German soldiers whom they wished to shield from the frenzy of the mob of French citizens who wished to take vengeance upon them for the sort of deeds just described. The mob was about to attack the French soldiers defending the church when the German shells began to fall upon it. Above the crash of the roof, the broken glass, the fall of statues, and the distant thunder of the German artillery, came suddenly the voice of a French priest standing on the steps of the building. "Stop," he said to the mob; "remember the ancient ways and chivalry of France! It is not Frenchmen who trample on the maimed and fallen foe! Let us not descend to the level of our enemies."

The French were different from the Germans. They did not burst into the Cathedral and slay the German wounded; they could not do to the Germans what had been done to their own loved ones. Most of the wounded Germans were carried amidst the flying stone and fragments of shell from the burning building to a place of safety, but a good many of them were slain, while they lay on the floor, by the falling stones and by the German shells. And there is to-day upon the pavement of that great church, and there will be as long as the ruins stand for men to see, a great dark stain—the burnt blood of the German wounded, slain by the barbarism of their own countrymen who fired upon the church to which these wounded had been taken as a place certainly safe. That great splotch will remain to subsequent generations as a stain upon German honor that will not be washed out, a permanent reminder of the way in which the Germans made war.

But it must not be supposed for a moment that such deeds as these were isolated instances or due merely to drunken soldiers. They were the execution of a set policy. It is that which makes them so frightful. They were systematically committed by the men under the orders of the officers. They were repeatedly done at the suggestion of the officers, though without their orders; constantly done before officers who made no attempt to stop them. The dreadful purpose of these atrocities was to terrify the French and Belgian people so that neither would dare to continue the war against Germany. The French government published after the armistice a letter written by the Kaiser, William II, with his own hand to his ally, the Emperor of Austria, early in August, 1914. "My soul is rent, but everything must be put to fire and sword, the men and women, old people and children slain, nothing must be left standing, neither houses nor trees. With such methods of terrorism, the only means of striking at a race as degenerate as the French people are, the war will finish in two months or earlier, whereas, if I consider humanitarian principles, it may drag on for many years. In spite of my repugnance, I have therefore been compelled to adopt the former system, which will, notwithstanding appearances, prevent such bloodshed..."

When it became clear that the French would not thus be frightened, the atrocities were continued to terrify the majority of people in Belgium and in northern France into working for the Germans. They could till the ground and raise food for German soldiers. They could work in factories and make things German soldiers needed. They could be sent to Germany and work in the fields and factories there. They must help the Germans carry on the war. They refused. They preferred to die.

A third purpose, more terrible than either of these, was the German intention to kill so many Belgians, French, and Poles in Poland, where this same terrorism was used, that the Belgian and Polish nations would be destroyed, and the French so weakened that when the war was over no resistance to Germany would ever be possible. There is no doubt of these facts; we have the German War manuals describing this and positively ordering it. We have the original orders of the German generals; we know from witnesses that the officers carried them out; we have diaries found upon dead

A BIT OF TESTIMONY ABOUT PUBLIC OPINION IN GERMANY UPON ATROCITIES. AN "ARTISTIC" TOY PREPARED FOR CHILDREN! "THE BOMBARDED VILLAGE."

German soldiers on the battlefield, telling why they committed such deeds. These methods of making war were adopted by the Germans consciously; they were not the disorderly conduct of a few men of whom their officers had lost control.

If it had not been for the immediate assistance of the American people, organized by Herbert Hoover through the American Committee for the Relief of Belgium, for the work of the American Red Cross and other organizations in northern France, for the most part within the German lines, it is probable that there would to-day be few left of the Belgian people. When these dreadful facts became clear at the outset of the war, the American nation demanded the privilege of saving the Belgians, and the Germans, bad as they were, could not in decency refuse, although they did what they could to obstruct the work of the Committee. America fed Belgium through the war; it clothed the Belgians; and of that fact we have every right to be proud. In a sense, it made the United States a participant in the war from the beginning.

Sea-Power and the Blockade

One of the most significant events at the very opening of the war was one of the quietest and least known. The British Grand Fleet was collected in the waters of the North Sea in anticipation of trouble, not so much because the British wished to fight as because they knew that part of the German plans involved a dash upon England. Each captain had in his possession a sealed envelope of orders, to be opened only after receipt of a certain signal. When it became clear that the war was a fact, the Admiralty sent out several hundred messages by wire to various ships, each of them consisting of a single word, "GO"; within an hour the exact number of replies came back, "GONE." No greater promptitude of action was displayed during the war. No more extraordinary case is known in history.

Sea-power had in past wars proved the decisive factor. Napoleon was defeated by the British navy; sea-power decided the American Civil War; and it was clear that the influence of sea-power in this war might also be decisive. As a matter of fact, it was. The British navy silently, quickly, without fighting a major battle, in a sense won the war.

The war was really won by a good many factors, not one of which could have been omitted. Thus, the Belgians in their first resistance saved France and therefore won the war; the French in the battle of the Marne threw back the Germans and decided the issue of the war; at the same time the Russians, by sacrificing their army in Poland, compelled the Germans to send troops east, and this allowed the French to win the battle of the Marne. The coming of the British army and of the American army were both events without which the war could not have been won; but, in a real sense, all of these must have failed but for the blockade established by the British fleet.

The great weakness in the German position, the very thing the Germans were fighting the war to correct, was their lack of raw materials necessary for German industry in peace or war. Nor could they collect in time of peace a sufficient store of cotton, wool, rubber, and copper without advertising their intention to fight a war. Some months' supply they might have on hand when the war broke out, but not more. A time would come, therefore, when it would be extremely difficult for them to get along without new supplies or without changing entirely their whole basis of living. They knew that if the British joined the war they would at once blockade Germany and stop the stream of supplies from outside.

It meant a complete transformation of German industry. Everything in Germany would have to support the war, because Germany would have to make everything she needed. Nothing should be made that the Germans could not themselves use, for otherwise it could not be sold and would therefore become waste. Substitutes they thought they could find for some things; enough supplies of others they thought they could smuggle through the British blockade with the help of the Dutch, the Danes, and the Swedes, who could claim rights, as neutral countries, to import such things for their own use, and who would then of course ship them to Germany. At any rate, the Germans thought their army would win the war before this economic pressure created by the sea-power could cripple them enough to bring the war to an end, They might have to get along without some things, eat food they did not particularly like, but there would be enough to eat and to wear and to fight with, and the end would be glorious. The British should be made to pay when the war was over.

The Germans thought it possible, however, that they might forestall the blockade. Their own fleet should slip out before the British fleet sailed, and once on the open ocean it could give the British a chase—perhaps meet and defeat them. It would get its food and coal from the United States and other neutral countries; and by dividing the British fleet prevent the blockade of Germany. Fast German ships should be also equipped to capture British merchant vessels, and they would thus reduce the stream of supplies going to England, which was no less dependent than Germany upon raw material from outside if she was to continue the war. It might be that they could in this way, by these commerce raiders, sink enough ships to make a difference.

Then there were the submarines. They should attempt to sink battleships and thus break the blockade; sink transports carrying troops across to France, steal into British harbors and sink the ships at anchor. If German ships could not sail the seas, it would then become a simple thing to loose thousands of floating mines. They would float along below the surface and, if a ship should touch one of them, it would explode and sink her. They would be carried by the tides and currents down upon the British fleet and sink it.

Everything depended for the British upon the successful work of the fleet. It must keep open the ocean so that the supplies could reach England on which the continuation of the war depended. The food of the British people, clothes for the soldiers, everything necessary for the war, depended upon the British merchant marine and the ability of the fleet to protect it against German cruisers, submarines, and mines. The whole issue of victory depended upon the adequacy of the work of the fleet.

At the outset the British were too quick for the Germans. The famous order described at the beginning of this chapter sent the British into action just in time to prevent the German escape. The German fleet was bottled up in its own ports before the war really began. There were a few German warships in Pacific and South American waters. Several German merchant ships were transformed into commerce raiders and for some months these were able to elude the vigilance of British and Japanese ships sent in pursuit. The Emden had a particularly thrilling and adventurous career.

But by Christmas of 1914 the German warships had been captured and sunk, and all commerce raiders had been rounded up. Meanwhile, the great harbors had been protected and a steel net had been erected across the mouth of the Thames River strong enough to resist submarines. This was a great engineering undertaking and its success meant much. Similar nets were created at once for the other British harbors, and one was even built practically across the Channel so as to stop mines floating down into the passage between England and France. These nets were composed of movable sections which could be opened at will. It became necessary—such was the cleverness of the Germans—to change the passage through the nets very often, because submarines would be waiting to sneak through the moment the net was opened at the former spot.

Thousands of British ships were transformed into mine-sweepers to clear the sea around the British Islands, a very dangerous and difficult work. Patrol boats to watch for submarines were sent out by dozens and then by hundreds. A screen of destroyers steamed up and down in front of the Grand Fleet practically throughout the duration of the war to ward off submarines and raiders. Week after week, month after month, the steady patrolling went on. The work of the submarine in sinking ships on the open ocean we shall have to tell about as the story goes on, but the success of the British fleet was complete. The entire British army, millions of men, was transported back and forth to France, practically without the loss of a man. Never for a moment was the army in France, or the French army (also dependent upon the British navy), without food, clothes, or ammunition, because of lack of transport. Despite the enormous number of ships sunk during the course of the war by the submarines, the British factories never stopped work, night or day, because of a failure of raw materials with which to continue.

In Germany, on the other hand, the blockade was so successful that things went from bad to worse. As the war grew longer, the measures which the Germans had originally invented to create substitutes or to reorganize industries became less and less adequate. While probably few actually died of starvation, civilians, and even soldiers, were wearing clothes and shoes made of paper, and were not getting enough fats and sweets to keep up health. The war came to an end with the German army beaten and practically in flight. It could hardly have been brought to that situation without the pressure of the blockade. The work of the British fleet was one of the most important single factors in winning the war.

A Bird's-Eye View of the War

This war was so different in character from those that preceded it that most people find it difficult to understand. They do not at first watch for the right thing. This was in particular a world-wide war. By Christmas of 1914, it was being fought in Europe, on the sea, in Africa, in the Near East, and in the Far East. There was in France a long double trench-line, six hundred miles long, every yard of it occupied by men. In Poland and all down along the Carpathians, there was a similar trench-line with Russians on one side, and Germans and Austrians on the other. Again, for a couple of hundred miles, down in the Balkans and around Constantinople were more trenches, more troops.

The British and French fleets were down in the Mediterranean, getting ready to attack Constantinople. British fleets were fighting the Germans off South America. The Japanese were helping the British capture the Germans all through the Pacific. The Turks were fighting the British around the Suez Canal and down in Mesopotamia in the district of the Bagdad railroad. Up in the North Sea, amid the fogs of Scotland, was the Grand Fleet, hundreds of vessels, constantly steaming back and forth to prevent the German fleet from getting out or other ships from getting in.

The most important thing to grasp is that the fighting was continuous on all these fronts almost from August, 1914, to the day of the Armistice on November 11, 1918. This was not so in past wars. There would be fighting here and then fighting there. There would be months, and sometimes years, when in any particular district there would be no fighting at all. Indeed, even in such long wars as those fought by Napoleon, the steady fighting was short, confined usually to a few months. A whole campaign, with all its preparations and marching, might consume only a few weeks, and the actual fighting between the armies be only a few days during the whole period.

But in this war the fighting never stopped anywhere, night or day. Over every foot of the hundreds of miles in France, for four years or more, there was never a moment's real interruption. The fighting became simply more or less intense. Instead of sending over an occasional shell every little while to make sure that the enemy did not go to sleep, they might send over hundreds or thousands of shells within an hour, but the firing never wholly stopped. We have therefore not one story to tell, but half a dozen continuous stories to follow.

The firing was moreover *simultaneous* on all these fronts all the time. While we are describing what goes on in France, something was at that same moment happening in Poland, very often of even more importance. Something else was taking place in Italy; other things in the Balkans, in Asia Minor, in the North Sea with the Grand Fleet. Every one of them may have had a vast influence on the history of the war and its outcome. It is impossible to tell about them all at the same time, but we must not forget that important things are happening in several places at once. This is particularly essential, because the fundamental plan of the Allies was to fight the Central Powers on all fronts, at the same time, for long periods. The Allies had more men than the Central Powers and they expected thus to wear them down by what General Joffre called "nibbling." Very often the main point of the campaign was not merely an attack in one place, still less the fact that there was an attack in any place, but a simultaneous attack in France, in Poland, and in Italy.

The real trouble with understanding the war is this manifold character. "It" is multifold. There were really hundreds of wars, all of them as big as any of the past conflicts, hundreds of heroes, hundreds of experiences. The war cannot in any true sense be described. It was too big to see, in a sense too big to be understood. There was too much in it to be told in a single volume. Besides, we need to know at once everything that went on everywhere, and it is impossible to describe more than one thing at a time.

The bigness of the war was appalling. Here in Flanders were men making trenches in the mud, piling up sandbags, building timber walls to keep back the mud and to keep out the water; up to their waists in water, much of the time. Then there were men on the hills of the Aisne, where they had solid ground under their feet, and could make trenches with concrete some thirty feet and more deep in the ground. Up in the Vosges and in the Alps were men fighting in the mountains, with deep precipices in front of them and high mountain crags behind them, compelled to climb about like goats in order to reach such positions at all. They must drag great cannon up the mountain sides, and often have ammunition and food sent up on cables or elevators. Down in the sand about the Suez Canal were men fighting in the heat. Up in the ice around Archangel at the same minute would be men fighting in the cold. The ice in the harbor was broken daily with dynamite in order that ships might get in, at the same time that men were shivering in the mud of Flanders, stamping their feet in the snows of the Alps, and suffering with thirst in the heat and sand of the desert. Negroes in Central Africa, Hindus in India, the Japs in China, were also fighting the war.

Throughout the world, far from battle fronts, were millions of people also fighting the war. Some were raising beef and chickens, others were planting wheat, making automobiles, or weaving cloth. All were essential to keep the war going and were also as important, though in a different way, as the continual fighting in the trenches. Indeed, the people in France who baked the bread in bakehouses where a million loaves were turned out in a day; the women who sat hour after hour sewing sandbags, thousands of which might be needed at any moment to repair some trench broken by a German shell; or the men and women engaged in making shoes for the armies; all of these were in a strict sense fighting.

That is a new idea to most people, for certainly such occupations would have not been considered fighting in past wars. Even mending shoes—millions of them—was a part of the business of war, just as the selling of bonds, the buying of thrift stamps by children, subscriptions to the red Cross, the making of bandages. The world worked like a beaver. Every man, woman, and child for over four years did something which played its part in fighting the war on one side or the other. A moment's thought will show how impossible it is that any one mind should ever be able to see all that happened in detail, or that any one book could ever say more than that the stupendous affair took place.

The real fascination of the war for most people who fought in it was due to this very sense of bigness. It was a greater game than had ever been played before in the world. There had never been so many millions of men all trying to do the same thing at the same time. It had never been so important that no one of these millions should fail to do his task in the proper way. Over hundreds of miles of trenches, everyone must be alert. Battles lasted months. Single incidents consumed a week.

The dramatic quality of the old wars came from the individual exploits. There are few who do not thrill to read of Richard, the Lionhearted, clad in full armor, spurring his charger into the midst of the Saracens. Joan of Arc, dashing forward on horseback at the head of the charge, or Henry of Navarre, with a white plume in his helmet so that his men might see how far ahead of them in the press of the enemy the king was, are figures which kindle one's imagination. Their exploits were frequently the important fact of the battle. All was being lost, when some one individual, like the king, would do something which made the difference between victory and defeat. It became therefore the essential thing in the battle to describe.

But thousands of men in the present war have done things which required a great deal more courage than any of these exploits of the past because they incurred a much greater risk of death; but they do not sound so dramatic when described and really did not affect the issue of the battle as a whole, and therefore did not affect the outcome of the war. In this war no incidents or personal exploits form an important part of its history. The real conflict took place in movements so big that the individual was lost and his exploits were not even incidents. One hundred thousand men were very often concerned in a movement occupying perhaps a week's time, which will appear eventually in history as a very minor incident of a battle consuming months of time. We are indeed to watch charges made by a million men, more magnificent by a thousand times than the old charges of a few thousand, but too big for the mind to grasp, for the eye to see, or for the historian to describe, so that an ordinary imagination, which works in terms of individuals, can take it in at all. The campaigns of this war were in reality many times more exciting than those of past wars, but there were so many men concerned in them that they lose their personal appeal.

At the same time, the history of the war is very simple and not at all difficult to understand. There is really no more to describe in the movement of the armies in its whole four years, in France certainly, than Napoleon frequently accomplished in six weeks. In the American Revolution, Washington's armies were moving constantly, and five thousand men in the course of a single year gave the historian more to describe which is intelligible to the reader than the whole of the last four years in France. Battles then were battles of movement. Napoleon would march so many miles; meet some army; a battle would take place; there would be a further shift of operations; all of which is interesting to read about.

But the war in France was like a great football game where the two elevens fell into a scrimmage in the fall of 1914, and, without ever stopping the scrimmage, pushed and pushed for four years, neither side gaining much ground or losing a great deal. If we look at the movements in France over the battlefields as a whole and over the four years as a whole, it looks very much as five minutes of a football game might look, when the teams moved back and forth across the center of the field, first one a little in the other's territory, then thrown for a loss, and presently gaining again.

The dramatic quality of the war was due for the Allies to the consciousness of its rightness. In no war in history had more been as clearly at stake. Every Frenchman, every Englishman, and most Americans felt that the whole future of the world was in jeopardy. To most of them the war was a great crusade. When the men in the trenches felt that the war was dull or dangerous, they would remember the starving Belgians, beaten and abused by the Germans, the little children slaughtered by German soldiers simply because they got in the way. They would remember the face of a child floating in the green floods of the Atlantic after the sinking of some ship by a submarine. Immediately their fear and fatigue would fall from them.

Or they would remember the Zeppelins dropping bombs upon London, killing innocent children, old men and women, or they would think of the German aim to conquer the world and compel all people to copy German methods. The war would become important, exciting, and a glorious thing. A young French soldier and art critic, a man of extraordinarily sensitive mind and hatred of bloodshed, wrote to a friend soon after he went into the war: "I have no wish to die, but I can die now without regret; for I have lived through a fortnight which would be cheap at the price of death, a fortnight which I had not dared to ask of fate. History will tell of us, for we are opening a new era in the world." "A splendid thing it is to fight with clean hands and a pure heart and defend divine justice with one's life."

The general movement of the war was so simple that it can be told in a few paragraphs, although it is so complex that perhaps the world will never understand it. There was for four years in France this deadlock of the two trench lines which shifted only a few miles one way or the other until the very end of the war. Tremendous attacks were delivered by both sides, often for months at a time, without shifting the position of the line to a perceptible degree. That was one phase of the situation. Simultaneous with it we have a succession of tremendous German victories in eastern Europe. In 1914 and 1915 Poland was conquered and the Russian army really broken. In the fall of 1915 Serbia was crushed and laid waste; in 1916, Rumania; and in 1917, Italy was invaded. In the east, in the course of four years, all was lost to the Allies. The Russians, defeated and disorganized, ceased to be a factor in the war at all; so of the Rumanians and the Serbians. The Italians were badly beaten and forced back into a dangerous position; but Italy was never crushed nor defeated, though for a time in very grave peril.

Outside Europe proper the war also went on for four years, and, although the Germans and the Turks at first seemed to have won in Mesopotamia and Asia Minor, they were at the very outset thoroughly beaten in South Africa, in Egypt, in India, and in China. Then eventually in the latter years they were beaten in Armenia and about Bagdad and Jerusalem, and at the very end of the war Constantinople would have been captured, if the Turks had not surrendered. So for the four years the Germans seemed to be able to hold their great gains at the beginning of the war in France, to pile victory upon victory in eastern Europe; but were beaten everywhere outside of Europe.

On the sea, the Germans were defeated at the outset. The few warships outside German harbors were promptly destroyed or captured; the few commerce raiders were taken by the British and Japanese; and the blockade by the British fleet was made effective. Once or twice, the German fleet ventured out for a few miles, but found the British so extremely vigilant that it scuttled back into the harbor a good deal faster than it came out. The British in the last two years of the war did their best to tempt the Germans out by sending forth small squadrons of weak ships, apparently not protected or supported, in the hope that the Germans would try to capture them. Preparations of course had been made to pounce upon the Germans with a great force if they did come out, but the Germans were too wary. Eventually, the great German fleet sailed forth and surrendered without as a whole having fired a gun or fought a battle. It was one of the most colossal demonstrations of supremacy on the sea the world has ever seen. The Germans admitted British superiority to be so great that they did not dare to try the issue in battle.

Then in 1918 the Germans made a very great attempt to break the Allied lines in France, which nearly succeeded. The Allies attacked in their own turn in July, 1918, broke the German line, followed up the German retreat so fast and won so many battles that the Germans were forced to surrender. It would almost seem as if everything which happened outside of France had not been able to affect the end of the war at all. Whatever the Germans did in eastern Europe, they could not win. The important part of the war in France seemed like one long draw of four years, and then two battles, each several months long. We must therefore watch a great many things in a great many places, but remember, for all that, the important thing is the fact that the war was continuous and that the war was simultaneous. It was fought in a great many places in the world and it was fought all the time and at the same time.

BOOK III

THE WAR IN 1915

The Campaign of 1915

The first months of the war had absolutely upset all the German calculations. Their original plans were useless. Those same months had given the Allies courage and confidence.[2] Indeed both Germans and Allies were now positive that they held the upper hand, could take the offensive with decisive effect whenever they might choose. This belief on the part of both that they could now proceed to lay their plans for the final campaign is the key to this year of the war. First we must describe the German plan because they fought the war throughout as an aggressive war.

They had failed in their design of overwhelming France before Russia should move. They were now face to face with a problem which they had always felt most difficult—a war in the west and east at the same time. Their desire was, as always in the past, to fight on one front at a time. But which should it be? Their real enemy they felt was Russia. There on the east were one hundred and eighty millions of people who would always be hostile to Germany.

2   Properly speaking, the term, "Allies," which was so commonly used during the war, included the French, British, Russians, Belgians, and Italians, all of whom were allied together against the Germans and Austro-Hungarians. The latter came to be called the Central Powers. But in practice the terms "Allies" and "Allied Armies" referred only to the French, Belgians, and British fighting in France, and included of course such other troops as were fighting there — Portuguese, a Russian division, Italians. The reason was that the Russians fought really only in the east, and the Italians in force only in the south for the greater part of the war. Similarly, it was common to speak of the "Germans" when writing of the Polish and French fronts and of the "Austrians" when writing about Italy, though there were Austrian divisions in France, Germans in Italy, and Austrians and Germans always in Poland and Galicia, and Hungarian and Slav divisions in all parts of the Austrian army.

France was already only half of Germany's size and could never be in the future dangerous. At the outset it had been desirable to crush France before meeting Russia, because the Germans had thought that France could be crushed quickly and they knew that the Russians could not. They would now therefore leave France alone, fight a defensive war in the west, and throw their strength in eastern Europe. If they could beat Russia they felt that even defeat in the west would be of no consequence. They would have gained so much that, even if they lost territory to France eventually, the war would have been worth while.

As for England, they had been developing during the long years of preparation two instruments which they believed might of themselves win the war. The one was the Zeppelin; with it they would terrify the English. For hundreds of years no hostile shots had been fired on London; for hundreds of years no enemy had crossed the English Channel, and the English had begun to believe themselves so absolutely secure that the Germans believed they would be terrified, and perhaps give up the fight, when the bombs began to fall in the London streets. On what other basis the Germans supposed the Zeppelin raids would influence the result of the war it is hard to see. They certainly could not expect to transport an army on the Zeppelins and thus invade England. Perhaps they might have hoped to destroy the fleet, but at any rate they meant the English to learn that they were no longer safe in their "snug little isle," as they loved to call it.

The other weapon was the submarine. With it English battle-ships should be sunk; English harbors raided; merchant ships captured; food and supplies sunk. The enthusiastic Germans saw the English starving and in a few weeks ready to surrender. They therefore proclaimed a war zone around the British islands which should be blockaded by German submarines and should be tra-versed by ships only at their peril. They saw now that the war must go on for a while at least. The submarine and the Zeppelin would subdue England while they held France at bay with one hand and destroyed Russia with the other.

The Allied plan of operations for 1915 assumed that the German bolt had been shot, that the German strength had been exhausted, that the German military strategy had been defeated, and that the initiative in the war had passed to the Allies. This proved not to be true and was in part responsible for the Allied failures in this year. What, they asked themselves, was the thing the Germans feared most? A simultaneous attack in Poland and in France. The Germans had always said that they would not be able to meet such an assault. Very well, said the Allied generals, let us deliver one. Let us begin it early and keep it up late. We shall not at first make much progress, but a steady pressure, compelling them to fight everywhere at once, must in the end succeed. They therefore proposed a great attack in France, a great assault by the Russians in East Prussia, and a great assault by the Italians upon the Austrian rear near Trieste, along a little river called the Isonzo, which formed the boundary between Austria and Italy. This involved inducing Italy to join the Allies, and in May, 1915, Italy did enter the war.

None of these campaigns, however, on account of the weather could be begun early in the year. There was another thing most essential to accomplish if the war was to continue. The Allies knew that, although Russia had plenty of men, she had few factories for making cannon, ammunition, and clothes, and it was clear that without adequate supplies, she could not continue the war indefinitely. There would come relatively soon a time when there would be nothing more for the Russian army to wear or to shoot with. Indeed at that moment not all the troops had rifles. But the Germans had blockaded Russia. Their fleet at Kiel bottled up the Baltic, which was the only way to reach Russia on the north unless one went as far as Archangel in the Arctic Ocean. This was tremendously far off, was frozen solid the greater part of the year, and its use compelled the Russians to haul the goods by rail for hundreds of miles before they could get them into Poland. But it was not possible to open the Baltic while the German navy existed and refused to fight.

On the south the waterways to Russia lead from the ocean into the Mediterranean and thence into the Black Sea. This was, however, blockaded by the Turks, whom the Germans had brought into the war for this purpose. Constantinople controls the mouth of the Black Sea, and is itself approached by two narrow straits, the one called the Bosphorus and the other called the Dardanelles. A ship trying to get to the Black Sea had to pass first through the Dardanelles, a very narrow rocky strait, some miles long, where swift currents made navigation difficult. It was protected on both sides by forts, mounting very large modern German guns. A ship then passed into a small sea, the Sea of Marmora, and must then go through the Bosphorus, another narrow strait, only a few miles wide, protected by the great forts at Constantinople. The British thought that the Dardanelles might probably be forced by the fleet, which carried guns fully as large as those in the Turkish batteries. They might thus open a waterway to Russia and be able to supply Russia with the guns, ammunition, and clothes that she needed so badly, and would be able themselves to get from Russia what they also needed, wheat and petroleum.

There was another purpose. Austria was the most vulnerable of the Central Powers and on the south could be easily attacked. Her southern boundary was occupied by the Balkan States, as they are called, and at this particular time, the three important states, Bulgaria, Greece, and Rumania, were still neutral and were very obviously waiting to see whether the Central Empires or the Allies were more likely to win. Nobody doubted that they proposed to join the victor, if they could only find out which side would win. If now the Allies could defeat Turkey and open the Dardanelles, they thought the Balkan nations would all join them. A French and British army would then be able to attack Austria from the mountains with complete success and so end the war. There were

GERMAN SKETCH OF GREAT ENGLISH AND FRENCH NIGHT BOMBARDMENT AT SENUC, SEPTEMBER 22-23, 1915.

a great many in London and in Paris who felt this was the only way the war could be won.

If the Balkans should join Germany and the Allies should have to fight their way through the mountains, the majority felt such a campaign was impossible. It would cost too much and take too long. The Germans would probably win in France while the Allies were getting through the mountains. A great deal therefore depended upon the attack upon the Dardanelles. If it succeeded, the Allies might win the war in 1915. If it failed, the war might go on indefinitely. But if the Dardanelles were opened, if the Russians and the French should attack simultaneously, and if Italy entered the war, the Allies thought it possible that they might reach Berlin during the summer, but certainly would celebrate Christmas there.

It is possible to tell much more briefly what the results of the year's fighting were and it is essential to see them in this brief way, if they are to be understood. The Germans opened the year with Zeppelin raids on England, which failed absolutely to do anything except stimulate British recruiting. By this time the British had undertaken to create an army of several million men. The submarine also began its operations, and with some effect. The great attack delivered by the British and French fleets in February and March on the Dardanelles failed. Then, in that same month, the British and French delivered great assaults in France, which the Germans, in accordance with their plans, merely tried to defeat and in which they were successful. The Germans themselves in April began a tremendous campaign in Poland, and another in Galicia in May and June, all of which were so successful that on August 4, the Kaiser entered Warsaw in triumph. Poland was conquered, the Russians crushed.

Meanwhile, Italy had entered the war at the end of May and had delivered an assault upon the Austrians at Trieste; but this, too, failed. Bulgaria now, in the autumn, joined the Germans. Having succeeded so well, the Germans and Austrians felt that they could take a little time to complete the conquest of Serbia and occupy territory so essential to the control of the great railroad from Berlin to Bagdad. They attempted to exterminate the Serbian nation. Their object was to leave behind a body of people too small to hope in the future ever to oppose their designs. Greece was kept from joining the Germans only by the landing of an Anglo-French army at Saloniki. So ended the campaign of 1915. The cause of the Allies looked more hopeless than before and victory farther away on the horizon.

The Character of Modern Warfare

The reason why the Allies failed in 1915 was the extremely complex character of the new warfare. They at first did not understand it, partly because it was new and partly because it was so complicated that it took time to analyze it. What the Germans had needed thirty years and more to think out, it was not to be expected the Allies would understand in a few months. What the Germans needed thirty years to get ready to do, the Allies could not prepare to duplicate in six months. That is the chief reason why the war lasted four years. The Allies had to fight under the new conditions. They were able at once to prevent the Germans from winning, but how to win themselves was not a thing so easy to learn. In fact, it was not until 1918 that they worked out a successful technique for the offensive. Much of the history of the war therefore is a story of experiment, of experience, of relative success, and relative failure. There are new methods and new weapons. The Germans invent one, and the Allies neutralize it. The Allies create one, and the Germans offset it.

This was the first great war fought with the new weapons which science had provided. The Russo-Japanese War had, to be sure, tried them out somewhat and the Boer War had shown some things, but in the main the result upon warfare of the new artillery and the new rifle was not fully appreciated even by the Germans. One

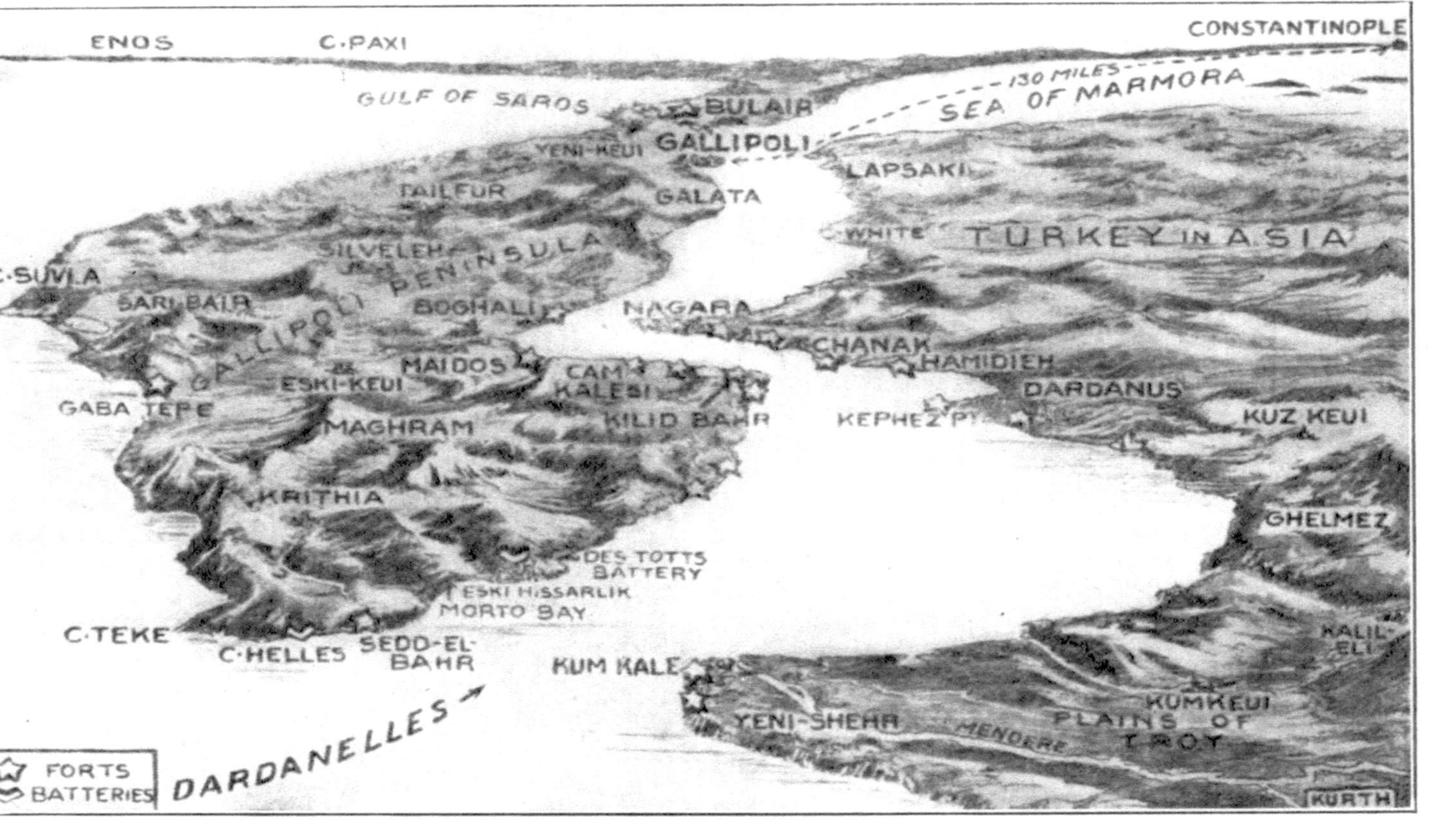

THE GALLIPOLI PENINSULA.

of the discoveries was shrapnel. This was a shell, thrown from a short-range gun—and a gun firing no more than three miles was short-ranged—timed to burst in the air and scatter over a wide area a great number of bullets or jagged fragments of iron. Flesh and blood could not resist it.

One of the great German surprises was the high explosive shell loaded with one of the super-powders or super-dynamites. The explosion was so tremendous that one shell falling upon a regiment would annihilate it; landing upon a trench it would simply wipe it out. Houses crumbled like cardboard and the most elaborate steel forts in Europe were turned upside down. There was only one way to meet that kind of shell and that was to keep out of the way. Then there was the machine gun, sending forth a stream of bullets, covering a wide area as fast as a man could turn a crank. The bullets were deadly and the stream was continuous.

The new cannon projected these shells and bullets astonishing distances. Rifles hitting at more than a mile were common; shrapnel was effective at great distances; and high-explosive shells could be shot with accuracy from five to ten miles. Eventually the large guns threw projectiles twenty miles or more, and one German freak cannon hit Paris from a distance of over seventy miles.

The result was that fighting in the open simply came to an end. Men in the open would positively be killed. A body of troops advancing across a field miles away from the German lines could be wiped out by high-explosive shells, if they were seen from a German aëroplane or balloon. Once they came within eyesight of the German batteries shrapnel could annihilate them, and long before they could get near enough to take a German trench, the machine guns could kill them all. They could not escape the three. At the end of the battle of the Marne, both armies were digging furiously to get into the ground out of sight. Nothing but Mother Earth could protect them from the new artillery. There came to be, therefore, in France, and to some extent in eastern Europe, nothing but a trench line from the mountains to the sea, in which

FRENCH OBSERVATION BALLOON. NOTE TRANSPORT WAGONS, HORSE LINES, CEMETERY, ETC. THE PICTURE GIVES MULTIFOLD DETAILS ABOUT THE AREA BEHIND THE LINES.

both armies burrowed like moles in a desperate anxiety to get as far out of sight as quickly as possible.

It may be interesting to give a typical description of an approach upon the battle line from the open country at the rear. The first thing we come to is the army of supply which supports and keeps alive the army in the trenches. It is a city of huts and horse tents something like a mammoth circus. Passing through long stretches of it we come to the supply lines. Here we find the roads filled with motors, carrying all sorts of things, and small railroads, with little dummy trains puffing back and forth on tracks running out here and there like veins in the landscape.

Far away on the horizon, miles away, is a ridge with a row of charred trees, standing out gloomily etched against the sky. That is the battle line. We do not hear anything, but we see some fleecy balls of smoke. Those are the exploding shells. Suddenly from above comes a roar of noise and we see an aëroplane, or perhaps half a dozen of them, starting out for a trip across the lines or coming back from one. Up in the air out in front of us are floating around a number of fat sausages. They are observation balloons, in each one of which is a man with a glass trying to see where the German batteries are.

On we go an interminable distance, several miles perhaps, and we come presently to a plain which was once a wood. A battle was fought here some time ago. The trees have all been mowed down as if by some giant scythe or tremendous mowing machine; here and there a solitary tree trunk, which somehow was missed, sticks out of the ground: Presently we come to a sort of slit in the ground and begin walking downhill. Now the surface of the ground is up to our knees, presently it is up to our waist, and pretty soon over our heads.

We do not march straight forward, because the trench is not straight. It curves and zigzags and goes round sharp corners until we are dizzy and have lost all sense of the way in which we are going. That is so that a machine gun of the enemy would not be able to fire the whole length of the trench, in case they should happen to get in front of it. It also protects the people walking along the trench from the tons of chance bullets which the Germans and Allies were both continually shooting at each other in the hope that one of them might kill a man. Nothing but large masses of Mother Earth stops bullets.

We come presently to a line of trenches that runs at right angles with the one we have come through. These are the support trenches and there are sometimes several lines of them. We proceed from one of these lines to another, all of them more or less parallel, by means of communication trenches which zigzag back and forth from one to the other. No one sticks his head above ground if he can help it. He would be likely to lose it.

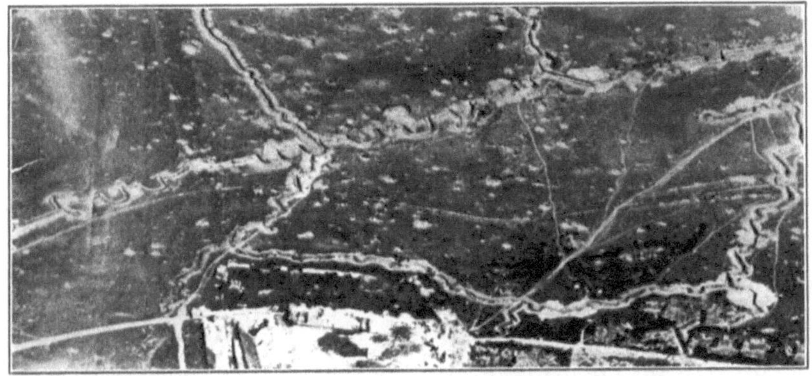

AEROPLANE PICTURE OF GERMAN TRENCH
LINES AT MALMAISON, DECEMBER 1917.

The front trenches are like the others, except that they are worse. Every once in a while a German shell blows out a section of them. In front of these a mound of earth has been thrown up or sand bags have been piled to make a sort of low parapet. Through cracks in this a soldier looks out to see if the enemy is coming, or he uses a periscope, exactly the same as the submarine uses. It is really an arrangement of mirrors, and is intended to allow one to look around a corner or over a wall. Looking through the periscope we see outside in front, a few yards away, a series of barbed wire fences. They are Allied entanglements to stop or delay a German charge. Some further distance off, in some places a long distance, in others only a hundred or two hundred yards, are other fences. Those are the German wire fences. The ground in between looks as if it had been stirred with some giant egg beater and churned up into mud. It is pitted all over with enormous holes where the high explosive shells have struck.

There in these trenches in the ground, looking through periscopes, sit the Allied soldiers, watching another series of holes where the Germans are sitting. A certain amount of shooting is going on all the time and the humming of rifle bullets and the scream of shells is constant. Then will come a great scream, announcing the arrival of a big shell. All the noise in the world seems concentrated on that spot and the earth shoots up like corn popping in a pan.

At night the trench line looks like a continual display of fire-works. Darkness is the most useful thing in modern warfare because at night it is more difficult to see people. Then the soldiers come out and repair the barbed wire, mend trenches, and go back and forth to the rear without much danger. In the day-time even an automobile moving along a road so far away that the cannonade sounds like little more than a rumble is in danger of being hit. To prevent the enemy from rushing, the trenches both sides keep sending up lights called star shells. Little balloons also are sent up carrying lights which float around and burn a long time. Some of these are so very brilliant that they light up whole sections of the line almost like daylight. When the artillery fires at night, the flashes make a magnificent spectacle. In the day-time trench warfare is not very picturesque; at night it is magnificent.

This was all the result of the necessity of getting out of sight and it at once transformed warfare. The old battle had been one of movement. One formation of troops marched against another. One general tried to get his army on the flank or in the rear of the other general's, and it was always possible because there was plenty of open ground to move over. But the number of troops engaged in the present war was so enormous that they spread out over miles of ground. The German invasion advancing into France was over one hundred miles broad, and when that number of men began to dig into the ground to get hidden, it took an extraordinary number of miles of trenches to hide them. The battle line started in half as wide as France and presently was continued all the way to the sea.

Movement in the old sense became impossible: there were only two ways to move. One was forward and the other was back, and both sides only wished to go forward. This meant that the only possible attack was a direct frontal attack upon prepared positions. The only thing either side could do was to charge straight at the other and attack the enemy exactly where he was expecting to be hit, exactly where he had concentrated his guns, was ready to do the most damage, and receive the least injury.

The Germans at first believed (as the Allies also did) that, if only enough men were sent out to rush the enemy trenches, they could capture them. It would cost a good many lives but it could be done. But presently the idea had to be given up. There were too many ways of checking the charge long enough to kill every man who started. The big guns could begin with the charge when it first left cover a long distance away, the shrapnel could continue the work as they came nearer, and then the machine guns could open up. The barbed wire would effectively prevent their getting at the front trenches until they had been riddled with bullets. Hand grenades, or small bombs thrown by hand, could be tossed out into the advancing troops by the defenders and would kill numbers of men. Then mines could be laid out in front of the trenches and exploded by electricity when a whole regiment of the foe was standing on them. Flesh and blood could not overcome such resistance. Some other method of attack had to be found.

Spreading the men out on the field instead of allowing them to advance shoulder to shoulder was promptly tried. The difficulty here was that more men got through out of those who started, but that not so many could start, and the weight of the charge was likely to be lost. It is just the same problem as that of a football eleven which spreads out five feet apart and then runs at its opponents. The men cannot go so far as when massed together.

Then the accuracy of the artillery fire became so great as the first months passed that a sort of attack which was very successful at the beginning of the war was destroyed before it had gone a hundred yards after the war was a year old. The shrapnel fire became absolutely accurate, the machine gun fire sure death to anything within range, and even the big guns, miles away, soon were able to hit a moving object with great frequency. It was difficult to get out of the trenches without being annihilated; it was almost as perilous to stay in them. Both sides experienced the same trouble.

It was clear that the decisive factor in the new warfare was the artillery and that the large artillery played the most important part. It was absolutely imperative to defend the Allied trenches from the German artillery by keeping it back out of range. The big Allied guns must be sufficiently prompt and accurate to wipe out all small German guns which were likely to fire upon the infantry at short range. They would never be able entirely to clear them out, but unless they demolished a considerable number, the Allied trenches could not be held. Of course, small guns of all sorts and kinds could be kept, and soon were, within the battle area by both sides, provided they did not reveal themselves to the foe by firing. This came gradually to be the rule: guns within range of the enemy's big artillery must be thoroughly concealed or must keep quiet until an infantry attack should take place. Then the enemy's large guns must stop firing to allow his own infantry to move into that area.

On the offensive, the artillery was absolutely the essential factor. It must first accurately blow out of the ground the barbed wire entanglements of the enemy. Otherwise the Allied troops would be held up and killed. It must also destroy the bulk of the machine guns and small artillery within the entire area the Allied troops were to attack. If it did not succeed, they were absolutely certain to be killed. If the artillery did its work properly, the infantry could then move forward and occupy as much territory as the artillery could "prepare," as the phrase went. It was demonstrated early in 1915 that it was perfectly easy to destroy any section of the enemy front line by artillery fire and then occupy it at some cost of life so long as the infantry kept within the protection of their own artillery.

It was merely a question of the amount of ammunition which had to be fired in order to destroy the enemy defenses. To be sure, that amount turned out to be extraordinarily large, but the real cost of taking the other lines was ammunition, not lives. But if enough ammunition was not spent, the price in lives was sickening. Even after proper artillery "preparation" it was not at first possible for the infantry to go forward more than a few hundred yards. Every step they advanced beyond a certain short range, they were leaving their own guns behind and running into the range of the German artillery which their own guns had not yet been able to destroy.

INTERIOR VIEW OF FRENCH CONCRETE MACHINE GUN NEST.

It was soon clear that the artillery could not move forward as fast as the infantry did, but it was also clear that the infantry would be exterminated the moment they went faster than the artillery. It was easy to go a short distance, but not particularly worth while. Days and months were necessary by this method to move into the enemy's defense for a few miles, and the trenches were of such a simple nature that he could dig new ones almost as fast as the Allies could take the old ones. A zone of trenches several miles wide, the Germans calculated, would be a perfect defense,

GERMAN CONCRETE HOUSE ABOVE GROUND ON
THE HINDENBURG LINE WHICH SURVIVED THE
FINAL ALLIED ARTILLERY ATTACK IN 1918.

if prepared in advance and protected by artillery. Human beings
could not enter it and live.

The Germans now began to systematize the new warfare. If the
game was to destroy the trenches, the machine guns, and small
artillery within a certain area, so that the infantry could then
come over and occupy it, the answer was simple. Even the largest
shells did not penetrate into the earth more than a few yards. If,
therefore, fortifications were built of concrete and timber thirty
or forty feet underground, the Allies might pound them with as
large shells as they pleased. They could not destroy them. Protection
was merely a question of depth. When the Allied artillery began
to fire, all the Germans needed to do was to retire to the underground forts and wait, playing phonographs, eating, or sleeping

until the enemy should get through. The Allied guns would have to stop firing to allow their own infantry to advance, and, when the silence began, the Germans would know that the Allied infantry was coming. They could then climb upstairs and annihilate them with machine guns.

Of course, it was true that the Allies could and did play this same game. By it, they could prevent the Germans from winning the war, but by it, undoubtedly, the Germans could also prevent them from winning. Modern warfare had produced a deadlock. Neither side seemed to be able in 1915 to make any progress nor did either of them make in France any real progress for three years.

The Machinery of an Army

The most complex thing in the whole world is a modern army. In order to keep alive at all it has to do for itself everything that the ordinary community does, and it then organizes, in addition, a machinery for fighting which is as much more exact and complex than anything else any nation does as it is possible to conceive. Most governments in the world are satisfied when they get a part of the things done that are desirable and when they do them fairly well. But it became clear at the very outset that the army could not be satisfied with any such standard. The omission of anything, however small, might cost anywhere from ten to ten thousand lives. A moment's carelessness or heedlessness or forgetfulness on the part of a single man, even no better than a private, might allow some German attack to succeed.

When the armies dug in out of sight and began to take elaborate measures to conceal themselves, a successful defense, to say nothing of a successful offensive, depended upon seeing something of what the enemy was doing and where he was. There was only one eye that the army could use which was of any value, and that was the aëroplane. To a man standing on the ground and looking across country there would be absolutely nothing in sight. The trenches themselves would not be visible. All the guns could be easily concealed by screens of trees or leaves. Indeed, at times while a battle was raging, it was not possible in the daytime to see anything except scenery and absolutely not a sound was to be heard. Yet along the hills and valleys there might be half a million men watching each other, waiting for each other to move.

But when an observer rose in an aëroplane and flew over the enemy's lines, a great deal became perfectly clear. The trenches could not be concealed completely. There was always that tremendous weapon, the camera, and a picture faithfully reproduced everything. It could be developed and enlarged, and then, with a microscope and a ruler, the officers could determine the exact location of nearly everything the enemy had prepared. Balloons were also sent up from which an observer could see several miles and

FRENCH TRENCH
WITH PERISCOPE AND
FIELD TELEPHONE.

from which, of course, the enemy batteries within close range could be detected by the puffs of smoke when they fired. The man in the balloon would identify the spot on his map and then telephone the location to his own batteries beneath him.

All this machinery of aëroplanes, balloons, observers, telephones, and wireless was absolutely essential to hit anything, whether for defense or offense. Of course, an aëroplane flying over the enemy lines could see whether the trenches were full of men, and therefore ready for an attack; discover whether or not large numbers of reënforcements were coming up, and therefore give the only warning which was at all dependable of the time and whereabouts of an assault.

The function of the aëroplane was also to put out the enemy's eyes. It must prevent his aëroplanes from cruising over the Allied lines. It must shoot down his balloons; it must kill his observers. Obviously, if either side could get complete control of the air for a time, it might win a great victory, and perhaps the war.

BRITISH ADVANCE ARTILLERY OBSERVATION POST, WITH PERISCOPE AND FIELD TELEPHONE.

When the army came to consist of millions of men, an ordinary voice became useless for giving orders and any of the older methods by dispatch riders became impossible. Ordinary ears were no longer useful. The war was necessarily fought by wire, by telephone, telegraph, and wireless. From the slightest thing up to the most important order, everything must go over the wires, and the electrical department of the modern army was its most important factor, because it was its voice and its ear. Headquarters looked like a telephone exchange. It would probably be located in some perfectly quiet village quite out of range of any possible gun fire, and even during a great battle no sound would be heard there but the song of the birds and the humming of insects, the low tones of the officers, and the buzzing of the telephone.

No aëroplane was without its wireless, no balloon without its telephone or telegraph, no listening post was created out toward the enemy lines without its wire. And the artillery observer, crawling on his stomach to the top of some hill miles away from his own battery, or perched on top of a tree somewhere, carried with him the invariable wire; otherwise he was lost. But with that wire he might talk to the commanding general himself. The ears of the army spread in all directions and a whisper from the front trenches could reach anywhere.

It was imperative, too, when millions of men went into the field, that the brains of the army should be multiplied. No one man could remember everything; no one man could attempt to make all the decisions; nor would he dare be responsible for everything. An apparently simple order from the commander-in-chief would involve hundreds of detailed orders for its execution, and the execution of that order was the important thing. Foch might decide to attack with a million men on a certain morning. It was the business of the general staff to get a million men there and see that they attacked. The number of orders and details involved was simply incredible. No civilian can possibly imagine what it meant.

The general staff of every army was therefore composed of a great many officers, each of whom had charge of certain parts of the work. Some of them made a specialty of knowing the map; others of watching the location of troops; others had charge of the railroads or of the artillery. Outwardly, the general staff consisted of a little group of gentlemen, living quietly in an inconspicuous house in some perfectly peaceful place miles away from anything that looked like war. The modern general never leads the attack. He is not even within sound of the battle. Indeed, his real work is probably done a week or a month or more before the battle is fought. Hours and days may go by without there being any occasion for him to change an order. He is merely waiting until certain things already decided upon can take place. In the meantime he occupies himself as best he may. He plays tennis or golf or goes fishing. He has to eat his meals and get his sleep even if the battle is going on. He is always in touch with it through the telephone, but he has to see and hear by wire, and he has a general staff whose duty it is to do most of the listening and watching.

The legs of an army of millions cannot be physical. Where the battle line covers hundreds of miles, there is no time to wait while men walk from one part of it to the other. Steam and gasoline were the legs of the army, and in the summer of 1918 the question of victory became almost the question of gasoline. If the supply could be increased, the movement of the army could continue; if the supply gave out, the great offensives which were driving the Germans out of France would come to an end. The gasless Sundays and holidays in America in the summer of 1918 played their part in crushing the Hun. The motor car was one most important leg of the army; the other was the railroad. It was not merely true that everything the army had came by rail or motor car and that it could not be maintained without them; the fact was that the moving of troops in actual fighting from one place to another was made by motor cars and railroad trains. The American Marines charged on motor cars from a point over seventy miles distant from the battle line.

The stomach of the army, as Napoleon pointed out in a famous remark, was its most important organ. "An army fights on its stomach," said he. A hungry soldier cannot fight well and he certainly cannot fight long. If the modern battle was to continue for weeks and months, it was essential that the men should be carefully fed and carefully rested during the battle itself. There must be no interruption in the supply of food and it must be hot food. Think of the amount of food that a million men would eat three times a day and the extent of an organization necessary to deliver that food to each man, wherever he might be, hot and appetizing.

That was one of the greatest tasks that the modern army had to perform. It meant the baking each day of tons of bread, the cooking of tons of meat. Whole railroad trains full of supplies were consumed daily. Bakeries covering acres of ground had to be erected. Storehouses, literally miles in length, with acres of space, were built

SKETCH FOR *L'ILLUSTRATION PARIS* OF FRENCH CHARGE IN FALL OF 1915.
NOTE RAPID WALK, CLOSE FORMATION, AND FILLING OF GAPS BY RESERVES.

and the task was done and well done, both by the Germans and by the Allies. One of the most remarkable things the American army did was the institution in a few weeks of a great supply department adequate to care for the hundreds of thousands of men whom the United States was rushing to the battlefield in 1918.

The important thing, however, which the French and British had to learn at the beginning of the war, was the need for absolutely exact cooperation between every part of the service. The infantry and the artillery must act together. Every infantry division must cooperate exactly with every other division and with every artillery division. Nothing could go wrong; not a man must fail to perform his task. Not a battery of the artillery must fail. The eyes of the army must see and see accurately. The ears must hear and they must not make mistakes. The voice must repeat over the telephone the exact number and not something else. The brain must be infallible; the legs must never get tired; the stomach must always be full. Otherwise the attack would fail, and because in 1915 all of these various elements of the army did not work together as one organization, some of the attacks did fail.

It would take time, the French and British saw, to perfect the machinery of the modern army and yet nothing short of perfection would suffice. "Muddling through" would not do; "pretty nearly right" was fatal; doing something "to-morrow" probably meant the death of thousands of men. The watches of the generals and the watches of the lieutenants must all read exactly the same and must correspond with the watches of the artillery. If a certain thing was to be done at exactly five o'clock, every watch of every man cooperating in that movement must correspond. For one set of guns to be a minute too early or a minute too late might throw the whole movement into disorder. For an infantry company to leave its trench a minute too soon might result in the death of every man. Literally no detail, however small, could be forgotten.

All these matters were more important and more difficult to achieve than the Allies thought in 1915. They were also more difficult than the Germans thought at this same time. That is one reason why the war lasted four years. So elaborately exact a movement on the part of so many millions of men, in which the failure of one man to do exactly right any one of twenty things might be fatal, took years to learn what to do, years to learn how important it was that it should be done. That part of the history of the war is extraordinarily difficult to appreciate, yet upon it depended the eventual victory.

The Personalities of the War

This war will seem to many to lack the personal element, but no one can study its history in detail without being impressed with the fact that the war itself was so huge that it became impersonal. It is possible that another Napoleon, Luther, or Bismarck might have dominated its events, as they did the great periods of the past, but to the men who lived through the war there was on neither side a man of that supreme caliber. To the extent that those men directed the trend of events no individual controlled them. Great men we have had, perhaps in some number, among whom certainly our own President Wilson will rank with the foremost, but in general opinion, the man of transcendent genius did not appear.

It is probably true that the war was this time too extraordinary in its scope for any single individual to play a truly dominant part in it. Modern society is now too complex in its organization; it requires the cooperation of too large a number of men to accomplish anything to allow events to be influenced decisively by a single personality. The democratic organization of the Allied countries was, alas, suspicious of power or responsibility in the hands of a single individual. In Germany, where such power might have been entrusted to one man, there was the fear that the individual might not possess sufficient ability to decide wisely.

The war indeed was not fought by individuals but by committees, by multiple executive bodies, called cabinets, councils of state, ministries, general staffs, many of them composed in their turn of committees. While, therefore, men like Lloyd George, Clemenceau, and the Kaiser had a larger personal influence than others, the real political decisions in all countries were the result of the thought of many men. So too of the generals. President Wilson and Marshal Foch perhaps had a greater power to act in matters of importance than any other individuals and both properly exercised it upon occasion. But Marshal Foch himself said, "The whole war has been one giant orchestra—I merely happened to hold the baton, to be the orchestra leader." At the peace conference President Wilson seemed to some the dominant character, but others declared vehemently that he was only one of many. No one man in this war has been able to decide, as Napoleon did, the issues of war and peace for himself. In writing, therefore, a book as brief as this, it seemed better to reproduce the impersonal quality of the war, rather than to attempt to emphasize the parts played by individuals, and thus introduce names into the text whose part in the conflict could not be properly described.

At the same time it is essential to make clear the extraordinary influence which personality had upon the history of the war. After all, men fought it. The quality or lack of quality in these particular men must be one of the most important elements in its history. Many foreign students have contended that the Allied failures in the first years were due to the incapacity of statesmen, staff officers, field generals, and the like. They were unequal to the responsibility placed upon them. Primarily, of course, they were lacking in experience.

The Germans had developed a military and administrative machine whose prime object was to eliminate possible failure, as the result of individual incompetence. So careful had been their work that their machine was at the outset superior to that of the Allies. On the other hand one of the most conspicuous reasons for the German defeat was the failure of individuals in Germany to judge correctly the British and American people and to understand the deep ethical convictions of the modern world. The sinking of the *Lusitauia*, the execution of Miss Cavell, the atrocities in France and Belgium are from any proper point of view individual failures.

In all countries the political and industrial situations played the most important part in the fighting of the war and the relations of individuals to each other had a most important effect upon the progress of the war. Human material was a vital factor but it cannot be described briefly, nor can it be truthfully said that any success or failure can be credited to or blamed upon one man. The war was intentionally organized to prevent a single man from playing any such role as the conquerors of the past had enacted.

GALLIPOLI

The execution of the plans for the opening of the Dardanelles was at first entrusted to the French and British fleets alone. Here was this narrow strait, protected by forts, the waters sown with mines, and nowhere more than a few miles wide. Some miles above the mouth of the passage came the Narrows, where it was not over two or three miles in width. Here were the chief defenses. It was supposed, however, that the range of the guns on the large British warships was greater than those of the forts, that they would be able to silence the latter, and would then be able to protect their own mine sweepers while they cleared the Channel. The real question was the effectiveness of a long-range attack by battleships. On February 19 and 25, 1915, fleet attacks were delivered upon the outlying forts, which were first silenced and then destroyed by landing parties. On March 6, a preliminary attack and on March 18, a concentrated assault, were delivered against the forts along the Narrows by the largest Allied battle-ships.

But it became evident that the fleet could not succeed alone. The passage was so narrow and so tortuous, the current so swift, that navigation of such large ships was very difficult. The mine sweepers were unable to clear the waters until the forts had been silenced and the fleet could not come up until the mines had been cleared. But the nature of the ground made it so easy to conceal shore batteries that the observers for the fleet were not able to detect their location, and therefore the fleet could not, as had been hoped, destroy them at long range.

The cooperation of an army was essential. The forts controlling the Narrows must be captured from the rear. They were located on the Gallipoli Peninsula, a very difficult position indeed to attack, but there was no other possibility because these very forts controlled the Asiatic shore and therefore could prevent the erection there of Allied batteries strong enough to reduce them.

The desperate character of the expedition lent to it an extraordinary interest, and has caused the British people to think of it "not as a tragedy, nor as a mistake, but as a great human effort which came more than once very near to triumph, achieved the impossible many times, and failed in the end, as many great deeds of arms have failed, for something which had nothing to do with arms nor with the men who bore them."

Here was a tongue of mountainous land fifty-three miles long and from two to twelve miles wide, gay with beautiful flowers in spring, drab in summer and in fall, when the heather and the scrub pines and dust made it desolate and drear. It was all but roadless, rough, waterless, and commanded throughout by the hills in the interior. Only a few narrow beaches existed on which a landing was possible and they were all positions on which a landing was thinkable only if the enemy could be surprised.

But it was impossible to surprise him. His preparations at these few spots had been so complete that it seemed hardly within the power of flesh and blood to overcome them. The beaches and the sea itself were covered with tangles of barbed wire, ranged by cannon, swept by machine guns at close range. The troops must push their way through all these obstacles under galling fire, clamber up the hills and gullies, still under fire, and dig themselves in upon a waterless, torrid hill, while the Turks raked them with fire from all sides and charged them with bayonets.

On April 24, the transports moved out of the great harbor of Lemnos, crowded with soldiers. The cheering of the sailors and the returning cheers of the soldiers, going as they knew to all but certain death, was one of the impressive moments of the war. Attacks were to be delivered at all possible points, but the main attempts were confined to two: one at the top of the peninsula against Sedd-el-Bahr, and the other, farther along the outer edge of the peninsula, at a place henceforth immortal as Anzac.

The plan at the former was to run aground a collier, the sides of which had been especially cut down and reconstructed so as to form a sort of landing stage, to tow in between her and the shore with motor launches groups of flatboats, over which the troops in the collier should rush ashore and carry the first Turkish trenches. The collier should then become a landing stage at which the other transports should leave their loads. The collier was grounded, the tows drew in ahead of her, and then the Turks opened fire. They could not miss. From one hundred to three hundred yards away, in clear daylight, were thirty boats all bunched together and crowded with men, and a good large ship. Thousands were killed at once, a few reached cover on shore, but the bulk who were not at once destroyed were forced to wait until nightfall before they could land. Despite the awful slaughter the landing was made, the first trenches were carried, and a footing gained.

Farther along the peninsula, the Australian and New Zealand troops forced a landing at Gaba Tepe, now called Anzac, from the initials of Australian New Zealand Army Corps. Here they approached a small narrow beach, mined, covered with barbed wire, ranged by Turkish guns. The men leaped into the water from the boats, holding their guns and ammunition above their heads, and rushed on shore. After a terrific struggle of two days and nights they made good their grip on a little strip of beach, by that time soaked with the blood of thousands of as gallant men as ever wore uniform. They were not only compelled to land under fire, but to bring ashore *on their backs* from the boats *under fire*, every gun, every bullet, ever scrap of food, ever drop of water they were to use. They carried up the hills on their backs the machine guns, the ammunition, and the food to the men in the trenches.

They had not merely to fight in a more dangerous position than most troops during this war or any other but to perform as well, under the most extraordinary difficulties, the services of supply and transportation. Without rest, improperly fed, drenched by rain, burning with heat during the day, chilled to the marrow by the cold at night, these same men must not only hold the trenches but make piers, dig shelters, bring on shore the food, water, ammunition, and heavy guns.

For ninety-six hours they fought continually with little or no sleep. And this they endured "night after night, day after day, without rest or solace, nor respite from the peril of death, seeing their friends killed, and their position imperiled, getting their food, their munitions, even their drink, from the jaws of death, and their breath from the taint of death, and their brief sleep upon the dust of death." No such undertaking was ever set an army before; no army ever performed such a task.

Their first landing came on April 25. A battle was fought on May 1, and a desperate general assault on June 4 from all the various stations gained a total of some five hundred yards. In the middle of August another landing was effected at Suvla Bay, but in September Turkish counter attacks were successful enough to show that the enterprise could not succeed.

The truth was that the troops were outnumbered, insufficiently equipped with artillery and munitions to be able to make headway against the Turks, admirably equipped with everything and ably led by German officers. The nature of the ground made conceal-ment of artillery simple for the defense and all but impossible for the assailants to detect or destroy. The fleet did what it could to blow the Turkish trenches out of existence, but was deficient in information or in accuracy of fire or in both. The Allies learned here at great cost the lesson that a charge on machine guns is mere slaughter. The real blame must fall on the English and French political leaders who ordered the expedition despite the all but insuperable obstacles which their military and naval advisers pointed out.

The decision was taken in the fall of 1915 to withdraw the army, but it was by no means clear that the army could escape. To land under Turkish fire had been slaughter; to embark under the same fire would be no less certainly slaughter. And yet by a miracle of organization the entire British force, with all its wounded and supplies, was taken off during December, 1915, and January, 1916, without the loss of a man. The embarkation necessarily took place at night. The transports would steal in after dark and the loading proceeded, night after night—horses, stores, motors, guns—in absolute silence. The Turks had the range to a nicety and could have fired as accurately in the dark as in the daylight. During the day great piles of empty boxes were landed to convince the enemy that the British were intending to spend the winter.

At last only the active men of the final contingent remained. During the day bombardment of the Turkish lines was continued and wireless automatic bomb throwers, with automatic candles and dynamite charges, were arranged to go off at intervals during the night to imitate a desultory fire. All through the hours while the last troops were boarding the transports, this display continued. At last at 4 A.M. all was ready and fire was set to the great piles of boxes so as to destroy what could not be moved. The great mass of leaping, roaring flames threw a red glow over the heavens and lit up the whole scene. The empty boxes burned furiously and the Turks began pounding everything in sight—the empty, vacant trenches, the piles of boxes, the vacant landings. And the British troops, safe on the ships, began shooting at the same target to make doubly sure of the completeness of the destruction. The army had escaped!

With Hindenburg in Poland

After the failure to crush the French at the outset of the war, after the battle of the Marne had resulted in the establishment of a deadlock in the west along the trench line, the German general staff transferred its activities to the east. It made up its mind to crush Russia first, allotted the months of 1915 to that task, and entrusted it to General von Hindenburg. It will perhaps be clearer if we pass in review the entire strategic movement in Poland from the outbreak of the war to the final German victories, even at the risk of some repetition.

The boundaries between Russia, Germany, and Austria were based upon military and strategic rather than upon racial considerations. They were the result of an attempt to strike a balance which would give some advantage to each of those powers in the event of war and place them all in a certain degree of peril. Russian Poland was thrust in between Prussia proper and the Austrian province of Galicia. It might menace the approaches to Berlin but was itself threatened in turn on either flank. Before the Russians could use Warsaw as the base of an attack upon Berlin, they must first clear East Prussia and Galicia. Nor could the Austrians attack from Galicia without exposing Cracow, the key to Vienna, itself easily assailed by the Russians. On the other hand, the Germans could advance on Warsaw direct, only at the imminent risk of being caught between the Russian armies maneuvering in Poland. Attacks upon Warsaw from both flanks by the Austrians and the

Germans would have to be made in great force because the Russian position in Poland was very strong.

These conditions explain the character and nature of the first campaigns. We find Warsaw the German objective and Berlin the objective of the Russians. But we find them both campaigning in Galicia and in East Prussia. In Galicia, too, there were great wells of oil, exceedingly useful to the Germans and Austrians, and no less useful to the Russians. These eastern campaigns threatened as well the great German industrial district of Silesia. At the same time the prime object of the first Russian campaign was not strategic at all. It was to compel the Germans to transfer both men and munitions to the eastern front and hence to relieve the pressure on the French until the British could arrive.

The Russians therefore advanced early in August, 1914, along both flanks into eastern Prussia and into Galicia in considerable force and with great rapidity, despite their very inefficient equipment. Both provinces were rapidly overrun. In East Prussia toward the end of August and the beginning of September Hindenburg, as already related, defeated the Russian armies in the battles of Tannenberg and of the Masurian Lakes. To the south, in Galicia, however, the Russian advance went on unchecked, meeting apparently no real resistance. Lemberg was captured; Cracow even was threatened, and many of the passes of the Carpathians fell into Russian hands, so that by January the greater part of Galicia had been overrun, and there seemed to be some possibility that the Russians might be able to capture Przemysl and even invade Hungary.

Long before this juncture, Hindenburg attempted a direct assault upon Warsaw. Having gotten possession of East Prussia and having thus made safe his flank and rear, he did not at this time propose to pay any attention to the Russians in Galicia, knowing full well that if Warsaw should fall Galicia would be a death trap for the Russian army. From October 20 to October 27 he delivered a tremendous series of direct assaults upon the Russian lines before Warsaw and was everywhere defeated by the Grand Duke Nicholas, whose masterly retreats and sudden counter-assaults checked and slowed down the German advance and often imperiled the whole German position. With inadequate artillery and a very small supply of ammunition, he fought a masterly series of actions, which did gain the time then so essential for the French, and which did prevent the defeat of his own armies by the much larger forces of his very much better equipped foes.

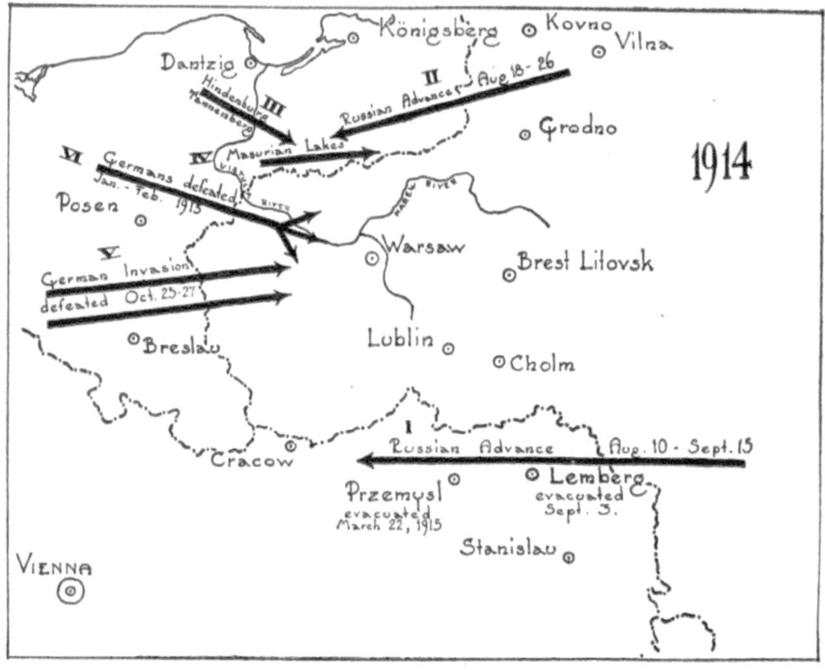

POLAND, 1914.

General Mackensen then undertook a new assault upon Warsaw from the northwest, advancing on a broad front between the rivers Warta and Vistula. The Russian armies were of course using the Vistula as a defensive barrier but its passage did not seem difficult to the Germans. From November to February the pressure went on but without real success. The loss of men was heavy and the fact was only too conclusively established that the Vistula's heavy floods were too great a defensive barrier, when utilized by a general like the Grand Duke Nicholas, to be overcome by any direct frontal attack.

Hindenburg therefore gave up the attempt and took time to prepare a tremendous series of movements, which should sweep all before them and crush the Russian army for good. He became convinced that he had been operating on too small a scale with too few men. The full strength of the German army must be thrown upon the Russians in a series of all but simultaneous assaults. He must smite them hip and thigh. He must also campaign behind the Vistula and therefore must assail Warsaw from both flanks. He could easily cross the Vistula in East Prussia, and by advancing through Galicia in the south he could march round the great river.

The Russians had meantime made good use of their opportunity in Galicia. Przemysl had fallen on March 17. The Russian armies could now safely cross the Carpathians and assail the defenses of Cracow itself. Already in London and Paris they had begun to hope that the invasion of Hungary and an assault upon Vienna might be the next news.

Hindenburg, however, proposed to take full advantage of the large number of men the Germans could concentrate at a particular spot and especially of the greater efficiency of the German artillery. He had plenty of munitions and he knew the Russians had not. The new campaign was to be an artillery battle. He would overwhelm them by mere weight of metal thrown. He would concentrate so tremendous a fire on them that their defenses would be wiped out, and he well knew that they had not a sufficient supply of ammunition to crush his forces in the same manner when his infantry should advance. It was a mathematical calculation—so many Russians, so many guns, so much ammunition; then the infantry could stride forward over the corpses so many miles. The process could then be repeated. They could advance as fast as the German artillery could be moved forward.

By these tactics he would cut through the Russian right flank in Galicia, separate it from the Russian armies in Poland, and thus

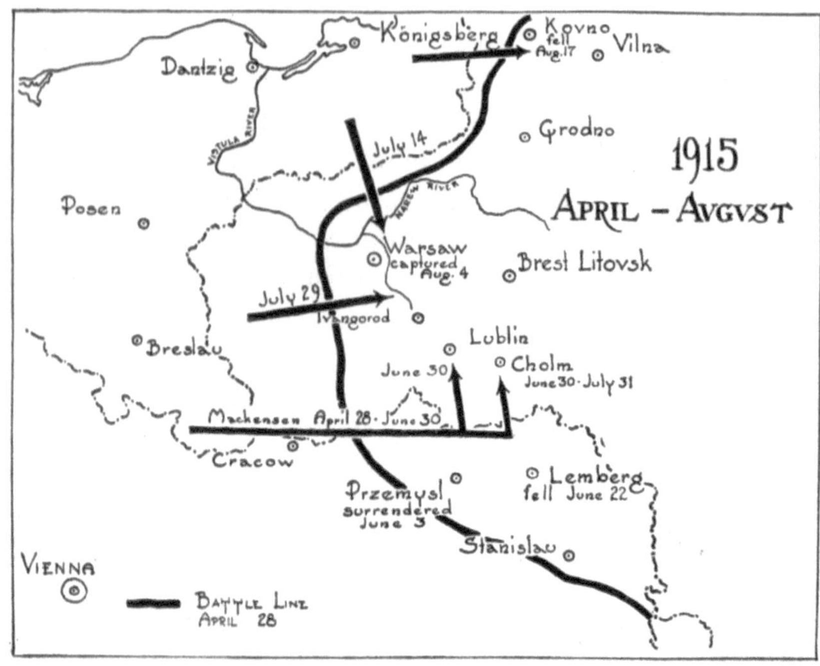

THE POLISH OFFENSIVE, 1915.

outflank the rest of the Russians in Poland and compel them to retreat on Warsaw to save themselves. The same movement would outflank the Russian center and left in Galicia and the Carpathians, which had been foolishly thinking of a descent upon Hungary. They would be compelled to retreat on Lemberg and would thus surrender without a blow the whole of Galicia and southwest Poland.

The movement was a complete success; it proceeded on schedule time, so many miles a day. Przemysl fell June 3; Lemberg was evacuated June 22; the whole of Galicia had been cleared by June 30. Cracow, Vienna., Berlin were safe; Warsaw itself had been flanked and was in real danger.

Now, therefore, came a change in tactics. The time had arrived to begin to draw the strings of the net together. Hindenburg hoped to entice the Grand Duke Nicholas into Warsaw by not attacking in the center and by remaining up to this period quiet in East Prussia. His troops in East Prussia were already far east of

Warsaw; Mackensen beyond Lemberg was also east of Warsaw. If only the Grand Duke would stay in Warsaw, the German armies could advance, the one south and the other north, and they would infallibly cut him off and destroy or capture his whole army. Thus told, the operations Hindenburg had in mind were simple in the extreme. But when such a movement had to be executed by more than a million men in a series of battles which must necessarily consume some weeks, it involved the most extraordinary foresight in planning and the greatest precision in execution. It also assumed a certain element of surprise. He had been quietly collecting enormous forces in East Prussia while Mackensen was pushing through Galicia. He had also collected a very large army in extreme East Prussia, which should be ready to assail the Russian railroads leading to Petrograd and Moscow as soon as Warsaw should fall.

On July 1, therefore, Mackensen turned north and began to press on, so many miles a day, schedule time, towards Warsaw. On July 14, the Germans moved from East Prussia south on Warsaw, being now well behind the Vistula. Thus they were approaching Warsaw in overwhelming force and with great rapidity on both flanks. The Grand Duke instantly began the evacuation of the great city and of all the Russian lines. On July 29, Mackensen reached the Lubin-Cholm Railroad on the south. Hindenburg crossed the Narew River north of Warsaw, and another huge German army was thrown across the Vistula south of Warsaw at Ivangorod. The Germans entered Warsaw in triumph on August 4, the Kaiser himself appearing for the function. The Russians evacuated of necessity nearly the whole of Poland. Hindenburg now struck southeast at Kovno, attempted to put an army in the rear of the retreating Russians. Starting August 17, the Germans pressed on toward Riga on the north and toward Vilna on the east.

For the remainder of the war some half-hearted attempts were made to push the lines somewhat further, and eventually Riga did fall into German hands. The fleet sailed up and captured some of the islands along the coast, and an attack upon Petrograd by sea

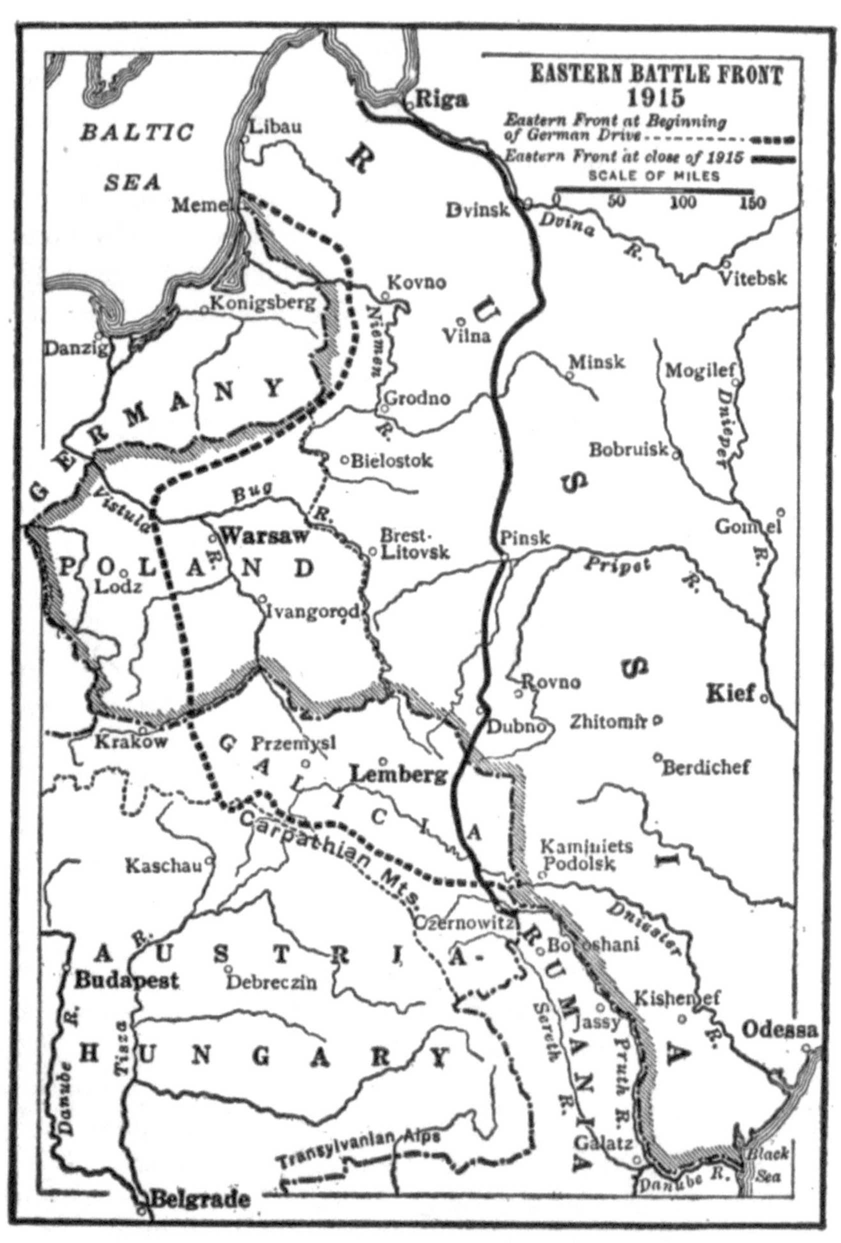

THE BEGINNING AND THE END OF THE GERMAN DRIVE.

was even considered. But by September, 1915, the German line reached in Poland practically the maximum of its extent until the Russian revolution in March, 1917, brought the real war in the east to an end. There was indeed little purpose in attempting to carry the war into Russia. The real foe was the Russian army, not the country itself, and the Germans believed that the army was broken and disorganized in 1915 to as great an extent as was useful to them. It was no longer dangerous, they thought, and could be further destroyed whenever they pleased. To pursue it into the marshes beyond the existing lines, to assail Petrograd or Moscow by invasion, would have been to commit the fateful error of Napoleon; to place their army at the mercy of Generals Winter and Hunger without accomplishing anything of military importance.

The Causes of the Russian Military Collapse

While the Russian revolution was the eventual factor which relieved the Germans of trouble in the east, the Russians really had ceased to be dangerous before the revolution occurred. The vital difficulty was not military but industrial. There were no adequate facilities in Russia for manufacturing guns, ammunition, or clothing, upon which a modern army depended. There was at the outbreak of the war no adequate supply on hand to equip the first troops that went to the front, and even if there had been the efficiency of the army could not have been maintained from Russian resources. The Germans calculated, therefore, that the Russians might fight with effect once, conceivably twice, but not longer. They might equip one army, but not two; surely not three.

Unfortunately, too, Russia lacked the essential railway facilities for the distribution to her own troops of the materials which she did possess or was able to secure from her Allies. Here lay the true significance of the fatality at Gallipoli. If the Black Sea could have been opened, the immense river system of Russia might have been utilized for some adequate system of transportation of the flood of material which the Allies could have shipped to her. Archangel and a new port on the Murman coast were both immediately utilized as ports of entry, and new railroad lines were built to Petrograd from both in 1915. American and British engineers were secured to operate the Russian railroads. The Trans-Siberian Railway was also to bring goods shipped across the Pacific from the United States, but the task was too great. The amount of material necessary to support Russia was really greater in volume than these railroad systems could possibly carry such distances. Miracles were achieved, but even miracles could not perform the impossible. Had it not, however, been for direct treason in the Russian ministry of war and in the Russian army, the worst might still have been avoided.

As it was, the Grand Duke could scarcely do more than dissipate the German efforts, compel them to employ great forces in the east which might have been able to force a decision in France. His strategy must be to save his army; to retreat from position to position, forcing the Germans always to pay the price in men and in time. He must sacrifice cities, provinces, states, if essential, conscious that Russia could not lose the war so long as the British and French were unbeaten in the west. Without equipment Russia could not hope to win the war as a whole in the east. She could not fail to win the final objectives in the east, when the British and French should win the final victory in France. Indeed, the British and French held from the outset that victory in the east could not of itself win the war.

At the same time, it must not be forgotten that the Russian defeat was due as much to the positive efficiency of the German army as to the comparative deficiencies of Russian equipment. The German artillery was not only tremendous in number, but extraordinary in efficiency. The Germans had also created on their eastern frontier a wonderful system of railroads which enabled them to deliver an army, direct from the western front, to any point along the eastern front or to transport it along the eastern front itself from point to point, or from one end of the front to the other with maximum speed. The element of surprise in modern warfare was no less useful than in earlier wars and the physical facilities at Hindenburg's disposal enabled him invariably to surprise the Russians with the number of men he could transport long distances in an extraordinarily brief time.

The German army was unquestionably the finer army of the two. Hindenburg again was a great strategist, one of the greatest in this war, Ludendorff was a remarkable organizer and strategist, as the campaign of 1918 showed; while Von Mackensen was certainly one of the greatest field generals that this war produced. The Russians fell before no mean foemen. Indeed, it is one of the miracles of the war that the Russian army without equipment could have fought so long against such armies so thoroughly equipped and so competently led.

FRIGHTFULNESS: THE LUSITANIA

Much of the story of the year 1915 is connected with the first concerted attempt of the Germans to show how horrible warfare could be made under the new science. Air raids were made by Zeppelins and aëroplanes with the intention of destroying innocent people who could not possibly be of assistance in warfare. Red Cross hospitals, clearly marked with great crosses, plainly visible from a great altitude, were frequently bombed and destroyed. Hospital ships with great crosses painted on their sides, illuminated at night by a great cross of electric lights, were sunk by submarines. There were no possible excuses for error. Besides, too many hospitals were destroyed to admit of accidents. The purpose was to frighten individuals by showing them how horrible war could be made and therefore influence them to surrender.

In the spring of 1915, the Germans determined to prove the great power of the submarine. They would sink the largest ship afloat—the *Lusitania.* They would give the world warning that they meant to sink her and they would then see that she went down. The German embassy in America warned Americans against sailing upon the ship, and thus gave notice of the German plans, but nobody believed that they could mean what they said. On the seventh of May at two o'clock in the afternoon, the *Lusitania* was steaming along the Irish coast. It was a bright clear day; the identity of the ship was known to every German submarine; she was also known to be unarmed and unable to defend herself.

There were on board no cannon and no explosives, nor was there any warning. She was torpedoed at least twice on the starboard side and began to sink at once; indeed, she floated only eighteen minutes after she was struck. There was no panic, although there was necessarily a certain degree of excitement. There was great difficulty in lowering the boats, due to the fact that the ship was leaning heavily on the starboard side into the water and that the leeward side was therefore lifted high above the sea. The ship also continued to travel fast through the water and it was difficult to lower the boats without capsizing them. How quickly the ship went down is clear from the following account by one of the survivors.

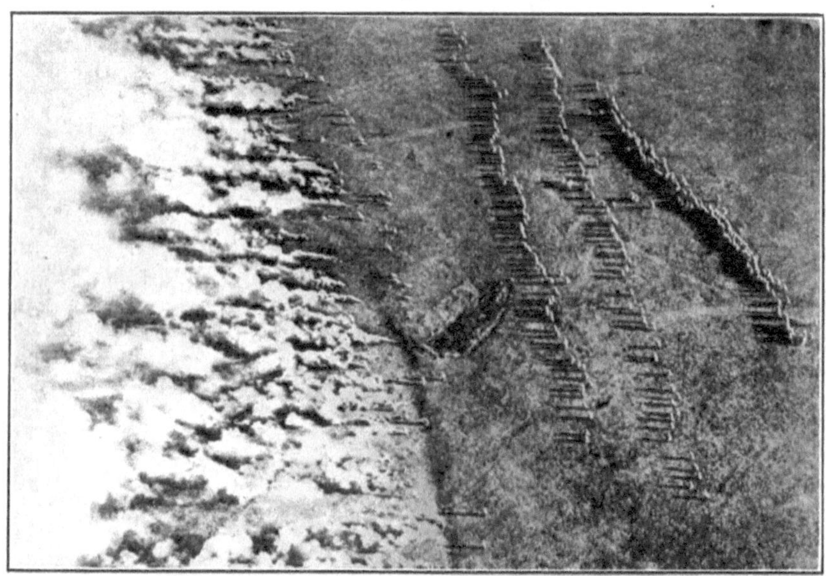

AEROPLANE PHOTOGRAPH OF GERMAN GAS ATTACK. NOTE TWO WAVES OF MEN IN OPEN FORMATION AND CLOSELY MASSED THIRD LINE, A FORMATION USED LATE IN 1915.

"I fell into a boat and we were slipped down into the water and over the side of the liner. The boat struck the water and after some seconds (it may have been a minute) I looked up, and cried out, 'My God! the Lusitania is gone!' The entire bulk, which had been almost upright just a few seconds before, suddenly lurched over away from us. Then she seemed to stand upright in the water and the next instant the keel of the vessel caught the keel of the boat in which we were floating and we were thrown into the water. I sank fifteen or twenty feet; however, I had my life belt around me and managed to rise again to the surface. Then I floated for possibly ten or fifteen minutes, when I saw and made a grab at a collapsible life boat at which other passengers were also grabbing. We managed to get it ship-shape and clambered in." A good many people were saved in life boats or by life preservers, but over a thousand lives were lost, over a hundred of whom were Americans. Many men of real prominence and importance went down with the ship, most of them in order to allow the women and children a chance for safety.

The Germans had thought evidently that the sinking of the ship would deter travel, frighten sailors, thus cut off England's supplies and bring the war to an end. Never were they more astonishingly disappointed. The condemnation of the act was universal throughout the world. Contrary to all rules and practices of three centuries or more, a great ship had been sunk without warning or without opportunity for her passengers and crew to escape. To sink without warning had been considered for three centuries the clearest evidence of piracy.

Six months later the Germans again astounded the world with an unparalleled act of cruelty. An English nurse, named Edith Cavell, had been arrested in Brussels on August 5. She had been the directress of a large nursing home at Brussels, where she had given aid impartially to German, Belgian, French, and English soldiers. She admitted that she had given certain assistance to Allied fugitive soldiers, with clothes and information about the roads to Holland. There was no claim that she had given any information to anybody that was of military importance or which in any way affected the issue of the war. The German charge was that of "conducting soldiers to the enemy."

According to this she was a spy and as such to be shot. Once more, as in the case of the *Lusitania*, they proceeded contrary to all accepted practices. While in a certain sense everybody who in any way, even by a cup of cold water, assisted any one not a German, did assist the enemies of Germany, it had been generally agreed that a man or woman was not a spy unless in disguise within the enemy lines and unless possessed of secret information of direct military value. Miss Cavell was therefore no more a spy than thousands of people during our own Civil War and all other previous wars who had performed acts of kindness for wounded and fugitive soldiers of both sides. Men had felt that to refuse simple shelter to a wounded man or a man in flight or in danger of his life was an act of inhumanity and not sufficiently dangerous to either side to be considered a crime. Nor had it been so treated.

The Germans proposed to execute this brave little woman for acts of common humanity to wounded and suffering men. But the horror of the world at her execution on October 12 was not due merely to her death for the performance of acts which the Allied world judged humane, but the manner in which the Germans conducted the whole case. They refused to allow her any legal aid or counsel. The American embassy made the most determined attempt to find out what was being done in her case and to render her assistance. Not only were they refused permission to aid her in any way, but the German officials repeatedly lied to them. Some time after she had been sentenced, in her cell behind locked doors, obviously that the fact might be secret, they denied on their honor that she had been sentenced at all. The order had been given to execute her at once during the night and it was only after the utmost pressure that the German officers were gotten to admit that the order had been given. All appeals for delay or for concessions of any kind were refused. She was denied at the end the common humanity of religious conference and prayer with her own chaplain. As Mr. Hugh Gibson, the secretary of the American embassy, wrote, "Her execution in the middle of the night at the

SKETCH SHOWING FIRST BRITISH CHARGE IN GAS MASKS. NOTE RAPID
PACE OF CHARGE, CLOSE FORMATION IN USE IN FALL OF 1915.

conclusion of a course of trickery and deception was nothing short of an affront to civilization."

The *Lusitania* and the death of Edith Cavell produced a tremendous impression in the United States and were among the prime causes which led this country to enter the war. We could not countenance for a moment the thought of victory for a nation absolutely lost to all considerations of decency, of humanity, and of civilization.

Why Italy Entered the War

In April, 1915, the Italians signed a treaty with the French and British, agreeing to enter the war in May. They were moved first and foremost by their own passionate attachment to democracy and their own love for civilization, as the French and British understood it. They realized that the German militaristic state and the methods it sanctioned would destroy all that they held most dear. While there were some considerable number of people in Italy who had doubts as to the way in which the general cause could be best advanced, there were very few outside of those bought with German money who differed upon the question of Italy's real interests.

In the next place, Italy had for centuries been oppressed by Austria, and the Italians had come to hate and distrust her to an extraordinary degree. Was she not the firm ally of the new Germany, committed to all Germany's schemes, and her accomplice in the very worst of her plots? Had not Austria opened the issue of the war by the extraordinarily severe ultimatum to Serbia? Was it not Austria who pushed the issue to war; who refused all compromises and declined to negotiate? Possibly the Kaiser and the Germans urged the Austrians on, but the Austrians at any rate yielded.

There had been a treaty called the Triple Alliance between Italy, Austria, and Germany, which had provided for mutual assistance between the three under certain circumstances. Many have therefore believed the German statements that the Italians broke the Triple Alliance and therefore themselves tore up a treaty by refusing to join the Germans and Austrians at the outbreak of the war. Nothing was further from the truth. The Italians had always declared from the very beginning that the Triple Alliance should never cover a war begun by the Austrians and Germans, and they had always insisted upon their right to reserve action in any dispute which the Austrians might have with Serbia. The very situation out of which the war grew was one which the Italians had foreseen at the time the treaty was signed; they had given notice then and since that they would not consider themselves bound by the treaty in any war growing out of a quarrel between Austria and one of the Balkan States.

Moreover, Austria still controlled a considerable section of territory in which the bulk of the people were Italians—Italy Unredeemed, *Italia Irredenta*. These Italians were most anxious to join United Italy and their compatriots were eager to free them from Austrian domination. Their freedom would add to the new Italy the last territory which belonged to her.

It was also true that this same territory contained the military defenses of Italy. The Austrians, when driven from Italy in 1866, had insisted upon retaining the military frontiers in their own hands, thus leaving Italy helpless before an Austrian assault. This was one reason why the great attack of 1917 was so successful. The strong position, the offensive position as we call it, the Austrians had always held. One reason, therefore, for Italy's entering the war was a desire to get possession of a frontier upon which she had some real chance to defend herself.

Nor was there much doubt in the minds of a majority of Italians in 1915 that, if Italy was to fight at all, she must join before the British and French were beaten. She had not moved at the very outset of the war because her army was not ready and because she rendered the Allies from the beginning a really tremendous service by declaring her neutrality and thus freeing the French from the necessity of guarding their own rear. If the Italians had joined the

THE SHADED AREA IS THE TERRITORY
THE ITALIANS DESIRED TO WIN.

Germans and had attacked France in the south at the same time the Germans moved in the north, the position of the French would have been indeed desperate.

By the spring of 1915, however, it was reasonably clear that the Allies could not win the war in a hurry, that long preparation might be necessary, that cooperation and unity among Germany's enemies would be essential to victory. The Italians therefore did not propose to wait until the British and French were flat on their faces before coming to their aid. It would then be too late. The great object which Italy herself had at heart would have been lost. They must act promptly and vigorously if the war was to be saved.

How Germany Fought the Blockade

In 1915 Germany adopted the most extreme measures to organize completely her whole population for the fighting of the war. The first great blow which was to have ended the conflict had failed. The British, contrary to expectation, had entered the war, had cleared the seas of German ships, and created a blockade of Germany. It was not yet absolutely rigid and might never become so. Great quantities of metals and fats were being imported into Germany in 1915 from Holland, Denmark, and Sweden, who secured these articles ostensibly for their own use, but the amounts were so enormous compared to anything those nations had ever used before that the Germans had no confidence the British would allow this so-called neutral trade to continue.

Germany must therefore expect to live during the war from what there was in Germany or in the territory of her allies. As long as they could live on what they had they could fight the war. The moment it became necessary to have other supplies the war must end. The question of victory or defeat, the Germans saw, might resolve itself into their ability to get along with what they had.

They immediately took official control of everything in Germany. All that was raised or sold or eaten or bought was at every stage controlled by the government. By forcing people to eat a little less, the existing supply could be made to last. To this end they issued bread cards, meat cards, and very soon cards for other sorts of foods. Nobody was to be allowed to eat more than so much bread or meat in a day or week. Every time he received any he must present a card to be stamped. It was a serious offense to get any more. In this way, by limiting the consumption of food it ought to be possible to make it last indefinitely. Certain products should be limited in their use; milk, for instance, should be kept for the sick, for children, and for the aged. Other people could get along with something else.

Then the most elaborate attempts were made to increase the amount of food in Germany. Every scrap of land on which anything could be grown should grow something useful. Little plots only six or eight feet square in front of the houses along the streets of German cities were dug up and planted with potatoes. All vacant lots were worked by the school children under the direction of their teachers in accordance with the orders given by the government. Planting potatoes was more important during the war than learning lessons, and the children represented just so much labor.

Great attempts were made to increase the number of cattle so as to augment the amount of milk, butter, and meat. The breeding of swine was encouraged because bacon and ham were the meats which kept best and were therefore most suitable for the army.

They did their best to think of everything that could be reserved, or increased, or portioned out so as to make it last. The British had expected that the blockade would very soon compel Germany to surrender for lack of food, copper, cotton, and rubber with which to continue the war. But the war ended because the German army was beaten, not because the German people were starving nor because they did not have enough war material to fight on. Somehow or other, substitutes were provided for things they could not get. Clothes were made of paper, bicycles and automobiles were given iron tires, or the tire was set on springs. "Coffee" was made from grain, and a soft sort of steel served the purpose of copper. The doctors told them that they had eaten too much in Germany anyway, had worn more clothing than they needed, and had kept the houses warmer than was good for them. They could just as well get along without. And they did. The German people at the end of the war were thinner than at the beginning, but they did not die for lack of food. At first the bread and meat cards were believed in London and Paris to be proof that Germany was weakening and would soon surrender. They were, however, merely German precautions, taken with the usual German thoroughness, to make sure that they should not be defeated from lack of forethought.

BOOK IV

THE WAR IN 1916

The Campaign of 1916

The fortunes of war in 1915 had taught the Allies that a speedy victory was perhaps too much to hope for. They had learned that the character of modern warfare required a sort of preparation which they had not had time to make. It required an unlimited amount of ammunition which the British had made elaborate plans to produce in May, 1915, but which could not arrive on the battlefield for some time. The British army was training rapidly and rounding into form but experience had shown that it was not yet the sort of offensive instrument the Allies were going to need.

The Allied generals and statesmen were more convinced than ever that the advantage of numbers lay on their side. General Joffre, who was still in command, thought that "nibbling" was a possibility still and sure to bring results. If the Germans would only attack, the French could kill a few more Germans each time than they lost themselves and thus the German army would wear away little by little. The initial success of the Germans was ascribed to superiority in numbers and not to superiority of equipment, preparation, organization, or training. Now as the new British and Russian troops arrived, the Allies would grow stronger each month, and the Germans, inasmuch as they were being killed, must be getting weaker each month. There was therefore some disposition among the Allied generals and statesmen to play a waiting game, to let the numbers pile up a little; to wait until unlimited ammunition should arrive; until the new big guns should be finished, and the new British army should be thoroughly trained.

Much also was expected from the blockade which, by the end of 1915, was extraordinarily efficient. The fleet in the North Sea was doing its work well and the German submarine did not seem as yet to be particularly dangerous. Certainly no one believed in England that the submarine could break the blockade. As time went on, therefore, the German supplies of all the things they did not produce must be getting lower and lower. The rubber, cotton, and copper were being used up. The food supplies were diminishing. The majority in London and Paris felt that a moment must come when the economic pressure must make itself felt on the German battle line and weaken the strength of the army for attack and for defense. When that moment came the Allies would know that victory was at hand. For this reason also there was a certain disposition to wait and not to attack too soon in 1916. There was as well the tradition of the Marne. By not forcing the issue, by not attacking too soon, by choosing the right moment, Joffre had in the end won a smashing victory. The same sort of tactics men thought would have the same result in 1916.

But when the British army should be ready and the ammunition should arrive, the Allies proposed to deliver a simultaneous attack on three fronts, and they proposed this time to keep it up, week in and week out, until they broke through the German defense. If the attack only was simultaneous, if there was only enough artillery behind it and enough men, and if only it was kept up long enough, they did not believe that the Germans could resist it. The sustaining of the attack until the Germans broke was to be the great factor.

The German plan for the year was based upon the knowledge, brought them of course by their spies, that the British were not ready to fight. Probably, too, they were aware of the Allied decision not to open the offensive until summer. They also felt that the Russian army had been beaten in the preceding year and was no longer dangerous. They could therefore afford to draw consid-

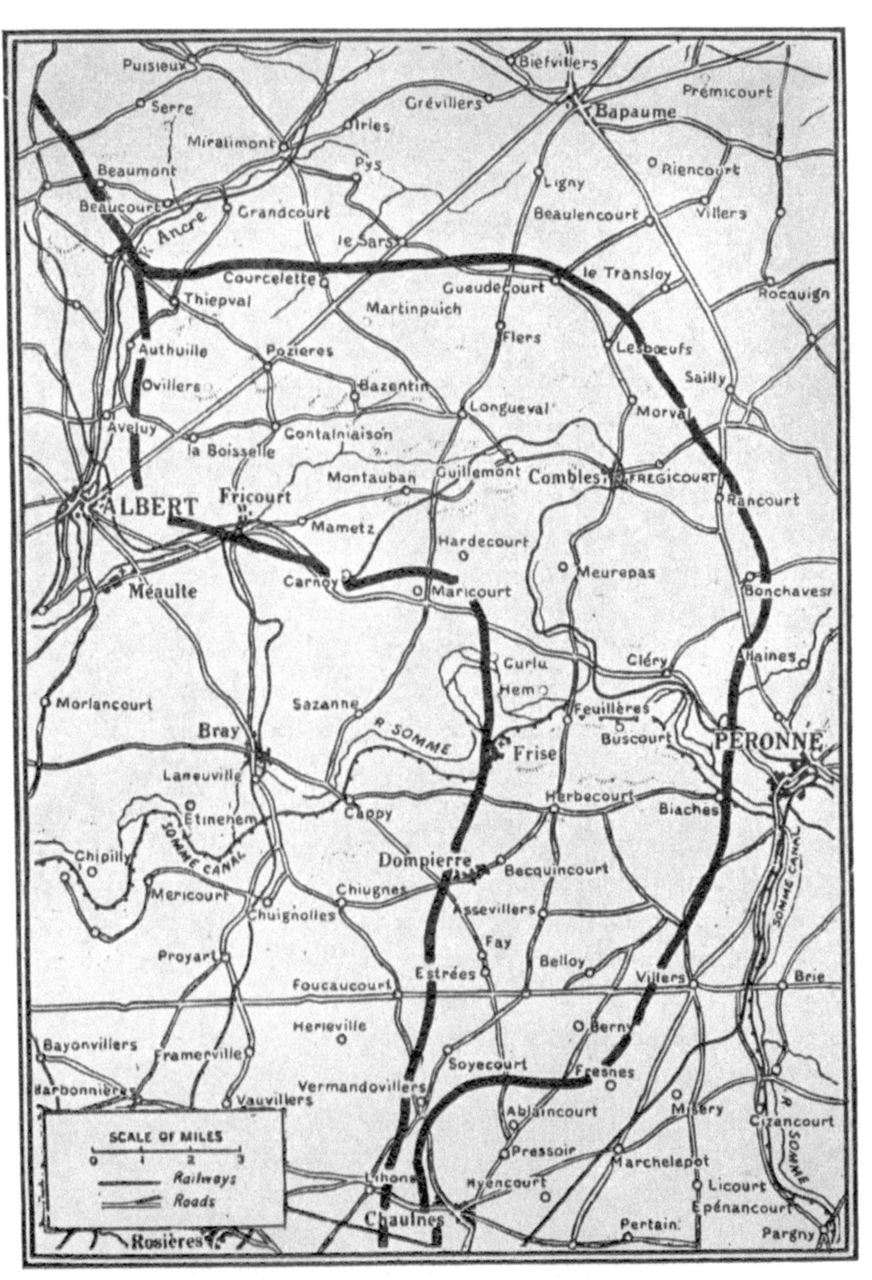

DETAILED MAP OF ALLIED GAINS IN 1916.

erable strength from the eastern armies to use in the west, which should give them an effective superiority in men and in artillery. To deliver a smashing attack on the British, who were not yet ready, was of course possible and the result would probably be the defeat of the British army. But this would leave the Germans face to face with the strong, competent French army and would use up time and strength without promising to effect a decision. The German general staff argued that it was better to let the British alone and to throw the entire German strength upon the French. Once the better army was beaten and the bigger army was destroyed, the British would be at the mercy of the Germans.

The assault had to be delivered of course on the French prepared positions and it had to be a frontal attack. It would therefore cost many lives and a vast amount of ammunition, but the German generals felt that if only enough guns and men were available, they could not fail. Being compelled to attack the French positions from the front anyway, they decided to assail the very key of the French line—Verdun. Here the great fortresses constructed in the past had been rendered useless by the new artillery and the French had abandoned them. The Germans, therefore, would have to reckon only with defenses of a type universal along the trench line. To carry Verdun ought to be no more difficult than to break any other part of the trench line, while the results would be proportionately more significant.

The German spies also reported that the French generals were not in favor of holding Verdun in case a great attack should be delivered upon it. Verdun would cost a tremendous toll in lives to hold and was no better defense to Paris than the new positions to which the French could move without sacrificing a man. Probably, therefore, the Germans expected to get Verdun very cheaply and then to advertise the tremendous success which the valor of their armies had won. They therefore made elaborate preparations for the attack, put the Crown Prince in command so that he might

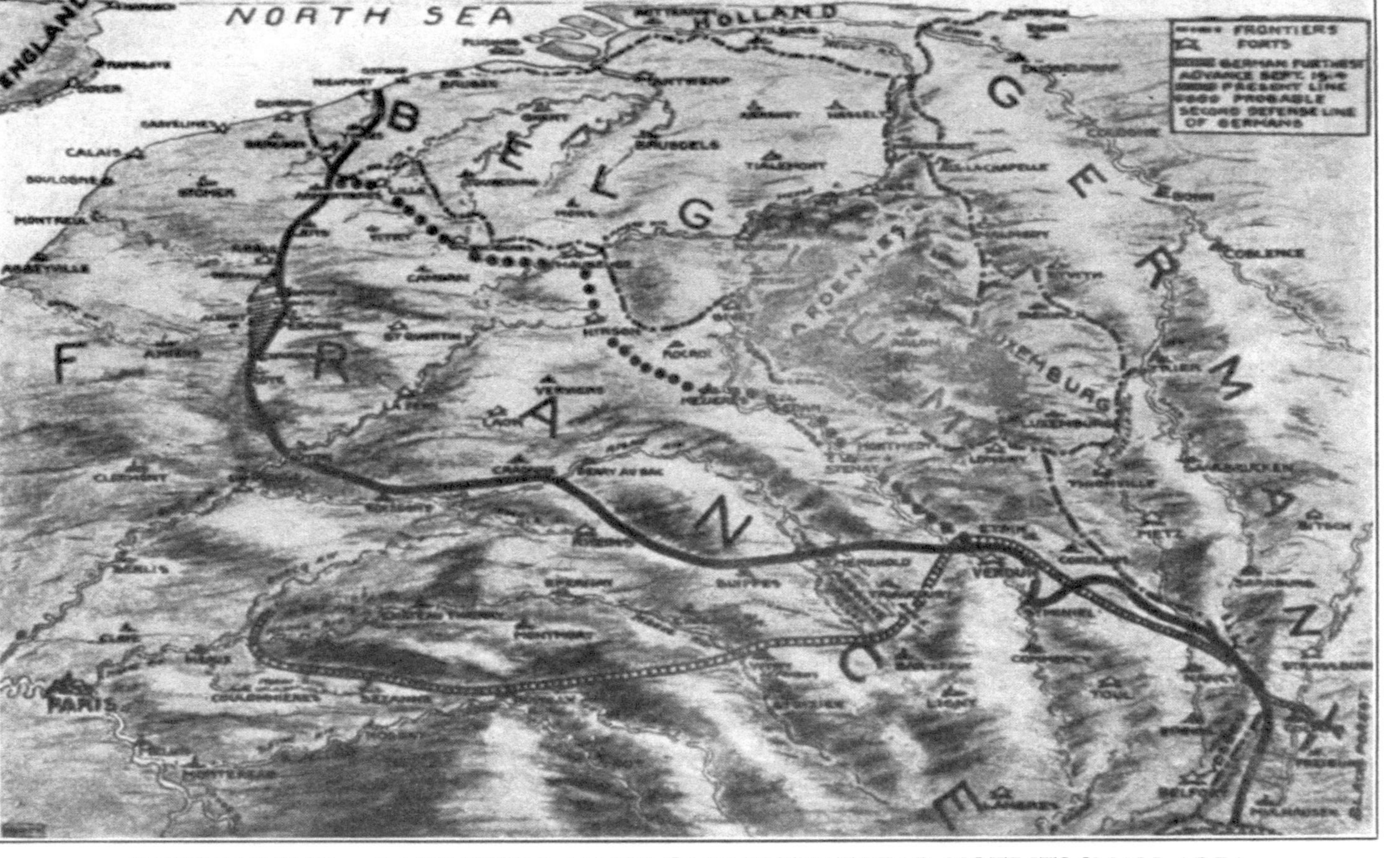

BATTLE LINE IN 1916 AND TOTAL ALLIED GAIN IN THAT YEAR. NOTE ITS SMALL AREA.

take the credit for the expected victory, and in February began a vast assault, miles wide, along the French center in front of Verdun.

The French statesmen appreciated better than the generals the moral effect of surrendering Verdun, even assuming that the generals were right that it possessed no military value which other positions did not have. It possessed a meaning for the French people which no other position could have. It had for centuries been considered the key to Paris, and the Germans would naturally advertise that because the key to Paris had fallen, the road to victory was open. It would not be true, but the French people might believe it and that would shake their confidence in the army. It would indeed be absolutely false, but the German people would also believe it and that would strengthen their confidence in their own army and in the Kaiser. Such moral results could not fail to be disastrous. Therefore the order went forth to hold Verdun at all costs. And Verdun was held. Month after month the German assaults broke upon it and failed. The famous watchword came true; they did not pass.

But when June came and the German attacks on Verdun still continued, the Allies deemed it wise to begin a tremendous offensive against Austria along the Carpathian front. In that month the Russians under Brusiloff made such progress indeed and defeated the Austrians so many times, that the Germans did diminish their efforts against Verdun in order to send men to the east. When, therefore, the magnitude of the German defeat was clear, the Allies felt that the German army in France had been tremendously weakened. Had it not lost hundreds of thousands of men before Verdun? Had it not sent hundreds of thousands to the rescue of the Austrians? Hundreds of thousands of British had now arrived in France; the English factories were pouring out an endless stream of munitions. The time had come when a great offensive must succeed if only undertaken on a sufficiently large scale and continued long enough. The Allies therefore launched along the river Somme a tremendous concentrated assault, which continued week after week, month after month, from July until November. All this time the Russian assault in the Carpathians was continued.

The Austrians had attempted in May and June to weaken the Allied resistance at Verdun by an assault upon the Italians. This they had had to abandon in order to send troops to the Carpathians and to resist the British and French along the Somme. In August, therefore, the Italians also took advantage of the German perplexity to deliver an attack upon the Austrians in Italy. Thus the summer of 1916 found the Allied armies fighting with tremendous intensity on all three fronts.

So confident were they that a movement had been at last launched which promised success, that they now made every effort to bring the Rumanians into the war. If only an additional push could be given the Germans on the east, something must crumble. Rumania, they thought, was in exactly the position to strike that blow. The Russians were already attacking in the Carpathians, and if the Rumanians came through the mountains into Hungary they would strike the flank and rear of the Austrians opposing the Russians. One of two things would be sure to happen, and either would be disastrous. The Austrians would be compelled to detach troops to meet the Rumanians, which ought so to weaken their armies facing the Russians that the latter would be able to win a victory. On the other hand, if the Rumanians were quick enough, they themselves might win the victory by striking the Austrian rear before the latter could reorganize their lines.

The campaign promised much for the Rumanians, for across the mountains in Hungary were some millions of people of Rumanian blood who had long wished to be joined to their compatriots. The Allies promised to add this territory to Rumania when the war should be won. At the end of August, therefore, the Rumanians did enter the war. They did deliver a great attack on Hungary, did penetrate the mountains, and did make some progress across the plains into Transylvania.

The magnitude of the peril aroused the Germans. Hindenburg

was now made commander-in-chief of the German armies. He at once changed many of the dispositions of the troops, and soon had the situation in hand. In September both the Russians and Italians were driven back; the Austrian lines were reorganized to meet the Rumanians; and the catastrophe for which the Allies had hoped never eventuated. In France the German lines yielded a little here and there but on the whole held stoutly. The British and French casualties were heavy; the amount of ammunition they expended was indeed unlimited; but the German defense system was not pierced, and the gains they did make were out of proportion to the cost in lives and material. If the war had to be won at that rate, they saw that the cost was going to be prohibitive. They could not ransom the soil of France by the expenditure of any such amount of blood and treasure. When the bad weather came, therefore, in November, and the winter set in, the British and French gave up the attempt along the Somme and settled down to another winter of defensive warfare.

Then, as if to avenge themselves for their drubbing at Verdun and for the terrible punishment they had received along the Somme for so many months, the Germans fell upon Rumania to rend her limb from limb. Her king had previously promised both Kaisers that he would assist them in the war, or at least remain neutral. He had not been able to keep his promise and the Kaisers proposed to punish him for it. The fields of Rumania were fertile, broad, and desirable. Great harvests of grain were ready for reaping and the hungry people of Germany and Austria would be able to use that food during the coming winter. There were also great oil wells in Rumania; gasoline was as useful to the Germans as to the Allies; and the Germans had no supply of it. There were a good many reasons why the Germans were anxious to get possession of the lower Danube.

They therefore sent south one of their best generals, Von Mackensen. He allowed the Rumanians to come as far into Hungary as they wished. Every mile they advanced they put themselves in his power. He then attacked their left wing at the Vulkan Pass with great force, pushed through the mountains with tremendous rapidity, and thus flanked the Rumanian army in Hungary. It was forced to retreat at all speed in order to save itself from capture. The Germans were moreover in a position which compelled it to retire on its own capital. No sooner had the Rumanians reached the defensive lines before Bucharest than Von Mackensen crossed the Danube on their flank and rear with another army and thus caught them between two fires.

The Rumanians were not expert soldiers and were none too well equipped. They had expected to fight a reasonably easy war in which the Allies in Greece at Saloniki and the Russians in the Carpathians were to do the bulk of the work. The Allied campaign in Greece had not amounted to much; the Russians had been beaten by the Germans; and the Rumanians were now left to pay the penalty. The greater part of their country was evacuated and the wheat fields and the oil wells fell into the hands of the Germans. Whether this conquest materially aided the Germans in prolonging the war has been questioned by Allied authorities, but, while it may not have resulted in as great accessions of food as the enthusiastic newspaper reporters in Berlin and Vienna led the people to hope, it must have been of real consequence and value.

Verdun

The tremendous assault upon Verdun fell upon the apex of the French defense system. It was not a single fort by any means, but a series of forts, supported on a twenty mile front by trenches, barbed wire, artillery positions, to such an extent that the French called it the Iron Frontier. They had learned long since from the experience of Antwerp that any fixed fort could be destroyed by heavy artillery. Verdun, the most important single point in the French line, must be an impregnable fort, and it must therefore be movable, nor must it depend upon any single position.

Every foot of ground for twenty miles was hence covered in a dozen ways by various grades of artillery, planted to sweep the roads, fields, and woods, as a fire hose sweeps a gutter. All the forests on the hills were labyrinths of barbed wire, so cunningly concealed, that if German spies, much less a file of men, should get in they would never find their way out. Bottles and pans were also hung on the wires so as to make a terrible noise, whenever any one unacquainted with the place attempted to move around in it. There would be no surprise at Verdun.

The strength of the new line was well known to the Germans, but its importance was no less clear, and when they concluded to crush the French army before the British could arrive in strength no spot was better adapted to their purpose than Verdun. It was the hinge between eastern and western France. It controlled all the roads from Germany to Paris; it controlled the great highway of the river Meuse; it was the center of the French line, and its key. Once lost, the roads to Paris would be open and the rest of the French army could be beaten at pleasure. The fact that the Crown Prince was given command showed that it was intended to be the decisive blow of the war.

The method employed in fighting at this time was to pave the way for the infantry by a prolonged bombardment of the enemy's fortifications, so long continued and so thorough that it was expected to break down all the barbed wire, blow up all the trenches, kill all the infantry, and prevent any other preparations being made to replace those destroyed. Such a bombardment lasted in this case for weeks. The effect of it is thus described by a French officer, caught for twelve hours in one sector by the bombardment.

"Alone, in a sort of dugout without walls I pass twelve hours of agony, believing that it is the end. The soil is torn up, covered with fresh earth by enormous explosions. In front of us are no less than twelve hundred guns of 240, 305, 380, and 420 caliber, which spit ceaselessly, and all together, in these days of preparation for attack. These explosions stupefy the brain; you feel as if your entrails were being torn out, your heart twisted and wrenched; the shock seems to dismember your body... Twelve hours alone, motionless, exposed, and no chance to risk a leap to another place, so closely did the fragments of shell and rock fall in hail all day long."

At night the firing slackened momentarily and he was able to make his escape from the hole, but passed five days in a cave underground with other men, packed so tight they were unable to lie down. They escaped then into a tunnel, where they stayed for two days, and then ran at top speed through the remains of what had once been a dense forest, through a hail of shell—to safety.

After the artillery preparations were judged complete, and the French troops and artillery destroyed, the German infantry came on in dense masses to the attack, surely expecting to occupy the territory from which the French had thus been driven. But the French had not been expelled from it. With artillery, with machine

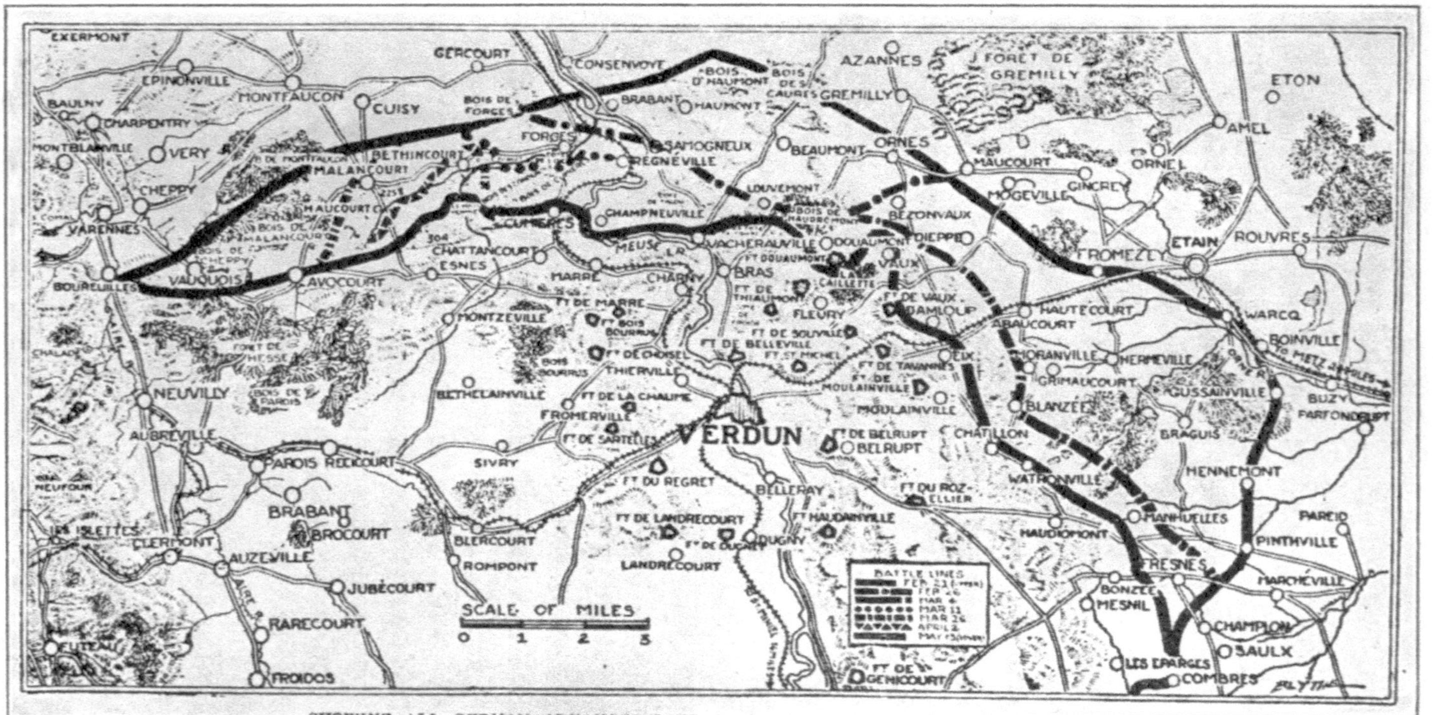

SUCCESSIVE GERMAN GAINS AT VERDUN.

guns, with rifle fire, and at last with bayonets, and even with their bare hands, they fought back the finest troops of the German army and defeated them. When the German infantry advanced, the German artillery had to cease fire or it would have killed their own troops. Then the French guns operated upon these vast masses of men proceeding across the fields.

A French officer describes such a fire. "We fired at full speed for twenty minutes. When 'cease fire' came, there was a heap of shell cases fully man high behind our guns. At the order I rushed to look out of the trench at the side of the battery. At the bottom of the ravine, on the edge of the plateau, was a great heap of Germans. They looked like a swarm of bees, crawling over one another. Not one was standing.... The whole ravine slope was gray with corpses.... The snow was no longer white... and the river ran past, dappled with great patches and streaks of blood."

For weeks and months this steady attacking by the Germans, the ceaseless bombardment, this continual reply of the machine guns and counter-attacks by the French infantry went on and on. At the beginning of the battle, the Germans won some considerable territory, first here and then there, but they did not reach Verdun. Toward the end of the year the French won back again more than they had at first lost.

Thousands of brave deeds, both by the French and by the Germans, were done during this tremendous battle. The following description of an eyewitness tells of the French counter-attack upon the Germans. "At midnight the concentration is completed and the armies are in their appointed places. Is the cannonade fiercer or less fierce? I cannot say. The noise is so deafening that I have lost the power of judging its intensity. I cannot even distinguish the explosions of the shells that fall nearest.... The searchlights throw patch after patch of trees into bright relief;... Not a yard of ground fails to receive the shock of a projectile. The solid earth bubbles before my eyes. Trees split and spring into the air. It is a surface earthquake with nothing spared, nothing stable.... The searchlight reveals the German redoubt... a wall of earth and tree trunks half buried in the ground. Now and again in the patches of brightness one sees tiny shadows running, falling, rolling over or flitting from trunk to trunk.... They are the soldiers of the Kaiser trying vainly to escape from the rain of death.

"Dawn breaks.... A shrill ringing startles every one. The captain springs to the telephone, listens for an instant, and murmurs, 'They're off'... Our guns still thunder, but they have lengthened their range, and the line of smoke blobs opposite leaps toward the horizon.... Some one grabs my arm and points northward. Down the slopes of Hill 304, a multitude of nimble figures are rushing westward. Their numbers increase; armed warriors spring from the ground, as in the old Greek. 'Our men,' says the officer beside me. It is the soldiers of France at the charge. For a while they are sheltered from the German fire by a swelling billow of ground. They mount its crest and pour headlong downward.

"Now the pace is slower; they advance singly or in scattered groups—crawling, leaping, running.... They pass the first trench without hesitating, as though it were a tiny brook... Now the whole mass is across... The charging men go straight forward like runners between strings, leaving open lanes along which their comrades can still fire upon the defenders. At last the edge of the woods is reached... It is hand to hand now... work for bayonet or revolver, for butt or club, or even for fists and teeth. Corpses are everywhere until the bodies form veritable heaps among which the living fight and wrestle."

At Caillette Wood an extraordinary exploit was performed by the Germans. They had found the work of holding the gains made by the troops during an assault extremely difficult because they could not fight and at the same time dig themselves in. After an attack had been sent forward successfully some little distance, the German commander determined to build a new barrier immediately behind it. Lowering clouds and the smoke of battle aided them. Behind the German assault columns came a corps of workers, three thousand strong, forming a long line across the fields. They passed from man to man, like firemen passing buckets at some old country fire, wooden billets, sandbags, pieces of steel, machine guns, and everything needed for the barrier.

To have carried the material across that field in any other way would have been impossible. The ground was too rough for wagons even had the artillery fire not been too intense. Only by such a human chain could the material reach its destined point. Cover was disdained. The workers stood erect, exposed to the sweep of the French fire. Again and again, great rents were torn in the line. Coolly, new men sprang from shelters to take the place of the fallen. Gradually another line began to double the line of workmen. It was a line of corpses, but, with the material they were piling, it did form the barricade they wanted. At last at a frightful cost, the new line was completed, At evening, the barrier still held, covering troops burrowing like moles into the hillside, strengthening the trench.

And then came a French exploit matching the German. It was eight o'clock and pitch dark. Volunteers from a French regiment crept forward on their stomachs, carrying with them dynamite with which to blow up the new fortification. In Indian file, the volunteer blasting corps advanced, the long line stiffening to look like corpses when the German searchlights played upon them, and crawling slowly forward when the searchlights moved away. When within a few yards of the new fortification, each man, lying at full length, began to scoop out with his shovel the earth under him, gradually making a shallow trench in which he sank out of sight.

Then the leader began to dig forward. Inch by inch, the file stole on, sheltered by this narrow ditch from the hail of German machine gun fire, which constantly swept the field. Hours passed. It was all but day, when the gallant remnant at last reached the barricade, placed the explosives in position, and crawled back along the ditch as fast as they dared. Suddenly came a roar, engulfing the sound of the cannon. Along the new barrier, fountains of fire rose skyward, hurling a rain of fragments upon the survivors of the blasting party. And then came to their ears the music of the cheers of their French comrades, dashing forward to the assault as they carried the position.

Another difficulty surmounted by the French during these long months was that of supplying the fortress and its defenders with ammunition and food. The German preparations had been carefully made and they had control almost at once of the only railroad leading to Verdun. There remained for the French only an automobile road and only one: over that for six months passed everything used in this tremendous defense. The Germans had calculated that Verdun must fall by reason of the inability of the French to supply it, but the French put in use every auto truck or car on the whole French front and started an endless chain of autos, running along that highway only a few feet apart at top speed.

For months that chain went on and on, day and night, never stopping, every car going in loaded with supplies and coming out loaded with wounded. If a car broke down, it was shoved off the highway in an instant, so that it should not block the line upon whose movement the fate of France depended. If it could be mended, a corps of machinists mended it and shoved it back into line; if not, they abandoned it.

The result of this long battle was a German failure. How many hundreds of thousands of Germans perished in this great assault is not yet known, but the number was exceedingly great, and in the end they failed to destroy the French army or to defeat it before the British could arrive with adequate assistance.

Of the fortress of Verdun nothing was left but the site where it had stood. Of the city nearly all was in ruins. As the battle went on, it became essential for the French to construct, deep in the earth, new fortresses which became, as time went on, a city underground, sufficiently large to house comfortably the entire army, with bedrooms, dining rooms, concert halls, theaters, long lines of corridors, to say nothing of the emplacements from which the artillery fired upon the enemy. Aboveground—not a blade of grass, not a tree, nor a yard of earth not churned up by artillery fire. Below—the French army, courageous, indomitable.

THE BATTLE OF JUTLAND

On May 31, 1916, there took place off the coast of Denmark the only engagement between the German and British fleets of the war;[3] and while it cannot be called in the strict sense a great battle, it does bring into relief the policies of the two navies and shows something of their relative competence. It was the only engagement, because it was the German policy to avoid battles. By great daring and skillful planning the Germans had brought into existence a fleet. They boasted that it was large enough to frighten the British navy, but they never so far deceived themselves as to suppose that it was large enough to conquer it. Indeed, they were pretty thoroughly of the opinion that despite its size and quality it would be inadvisable to risk it in battle. The existence of that fleet was more useful to them than a victory could possibly be. Even supposing that it won a great battle, it could not expect to do so without loss, and, inasmuch as the German fleet was smaller than the British, its losses would be relatively more serious.

So long as the fleet existed, the British were compelled to concentrate their own navy in the North Sea, both in war and in peace, and were therefore compelled to surrender the actual control of the ocean highways to their allies.

[3] There had been engagements in the Pacific and South Atlantic which had had the important result of clearing the seas of German raiders and cruisers, but which had not been in any sense engagements between the major fleets. There had been also skirmishes between the cruiser squadrons in the North Sea and some raids of the British coast by light-armed fast German craft.

The Germans could easily conceive that these allies might not always remain faithful. It was even thought in Berlin that the chances to take possession of the Pacific would be more attractive than the Japanese could resist, that possession of the Mediterranean would have an irresistible charm for the French, and that the United States would not be sorry to occupy the West India Islands. By all means, therefore, keep the German fleet in existence. It perpetuated a situation extremely dangerous to the British, one which had caused uneasiness in London for ten years.

This policy had also caused the Germans to locate the real base of the fleet in the Baltic at Kiel rather than on the Atlantic at Hamburg. The Kiel Canal, connecting the Baltic and the Atlantic, allowed them to use their fleet in both seas, gave them control of the Baltic, and enabled them to blockade Russia. On the Atlantic they erected at Helgoland and at Wilhelmshaven the most extraordinary variety of defenses, with great guns, mine fields, and all other devices they could think of, to prevent the British fleet from attempting, in Nelson fashion, to deliver an assault upon the German base. For they well knew that it would be British policy during the war, as indeed it was, to force an action between the fleets at all costs.

The British were so far superior in numbers and believed their fleet, ship for ship, so superior in quality, that they could well afford to take great risks and even suffer considerable loss to cripple or destroy the German navy. They were entirely capable of dashing into the German fleet at anchor, for, if they could sacrifice ship for ship and succeed, it would be well worth their while. The German base must be strong enough to prevent a battle without German consent.

For practically two years, therefore, the German fleet swung at its moorings, while the British fleet steamed restlessly up and down the North Sea, partly to make the blockade tight, but principally to be on hand to take instant advantage of the slightest opportunity the Germans might give for an attack. The British admirals knew at the outset that any attempt to rush the German fleet in harbor would be suicide; they must entice the Germans outside. They were also wisely anxious about mines and submarines. As Admiral Jellicoe has revealed since the war closed, the preponderance of the British in numbers in 1914 was not sufficient; the German calculations were correct; the British could not disregard caution. There was in 1914 the possibility that they might be defeated.

Nevertheless, they were anxious for an engagement, and on May 31, 1916, the British scouts reported that a battle screen of swift, German light cruisers had come into sight off Jutland, followed by five battle cruisers of the largest type. It was half past three in the afternoon, however; the day was relatively dark, and the light was therefore likely to fade between six and seven. If an action was to be forced, it must be done in a hurry. Nine fast British cruisers, followed by four of the largest battleships of the *Queen Elizabeth* class, started at once in pursuit. The details of this engagement as given by the British and the German accounts vary considerably, but it seems likely that the British account is the truer, primarily because it accords with the general policy of the two navies, whereas that of the Germans does not.

When twelve miles distant, the British battleships opened fire, but the Germans kept back well out of range. At 4:40 P.M. a destroyer screen was seen behind the German battle cruisers and behind it what the British believed to be the whole German high seas fleet, steaming ahead in three divisions. The British grand fleet was already in motion but was some miles away. Admiral Beatty did not hesitate for a moment. He saw before him the only opportunity in two years to force an engagement and he started at the Germans at top speed, his object being to engage them, lead them to attempt the destruction of his small force, and thus expose themselves to the full weight of Jellicoe's assault, which Beatty hoped they would not realize was so imminent.

A considerable amount of maneuvering took place. The Germans attempted to close around Beatty; he avoided them and kept clear his own retreat, while at the same time enticing them to pursue him toward Jellicoe. All this time a running battle was continued at long range between such ships as could open fire. For about an hour, therefore, Beatty's cruisers and the *Queen Elizabeth* were in contact with the German fast cruisers, and perhaps with a portion of the German high seas fleet. But the mists of the evening were rising, the smoke of battle added to the obscurity, the ships were firing at a distance of several miles, and marksmanship became extremely difficult.

The British grand fleet was coming up fast in three divisions, and by masterly maneuvering, Beatty so arranged his division as to keep in touch with the Germans and at the same time let the whole British fleet pass through upon them. Jellicoe seems to have attempted the Nelson touch, an attack in force upon the head of the column of advancing German ships. He seems also to have meant to get between the Germans and their own base, if possible. But the mists descended; darkness came; the whereabouts of the rival navies could only be determined by distant flashes. There was imminent danger that the British would fire upon each other in the dark. The Germans seemed to have profited by the situation and made good their escape, for escape it was.

Both sides at first claimed the victory; both claimed to have sunk the larger number of the other's ships and the greater tonnage. The British admitted the loss of fourteen ships, the Germans of eleven, though the British felt sure that they sunk some eighteen or twenty German vessels. The darkness and distance made it impossible, however, to dispute the German claims. There seems to be no considerable doubt now that the victory remained with the British. Technically it was theirs, because they remained in possession of the field of battle. Certainly too the Germans retired behind their defenses and never emerged again until they sailed forth to surrender.

The engagement showed the mettle of the British navy, its willingness to attack under tremendous odds, its great skill in maneuvering, but the fact is none the less clear that the real fighting took place between a few ships only of the second type,—fast, heavily armed cruisers. The battleship squadrons of both fleets were present, rather than in action, and certainly did not really come within effective range of each other until darkness had already fallen. The real result of the engagement appeared in the German unwillingness to attempt another. But the German policy, as the war displayed it in the field, in the air, and on the sea, was always the same, never to risk an engagement without practical certainty of victory. No victory could possibly be worth the risk of the navy's loss. When eventual victory came in France, the navy must be ready to go forth and conquer the seas. A victory on land and defeat at sea would be in the end an overwhelming defeat. They must win both on land and on sea, but they could not begin the battle on the sea until they had won on land.

LIFE IN THE TRENCHES

To those who have not experienced warfare, it seems a most thrilling and exciting adventure. We imagine something happening most of the time and certainly suppose it to be the most interesting experience which an individual could have. But on the majority of men who fought this war, life in the trenches left the same impression. War was dull. It was composed of long delays, of interminable waiting, of weeks and months in which nothing of consequence took place. The danger of being shot became too commonplace to furnish any excitement. The ordinary man spent day after day sitting or lying in little holes in the ground, either waiting for something to happen, or, if he was fortunate, watching another hole in the ground some distance off where the Germans were. While the year 1918 was one of almost continuous activity all along the front, such was not the case in the years preceding it. An individual might have a week or more of the most intense or exhausting activity, followed by months in which he felt that he was doing nothing at all.

The soldiers, moreover, were unanimous that war was uncomfortable. War was, first of all, mud; war was also wet, for it rained upon the Allied trenches as well as upon the Germans. In Flanders the greater part of the country had always been under water during the winter and spring months and the floods came during the war as at other times. The Germans and Allies also took great pleasure in devising measures for turning rivers into each others' trenches. On large sections of the lines throughout the winter the mud was ankle deep when it was not deeper. On some considerable portions, the men stood waist deep in ice water, sometimes for hours at a stretch.

War also was cold. It had to go on in winter as well as at other times. Men had to be on duty in the trenches during long winter nights when the sleet and snow descended as well as on pleasant summer evenings. It does not get cold in Europe as it does in this country, for in northern France the ground does not freeze solid for the winter, as it does in the northern part of the United States, and the snow is rarely deep and seldom lasts. But it is damp and foggy and the cold somehow seeps through one's clothes and flesh into the very marrow of one's bones.

War therefore was dirt. A soldier coming out of the trenches looked like a sort of animated mud bank, or, if it were a rainy day, like a man who had fallen into a sewer and had just been rescued. It was extremely difficult to keep clean, and while baths, dry clothing, and new clothing were provided, it was very difficult for the men to keep comfortable. The amount of food on hand at all times in the trenches and dugouts drew vast numbers of rats and mice who were very unpleasant companions. Dogs and cats were kept to kill them but it was never entirely possible to get rid of them.

All of these conditions made two things particularly essential in the trenches if life was to be endurable. First, what was known in the British army as "spit and polish." Whatever the conditions, however deep the water or mud, however long the rainstorm, the men must present themselves in the morning at inspection with the chin shaved, the hair cut, the gun clean, the clothes brushed, with all the buttons on, and with the leather shiny. The result might last only five minutes but the officers were insistent that it should be done. The purpose was clear. It was necessary if the men were to keep well. Unless a man is kept clean, he very soon becomes diseased and sick. Unless his clothes are clean, he accumulates vermin and also germs. The health of the army could not last long unless as great cleanliness were insisted upon as possible.

But why the polish? That had to do with the morale of the men. The tendency of the soldier is to say after a while to himself, what's the use of being clean I am as likely as not to be killed the next minute—why should I be polishing my boots—what difference does it make to me whether I am killed in a clean or a dirty shirt—whether I have two buttons off or two buttons on. Once an officer allows the men to become dirty, they begin really to believe that they probably will be killed the next minute. It was absolutely essential that the men should act as if they could not be killed; as if they were going to live forever. If the mud was deep, all the more reason to act as if it were not there. The effect upon the men was to keep up their courage and to keep them in good humor.

The other essential thing was healthy amusement. For the British and Americans this took the form of football and baseball, which the Americans began to teach the British. There were dances in which the men danced with each other, when there were no girls available, and movie performances which were regularly provided for the troops. The British created almost at once what were called Church Huts; the American Y.M.C.A. also began its work in the British army before we entered the war. The British Salvation Army undertook a vast work for keeping the men happy and amused. All of these organizations distributed a considerable amount of luxuries, particularly tobacco. The French do not care for games of the sort the British and Americans play, and the French government provided theatrical and vaudeville performers and moving pictures. The greatest actors and singers in France were glad to give all their time to the task of amusing the soldiers and their work was extremely important and successful.

It would be a very great mistake to allow any one to suppose that there was any lack of humor or cheerfulness in the trenches. The contrary was true, especially in the case of the British and Americans. The British in particular extracted a great deal of satisfaction out of French names, which they never were able to pronounce and which they therefore mispronounced intentionally. Ypres became Wipers; Meault became meaow, pronounced as we pronounce the mewing of a cat; Mouquet became moo cow.

A QUIET LITTLE PARTY.

The French early in the war began to refer to the Germans as the "boches," which is supposed to come from *caboche*, meaning thick head, but its real derivation is declared by the best authorities to be vague. The British promptly nicknamed the Germans "Fritz," just as the Germans called the Highland troops, with their kilts and bare knees, the "ladies from hell." The Americans also contributed to the army slang and nicknamed the Germans "Jerry," and termed their own motor corps the "gas hounds." One of the most peculiar words commonly used by the British and Americans was "blighty." It meant a wound sufficiently serious to invalid a man home and was supposed to come from a Persian word, picked up by the British in the east, which means back home, or going back home.

Almost at the outset, the French private soldier began to be called "poilu," which is said to be derived from a French word

POSTER OF AMERICAN ARMY
CAMP SHOW IN FRANCE.

meaning hairy, and refers to the fact that most Frenchmen wear beards, and that most soldiers therefore were hairy. "Tommy Atkins" was a term for the British soldiers which had been in use for a long time before this war, and is supposed to have come from some story or comic song. It is also interesting to know that the British and American soldiers used a great deal of that sort of private language which a good many American children think they invent, when they turn words hind side before or reverse some of the letters. The soldiers after all were nothing but great boys; many of them in fact were no more than seventeen or eighteen years old. It is therefore not surprising that they should have continued in the army all those practices which have been so long dear to the British and American youth at home.

Belgium—Scornful—Defiant

Throughout the war, although crushed beneath the German heel and helpless beyond all question, the spirit of Belgium never for a moment wavered. The loyalty of the people to their king and to the ideal of independence never faltered. Money, physical abuse, threats, torture, were absolutely unavailing to draw from them any admission of the right of the German cause or any cooperation with it. If they must go to prison rather than aid the Germans by working, to prison they went, and in prison they stayed. If they had the alternative of betraying their fellow countrymen or of being shot, they placidly and cheerfully put their backs against the wall and were shot.

The Germans could not understand it. It was the sort of logic which never appealed to the German mind. But the silent, continued, scornful defiance of an entire nation of truly helpless people did make its impression. There came to be lengths to which even Germans would not go. There was an extent to which an unresisting people could not be abused for loyalty to their country.

The very children in the streets carried on the war for Belgium. They mimicked the German soldiers' march to their faces. Nothing delighted the public or the children more than to see some German dignitary proceed down the street, followed at a safe distance by three or four ragged urchins, imitating his stride, and probably whistling the Belgian national air. The children made faces at the Germans, made to each other exceedingly uncomplimentary

PRINCESS MARIE OF BELGIUM.

remarks about Germans, which the soldiers could not help hearing, and kept it up month after month, year after year, despite the thrashings they at first received and the kicks and cuffs they always got when within range.

At first the whole population determined to show that it was not conquered, by wearing a little button or badge containing the picture of the king. Every man, woman, and child had one; every dog wore one on his collar; every horse had one on his bridle. They were stuck on the street cars and on the doors of all the German officers' houses; when possible, the little boys attached a button to the tail of the officers' coats. The movement was so absolutely universal that the German governor felt himself helpless; he could not send a whole people to jail. But after a while the buttons were forbidden.

All the newspapers, of course, were prohibited at the very beginning of the German occupation. All public meetings, speeches, songs, or any demonstrations in favor of Belgium were prohibited. Then one morning in February, 1915, there appeared on the streets of Brussels, a newspaper, *La Libre Belgique*—Free Belgium. The paper announced that it was to be "published regularly, irregularly"; it would be brought out whenever possible and would be distributed but not sold. Certain prominent Belgians had contrib-

uted the money and pro-
posed to issue this secret,
flaming, patriotic paper
under the very noses of
the Germans. The edi-
torials declared that the
Germans were assassins,
traitors, pigs, dogs, and
other names which their
high mightinesses did not
appreciate. It printed pictures of the German mili-
tary governor which made
him ridiculous; there was
even a cartoon showing
the Kaiser in hell.

From the first the
Germans were deter-
mined to put a stop to the
paper and they did their

FRENCH POSTER DESIGNED TO
SHOW GERMAN ATROCITIES.

best to discover how and where it was published. They turned
Belgium upside down, but the paper still appeared. The military
governor himself found a copy on his own desk or breakfast table
on the morning of its publication. Who put it there, he could
never find out, but it always arrived. Presently it began to contain
exceedingly humorous articles about the attempts to suppress it. It
showed its own printing plant installed in an automobile, touring
around the country, with the Germans running after it. Finally it
printed a picture of the German military governor reading the
paper itself. His rage when he found that on his desk fairly shook
the foundations of Belgium.

The search was redoubled. Every house that they could think of
was ransacked,—any house was subject to search at any time,—and
many people spent weeks and months in prison for possessing a

copy, but not one of them ever told how he got it. Some "confidences" were made to the authorities which resulted in making them more ridiculous than ever. In one case the plan of a house was sent and the location of the press was marked. With infinite care, the Germans surrounded the house, the soldiers, on tiptoe with expectancy and anxiety not to alarm the prey, went inside and proceeded to the spot marked—and found a small, dark closet. The hated newspaper knew about it and soon all Belgium was laughing over the ease with which the Germans had been gulled.

On another occasion directions were given of such an explicit character that the authorities felt sure they were at last going to catch the publisher of the forbidden sheet. They followed the directions to the letter and presently found they were to arrest an old statue in one of the public squares!

The greatest public demonstrations were naturally those on the Belgian national holiday, the twenty-first of July. Fearful of riots and demonstrations in 1915, on the first holiday after the war had begun, the German authorities forbade the people to celebrate it in any way. But word was quietly passed of a method to demonstrate to the Germans without breaking their rules the unity and determination of the Belgians. The entire population of the cities, particularly in Brussels, put on their Sunday clothes, closed the shops and houses, and walked up and down the streets quietly, slowly, peacefully, irreproachably from early morning until late at night. The German officials raged and fumed but not a single individual broke any of the rules posted for the day, and apparently not a soul in Brussels failed to turn out to demonstrate to the Germans that he despised them utterly and always would.

So complete was the lesson that when the next national holiday appeared in the following year, the German governor attempted to forestall this particular sort of demonstration, and required that no stores or shops should be closed, and, of course, that there should be no celebration or demonstration. He threatened any who disobeyed him with prison and a fine of five thousand dollars. As

BELGIUM—DEFIANT.

La Libre Belgique said, the fine did not matter, for the only people in Belgium who had five thousand dollars were the Germans, who had stolen it from the Belgians.

The twenty-first of July, 1916, dawned a wonderful, sunny day. The entire city was green. Every one had a green ribbon, signifying hope, in his buttonhole; every dog had a green ribbon round his neck; every horse had one on his bridle; every house and every store had green paper pasted in the windows. Every shop and store was open, but everywhere green was in sight. The Germans understood, but were helpless. One particular place in the city where the Belgian martyrs were buried gave the Germans especial concern. There a guard of soldiers with fixed bayonets had been placed to prevent any demonstration. The Belgians found the matter simple. The entire city of Brussels walked through that street sometime during the day, and, as they passed the spot where the martyrs had fallen, they simply bowed their heads. The rules did not cover this point, and all day the officers and soldiers stood there, witnessing this tremendous demonstration made in their very faces, without being able in the least to do anything.

At the churches, service was held and the crowds were so great that not an additional person could have entered one of the buildings. That was the point. The churches were so full that the police could not get in. At least twelve thousand people were supposed to have been in the largest church. The Germans raged but were helpless. At the Cathedral the ordinary service was held and then the Dean announced that at eleven o'clock a funeral service would be held for the Belgian soldiers who had fallen in the war. It was sung by Cardinal Le Mercier with great pomp and dignity. The Cardinal sang the service in a voice shaken by emotion and then delivered a patriotic address which stirred the very souls of the thousands present.

On the national holiday, despite the German prohibition, they were celebrating their resistance and the Germans could not interfere! They sang the national song, and suddenly there rang through

the building a shout—
"Long live the King!"
And despite requests
that no demonstration
be made, a tremendous
shouting and cheering
rose, swelled, broke, and
reechoed through the vast
spaces of the Cathedral.
"Long live the King! Long
live Belgium! Long live
the Queen! Long live the
Cardinal! Long live the
Army!" Hats were thrown
in the air, handkerchiefs
were wildly shaken, people
wept, laughed, fell on each
others' necks. The soul of
Belgium, repressed for two
years, suddenly burst the
bonds placed upon it by

BRITISH POSTER TO
AROUSE SYMPATHY FOR
BELGIAN REFUGEES.

the German government and gave voice to its true feeling.

The end of the war made known the fact that the principal
author and publisher of *La Libre Belgique* was M. Eugene van Doren,
aided by several Belgian journalists, the chief of whom were M.
Victor Jourdain and M. van de Kercheve. At the beginning the
printing offered no great difficulty because the Germans did not
know what was going on. The delivery of the papers was the great
problem. M. van Doren and his wife put them in envelopes without names on them and delivered them personally to a number of
people who distributed them personally to friends. No name was
put on the paper and only a very few people knew from whom it
came. They merely knew that their own copy came from a friend.

When the third number was printed, a new press had to be

found. The police had already discovered the identity of the first. M. van Doren bought the necessary material with great caution and installed the plant in an abandoned house in a little town outside Brussels. Two professional printers, the Allaer brothers, did the work. Phillipe Baucq delivered alone between four and five thousand copies of the paper each time, making the trips at night on a bicycle. When the Germans forbade the use of the bicycle, he had to walk and at one time walked two days without a rest. Presently M. van Doren decided to set up the type in his first plant but to print the paper in a second plant at another village at some distance. Here was the automobile feature. He was, however, very soon compelled to carry the matrix on a trolley car. One day, when he himself was carrying some four thousand copies of the paper, some German soldiers obligingly lifted the bundle for him and set it on his shoulder.

The paper was so popular and so many copies were demanded that it became necessary to have a larger printing press, and the problem to get that press set up and enough blank paper on which to print was difficult to solve. The printing was being done in a house fairly surrounded by Germans and there was a reward of twenty thousand dollars for the discovery of the office of the paper. To deaden the noise of the press M. van Doren built a brick room around it. He left for a door a little hole in one corner through which he crawled on hands and knees. This opened into what seemed to be quite an ordinary shop and was hidden there by a pile of boxes and old iron.

After the great celebration of the national holiday in 1916, the German spies ferreted him out. The plant had to be broken up in great haste and transferred. Some few more copies were issued, but then M. van Doren had to flee and take refuge with relatives and friends, lying in hiding for several months. But the paper did not stop. One man after another took it up, each for a short time. Baucq, who had so faithfully distributed it for so long, was captured by the Germans and shot, and many other men, who at one time or another had aided in the printing or the circulation, spent long terms in prison. But despite the extraordinary rewards offered and the terrible penalties dealt out, not one individual in the whole of Belgium, who had anything to do with the paper or who received a copy, ever in any way by word or look betrayed what he knew. Belgium might be crushed but she could not be conquered.

The War in the Air

The air service became, as soon as the armies dug underground, the most important factor in the war. The aëroplane became the eyes of the army. On it the artillery fire entirely depended at all times. Upon it the army must rely for knowledge of the existence and whereabouts of any assault. The all important portion of the air service was, therefore, its least dramatic and the one about which least has been said. The observation of the enemy's batteries and lines was undertaken partly by observation balloons, anchored within the Allied lines, and able to see with accuracy all of the smaller and nearer enemy artillery. The larger enemy guns, located, of course, several miles away, were ferreted out by the slow, heavy aëroplanes, carrying at least the pilot and his observer, and equipped with camera and wireless. This branch of the service was the fundamental factor, and performed what the British called "ceiling work." On it almost every phase of the combat depended.

Another phase of air work was the bombardment of enemy territory. Munition factories, railroad junctions, railroad yards far in the rear of the lines were commonly the targets, and a few well-directed bombs might do enough damage, it was thought, to prevent some movement at the front; might interfere with a stream of supplies or with the manufacture of munitions long enough to be of some consequence. It is not yet proved, however, that the bombardment from the air, undertaken by both sides, had any material effect upon military events.

The last phase of aviation, the most dramatic and most popular, was, from the point of view of the larger aspects of warfare, the least important. This was the aviation of combat. Its purpose was to protect the balloons and the observation planes of the Allies while they were obtaining the data upon which the conduct of the war depended. This made essential attacks upon German aëroplanes which were attempting to destroy the Allied balloons or observation planes. Another phase was naturally an attempt to destroy the German balloons and observation planes and often led to combats in the air with the German fighting machines sent out to protect their own observers. This work was always dangerous in the extreme and not infrequently important, though it is not yet demonstrated that either the Germans or Allies succeeded in getting control of the air for more than a very brief period or that any of the military victories was the direct result of the fighting in the air. Probably no military event of any consequence took place which did not have vital connection with the air service, but it is probable that the great successes were not due to any one arm of the air service.

During the last two years of the war extraordinary developments were in progress which might have resulted, had the war lasted longer, in great transformations of warfare itself. The aëroplane began to take a direct part in the fighting on the ground. Fighting planes did occasionally annihilate a German division marching to the trenches, or was able to rake a trench with machine gun fire from the air and thus remove the obstacle facing the Allied troops. The great gun batteries located far behind the lines were particularly vulnerable.

In the great offensive of 1918 whole squadrons of aëroplanes fought battles in the air, when hundreds of planes charged each other, laid down barrages of machine gun fire, and even attempted concerted assaults upon large masses of troops, advancing across open ground. Of course, the aëroplane, armed only with a machine gun, could never assault with success prepared trenches or dugouts, but once the troops left their defenses and started to charge across the open, unprotected by artillery, a single aëroplane might do great damage. Columns advancing to the support of the front trenches were also splendid targets for the aviators. The daring of some men was extreme. Garros, one of the first great French aviators, bombed trains, troops, supply depots, from a distance of only one hundred feet above them.

SKETCH FOR LONDON GRAPHIC OF AËROPLANE ATTACK IN RAIN STORM ON GERMAN TRENCHES. DECEMBER, 1917.

As the war went on, changes in the structure of the aëroplanes were no less remarkable than the increase in the skill of the pilots. Before the war the machines had been barely dependable, had lacked strength and stability, but as the war went on nearly all desirable qualities were developed, and in addition, motors were created capable of carrying heavy weights over great distances and planes were built able to fly in heavy winds or storms. Mechanics learned how to mend the machines while in the air, even repairing the engine itself. Hospital aëroplanes were created and minor operations were sometimes performed in flight. So great was the stability of the planes at the end of the war that part of the machine could be blown away by a shell and the machine would still fly. Bishop, the British aviator, landed with his machine in flames and escaped unhurt, largely because of his confidence that, although the machine was doomed, he would be able to control it long enough to reach the earth.

The real interest of the war centered in these fighting planes. They developed a speed of one hundred and thirty miles an hour, would climb into the air at the rate of one thousand feet a minute, and some carried as many as three rapid fire guns, able to fire four hundred shots a minute. Many great aces were developed on both sides, but although numerous personal exploits are extremely interesting to study, the general tactics of aviation as a whole are really of more consequence in the history of the war.

As always, German tactics reasoned out logically what was to be done and then proceeded to keep the individual within bounds. At first the Allies charged the Germans with cowardice because their aviators kept for the most part over their own lines, but the great German aces explained that if a German plane fell within their own lines the Allies learned none of the German secrets of construction. The object of the fighting planes in any case was to prevent Allied observation and to protect German balloons and observers. This could always be done within the German lines. It was therefore foolhardy to venture beyond them. Immelmann developed first among the Germans a method of attack upon an enemy plane which combined the maximum chances of success with the minimum danger. The aëroplanes were at first not armed at all and then carried guns which shot only between the blades of the propellers, straight in front of the machine. Let the aviator keep above, behind, below, or at either side of his adversary and he was perfectly safe. Immelmann, therefore, cruised around at high altitudes, preferably in the clouds; when an Allied plane appeared, he waited until it passed beneath him. He then shot straight down upon it, carried by the force of gravity at a terrific speed and intending to pass just behind it. When almost upon the enemy he fired as many shots as he could, and was then carried by the speed of his own flight below and beyond his enemy, protected from his enemy's fire, partly by his position and then, as he passed in front of him, by his speed. He would never wait to see whether the enemy fell or not, nor attempt to reengage him. To do that was to fight at a disadvantage.

COOPERATIVE ATTACK BY FRENCH TANKS AND
AEROPLANES IN COMBINED FORMATIONS IN
ONE OF THE LAST ACTIONS OF THE WAR.

Boelke, another great German ace, pointed out the advantage of fighting in pairs and later in squadrons. Several German planes would engage a smaller number of Allied planes, but preferably a single plane. This increased the chances of their success and diminished the danger. Commonly, if outnumbered, the Germans turned tail and fled. They did not propose to take risks; the pilot and machine were too valuable to be lost in such fashion. Richthofen, perhaps the greatest of the German aviators, invented camouflage in the air and developed maneuvering by a squadron of aëroplanes. His favored method was to attack in long file, he himself heading the tango circus as it was called. He scorned concealment in his own case, however, and painted his machine bright red so that it might always be known.

One of the most successful French aviators was Fonck, who destroyed ten German planes without himself being scratched. On May 9, 1918, he went up alone, as Allied machines frequently did, to meet three German planes, each carrying two men, and, therefore, more than doubly dangerous. Two he destroyed in ten seconds and the third five minutes later. That afternoon, he met five German planes in formation, dove into them from above, and sent down three, the remainder escaping. The whole six had been shot down with an average of six cartridges per plane. Bishop, the Canadian aviator, was ordered to return to England to take charge of instruction and went out for a last trip across the lines. He was gone twelve minutes and brought down five German planes. The true secret of success in the case of these exceptional men was primarily deadly marksmanship. Their skill as aviators was apparently a secondary consideration, although none of the tricks in flying was without its value and sometimes meant the difference between destruction and safety. Their coolness, confidence, and self-control under all circumstances were the great qualities which accounted both for their marksmanship and for their ability to fly.

The greatest of aviators, however, typifies the Allied methods and, as well, the romance of the war. Guynemer, a young Frenchman, physically rejected by all sections of the service more than once, only twenty-three years old when he died, exemplified the reckless courage and daring of the Allied tactics in the air. He courted rather than avoided danger, gloried in risks, preferred to fight several German planes at once, and commonly returned from a trip with his clothing and plane riddled with bullets. His favorite method of attack was to approach his adversary from below, perform the difficult tail spin, which stood his plane on its tail, immediately below his adversary, and bring him down with a stream of bullets through the bottom of his machine.

No single character of the war so attracted the admiration of the French people. He seemed to them to embody all that quality of French youth most precious to preserve. They seemed to say of him, "Here is the pattern of the young men of France; look upon it, and copy it: it is the best; it is France." While everything about him was burning truth, it seemed as if the truth was already legend. The subtle perfume of mysticism appeared to hang about him. He died in combat, September 11, 1917. The official citation read: "Like a legendary hero fallen in the full measure of glory after three years of ardent combat, he will remain the purest symbol of the qualities of the race: indomitable tenacity, fierce energy, sublime courage. Animated by the most unshakable faith in victory, he bequeathes to the French soldier an imperishable remembrance which will exalt the spirit of sacrifice and stir to the noblest emulation."

One of his intimate friends wrote: "I have known his intrepidity, his tenacity, his fascination. Duty of combat was for him a religion. He had an iron will. He was upright as a sword, pure as a diamond, and utterly absorbed in the struggle which he carried on to the detriment of a constitution already frail.... He was of a finer essence than ourselves, inspired with a sacred fire which passed our understanding. He fell amidst forty enemy aëroplanes, of which he had brought down one, one arm was broken, a ball was in his head, and a smile was on his lips."

BOOK V

THE WAR IN 1917

THE CAMPAIGN OF 1917

Despite discouragement and disaster the strategy of the Allies remained in 1917 what it had been in the two years previous. The Allied statesmen still believed that unless victory were won in France it would be worthless. They must not merely beat the German army somewhere; they must drive it from France and Belgium; a satisfactory peace could be signed only with the Germans across the Rhine. The trench line imposed upon the assault extreme difficulties and sacrifices, but they saw no real alternative. They prepared themselves therefore once more to deliver a simultaneous offensive on all fronts, on the theory that the previous logic was good, but that the earlier preparations had not been sufficiently elaborate. More men, more cannon, more ammunition, larger artillery, and better trained infantry must infallibly succeed. They proposed also to win back the ground lost in Asia Minor, where a very small British force had been defeated by a considerably larger Turkish army. The military positions were of no consequence to the issue of the war, but the British made it a point of pride to recover the lost ground before the war should end.

The German plans were, as usual, based upon their suppositions as to the plans and preparations of the Allies in France. Hindenburg still seemed in 1917 to cling to his original plan of holding the lines in the west, while all German foes in the east were beaten and victory then made final. Though the Russian army had been considered beaten in 1915, had been again demolished in 1916, its

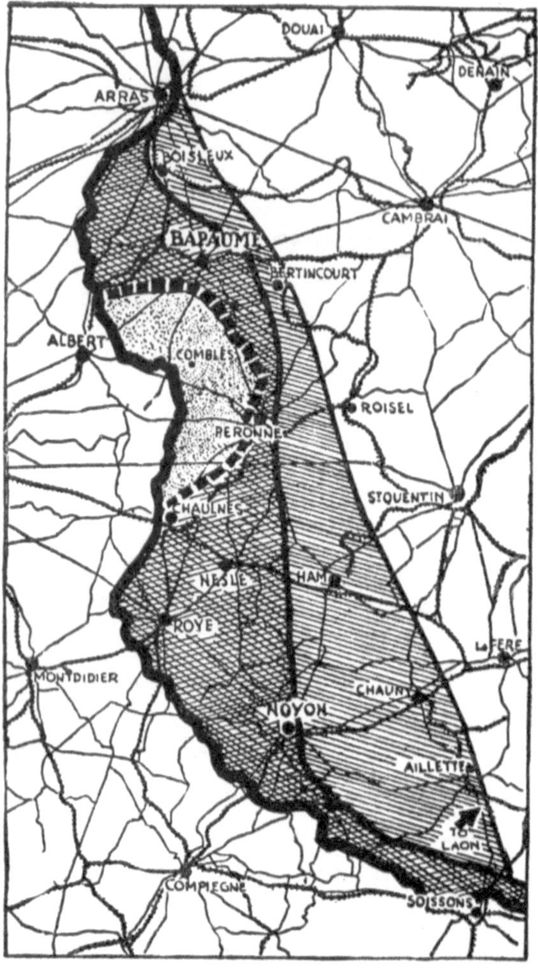

ALLIED GAIN IN 1917 IN DETAIL

continued existence alone compelled the Germans to retain a strong force of men on the eastern front. They therefore schemed in the winter of 1917 to remove Russia permanently from the conflict and to conquer her for the present and for the future. They precipitated the Russian Revolution in March, to put Russia definitely out of the war and to release the German armies on the east front. They would then throw large forces against Italy in the fall of the year, at the season most favorable for the campaigning in the south, and treat her as they had treated Poland and Rumania. They could then end the war in 1918.

Meanwhile Von Tirpitz was to attempt to bring England to her knees by means of unrestricted submarine warfare. For two years now the submarine had sunk British shipping where it could, but, despite their general lack of humanity, the Germans had observed some of the rules and practices of the past. They now announced to the world that from February 1, 1917, they would sink any and all ships that the submarines might meet. They declared a danger zone around the British Isles and the French coast within which no ship, however neutral, should be safe. They thus rescinded all the promises they had made to the United States and other nations of warning to vessels in order to allow the crew and passengers to escape. The new order was "Sink without trace": the ship must disappear—there must be no survivors to tell the tale of how she was lost. They promised themselves that England and France would be put to such straits by this unrestricted warfare that the factories would be unable to get the raw materials necessary to continue the war. Food would give out, especially in England, and the British would be compelled to sue for peace.

Meantime while Russia was being successfully revolutionized, while the submarine was bringing Great Britain to terms, the lines should be held in France with the least possible effort. They should maintain the defensive as cheaply as possible. Hindenburg knew well that the British and French had made extraordinary preparations throughout the fall and winter for an assault upon the German lines. Special railroads had been built all along the front to make easy the movement of troops, of ammunition, and of food so that men could be massed readily at any point, transferred elsewhere with rapidity, fed there, and supplied with ammunition.

In February and March, therefore, to render all these preparations useless, Hindenburg withdrew the German lines to the famous Hindenburg line, a new line of defense elaborately prepared, miles enough in the rear of the old line to prevent any assault upon it by the British and French from the positions which they had prepared so carefully during the winter. Moreover, the Germans destroyed every living thing, every building, every tree, every possible shelter in the entire zone, which they thus abandoned; it was laid waste with a thoroughness which only Germans can attain. The Allies must therefore attack them over a waste ground where everything

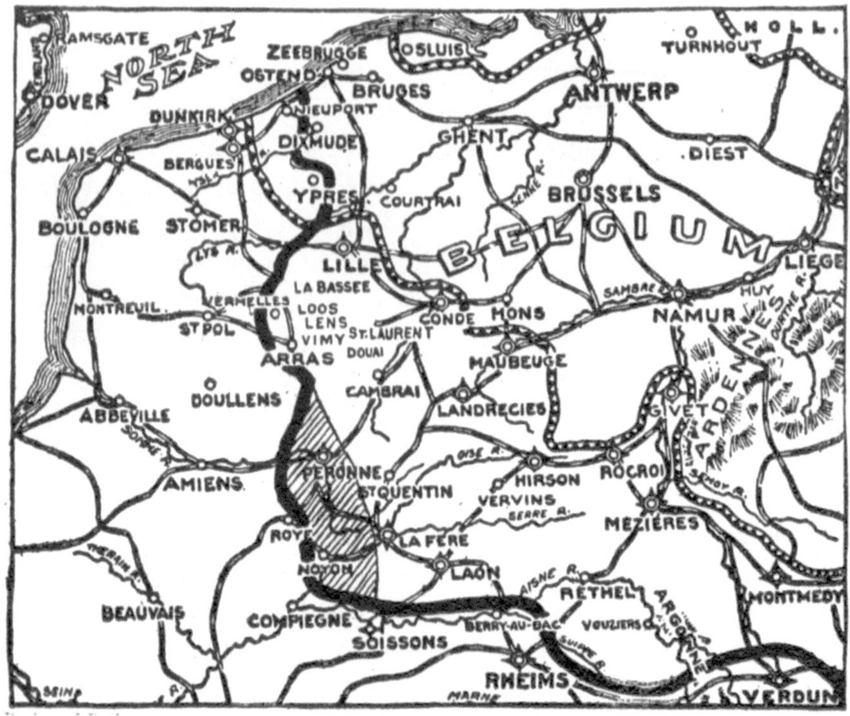

WEST FRONT IN 1917 AND TOTAL GAIN IN THAT YEAR.

would impede their progress to the maximum and where there would be nothing to aid them.

The results were not exactly what the Germans had anticipated. The United States promptly entered the war on April 6, 1917, and undertook with equal promptitude an extent of preparations which paralyzed the German statesmen and generals. Conscription was voted almost immediately and an army of millions was put at once into training. The United States government took over factories and railroads and began to build ships to transport the new troops to France. Indeed, we began to build from the bottom an army of five millions of men, with everything necessary to place them on the fighting line in France and keep them there indefinitely. The example of the United States was followed by declarations of war from a crowd of hitherto neutral states in South America and in Asia.

In a measure the new submarine menace was met by the seizure of German ships interned in American and neutral harbors. They were promptly repaired, despite the fact that the Germans had intended to injure them so that they could not be put into service for some years. In June, Greece joined the Allies, and the obstacle to an assault upon the Austrian rear, which had bothered the Allies for three years, was removed.

In April the British delivered a great assault on the German lines around the city of Arras, to the north of the new Hindenburg line in a position not affected by the German retirement. Although some territory was won, the battle failed to break through the German trenches, and in July the British began a determined effort, which was continued until December, to break through the German lines along the coast so as to reach the submarine base at Ostend and Zeebrugge. Not only did they feel that if they could capture the coast they might lessen the power of the submarine, which was already committing great inroads upon the world's shipping, but they might also turn the German right and compel the withdrawal of the whole line over a considerable area of territory. But the attempt failed. In the center an attack was launched on November 20, at Cambrai, known as the battle of the tanks, which did gain a larger amount of territory than the Allies had up to that time won; but some of it was lost again and in general the success failed to produce any effect upon the fundamental strength of the German position.

Meanwhile, the Italians had begun on the Isonzo in May a great assault against the Austrian army, intrenched around Trieste. The object was twofold; partly to put pressure upon the Germans on two fronts at the same time, and partly to win the Austrian territory occupied by people of Italian blood, which the Italians were determined to add to Italy when the war should end. They felt that there was small chance of its cession to Italy unless they should capture it during the war. They therefore made this determined attempt throughout the summer to capture Trieste. In October, the Germans and the Austrians delivered a well-timed and well-planned blow against the Italian army along the Isonzo. They broke the left of the Italian army before Trieste and won through the mountains into the valley below.

The entire Italian position was at once flanked and the great bulk of the army in great danger of being cut off and captured. To escape, it was necessary for the army almost to run; to abandon its artillery and baggage; and to make its way back at breakneck speed to some new front. Finally, in November, after a magnificent retreat, a new front was established on the Piave. British and French aid had been promised and had arrived. The French and British had marched on foot from France, had crossed the Alps, and joined the Italians. A furious attack was delivered by the Austrians in November and December, but the line on the Piave was successfully held.

Yet the net result of the year 1917 was extremely discouraging for the Allies. Russia was unalterably out of the war; all possible help from her army had evaporated. Italy was in the gravest danger thinkable. The submarine had been successful in sinking an amount of shipping which the Allies had not believed possible although it was far less than the Germans had thought probable. It had not prevented the supply of the British and French armies in France nor interfered for a day or an hour with the stream of ammunition, but, if the loss should continue at that rate, there was no knowing when the submarine would make itself felt on the battle line. England was building ships at furious speed; so was the United States; but the submarine was sinking them immensely faster than they could be built.

Meanwhile the Allies had failed to gain anything of moment in France. They had supposed that a simultaneous offensive on more than one front would expose the Germans and Austrians to certain defeat on some point. But instead the Germans had

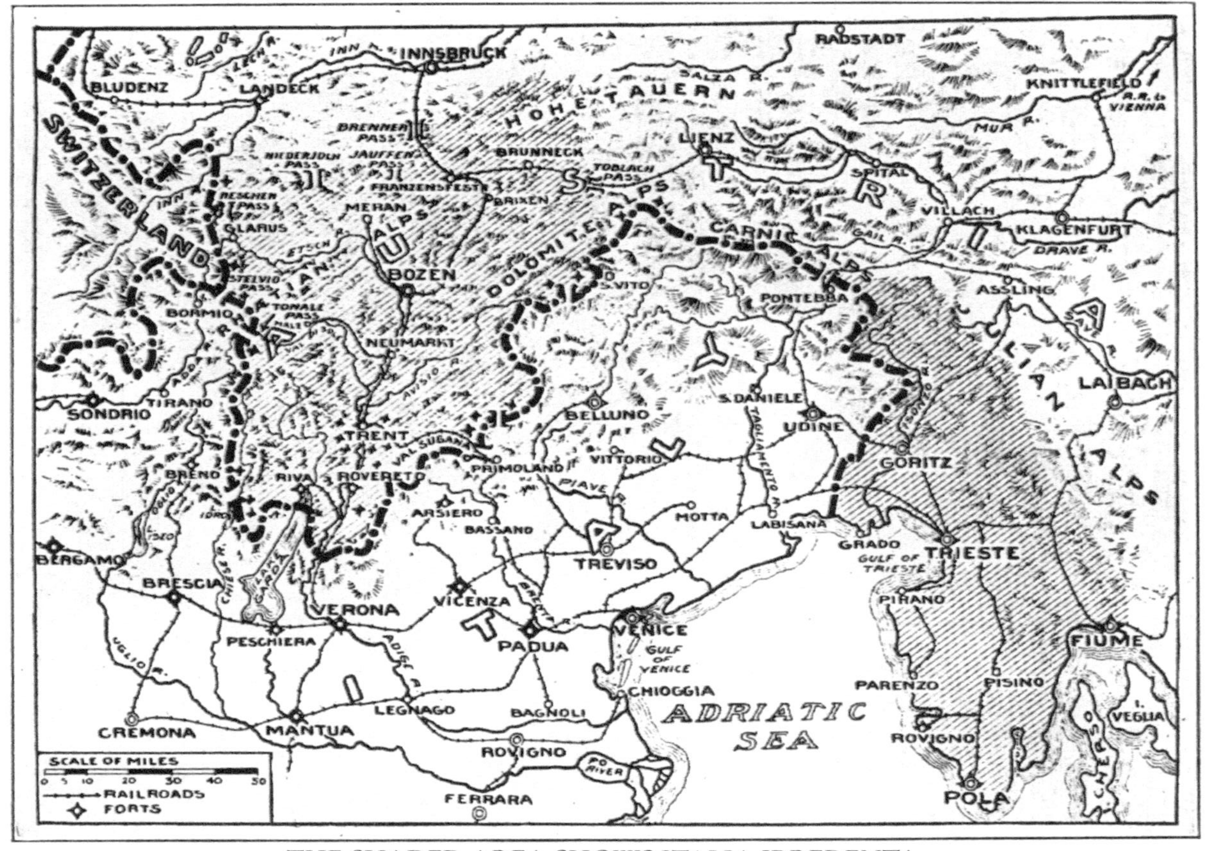

THE SHADED AREA SHOWS ITALIA IRREDENTA.

successfully held the lines in France and had won victory after victory elsewhere. The outlook was black indeed, for, although the United States had entered the war and had begun preparations of extraordinary magnitude, the American army could not in the nature of things take the field in great force for some months to come and perhaps for a year or more. The year 1918 every one foresaw would be the critical period of the war.

THE RUSSIAN REVOLUTION

One of the most important and dramatic events of recent decades was the Russian Revolution. In its results upon the war itself and upon conditions after the war in Europe it was one of the most significant events of a complex period. While we do not at present know with certainty much about it, we know enough to say that its causes were varied. We are really dealing with three revolutions, all simultaneous.

The internal condition of Russia had been for generations extremely bad and the government was still tyrannical, unjust, cruel, and oppressive. The conditions of life were hard. It was extremely difficult to make a living. Sweeping reforms had been put on paper but were still awaiting execution, so that, despite decrees, the peasants rarely owned the land on which they worked. They were bound to pay heavy taxes, heavy rents, and suffered greatly from the oppression and injustice of the proprietors, the local nobles, the local officials and clergy. They formed the overwhelming majority of the population and their dissatisfaction had been growing in recent years in intensity and readiness of expression.

FRENCH CARICATURES OF BOLSHEVIKI—1917.

These conditions had produced definite movements in Russia for reform. Various parties were organized to oppose or destroy the Tsar's government. The laws, however, were strict against holding meetings without permission or publishing criticisms of the government in books or newspapers. Secret societies became, therefore, the only way in which reform movements could be organized. To ferret these out was the work of the secret police, which became in Russia an exceedingly powerful organization. The penalty for opposition even in small things was exile to Siberia, where the most terrible suffering was experienced by political prisoners. Only by the use of the army, the officials, and secret police had the Tsar's government kept itself in power so long. Revolts had been planned in 1913 and 1914, but the outbreak of the war postponed them and united Russia for the time against the Germans.

There came to be an almost universal belief in Russia that the defeats in the field and the death of nearly four millions of soldiers were due to treason. The generals and officials were pro-German, had sold the nation to the enemy, and were sacrificing the army in the field. They prevented sufficient food from reaching the troops, failed to send the necessary ammunition, or ordered the men to make attacks prearranged with the Germans so as to insure the destruction of the regiments.

An economic crisis also developed as the war proceeded, due not so much to the Tsar's government as to the inability of the railroads to do the work required, but the result in the large cities was a great scarcity of bread and the possibility of famine. Reforms had been promised before the war, and, while some had been granted, the more important changes had not been made. As the war progressed more reforms were asked for by the Russian National Assembly, the Duma, but were again refused. In fact measures were taken by the government in the large cities to deal severely with any opposition.

This brought to a head simultaneously three independent attempts to overthrow the Tsar's government. There was first a strong body of Russian Liberals, headed by Milukoff and Prince Lvoff. The former was a college professor, an extremely well-educated and intelligent man, who had lived in America and had come to know much of our notions of government. He had long been the leader of the Intellectuals in Russia. Prince Lvoff, also an extremely intelligent and well-educated man, had embraced the cause of the peasants and had organized them so as to create better conditions and to prevent their oppression by the officials. His peasant organization had rendered great service to the government in feeding the army. These Liberals were in control of the Duma, wished to depose the Tsar, and frame a new constitution. They did not, however, propose to go beyond political reform and would have been entirely content to have the son of the Tsar as monarch.

A considerable portion, though by no means a majority of the population, had been organized in various groups called Socialists, Anarchists, Nihilists, who had long been anxious to overthrow the Tsar's government. They were radical thinkers and wished for something more than a mere reform of the political machinery or a change of the people who did the governing. They wished a complete social revolution which should shake society from top to bottom, and affect not merely the government but the ownership of property. It should put the control of the new state into the hands of the laboring people. This party controlled the army and comprised the majority of workmen in Petrograd and other large cities.

There was a third party hostile to the Tsar's government. The Germans were anxious to put Russia out of the war for good. They had beaten the army, but so long as it existed they must still keep a million or more Germans on the lines in Poland, whom they needed to win the war in France. Once overthrow the Tsar, the Russian army would be disbanded and they could then throw their entire strength against the British and French. They also foresaw that they might secure control of the new Russia and set up a government there in the hands of Germans, or of Russians in

STEET BARRICADE, PETROGRAD, MARCH, 1917.

German pay, who would organize the country in German interests and make it a German colony.

When, therefore, on March 5, 1917, food riots broke out in Petrograd, there occurred at the same time movements against the Tsar's government in the Duma and in the army. For three days the rioting in Petrograd went on. The police and the army were ordered to put it down, but the army joined the rioters who took possession of the imperial palace and most of the government buildings. With some few exceptions the whole city fell into their hands on March 11. The fact was that the Tsar himself was very weak as a sovereign, the government had no real roots, and was nothing better than a sort of block balanced on top of a pyramid; a very small push was sufficient to knock it off.

By March 15, the Revolution had been successful in Petrograd, Moscow, and Odessa. A provisional government was set up by the Duma in the hands of Milukoff, Lvoff, and others, although the city was practically already in the hands of the Soviets. The truth was that all these parties had acted together without knowing it and each apparently believed that the others were acting in cooperation with it, a fact which they all soon realized was untrue. They were all agreed in putting down the Tsar. They were by no means agreed upon the reasons for which they wanted to get rid of him or upon the situation they proposed to create when he was gone.

On March 15, certain generals visited the Tsar on his special train. He had been with the army at the time the revolt broke out and was journeying back to Petrograd. They stopped his train out in the country, there informed him of the situation, and requested him to abdicate. The scene was tense but very quiet, much like an ordinary conversation between men in a small room. The Tsar was very composed and abdicated in favor of his brother in order that he might keep his son with him. Two days later he was arrested and brought to Petrograd as a prisoner, whence he was sent to southern Russia and finally to Siberia. There he is said to have been shot by official order, though his family are still supposed to be alive.

The provisional government at once declared in favor of a constitution, assured the Allies of the loyalty of Russia, announced liberal reforms, and called for a constitutional convention. Meanwhile, certain committees had been organized in Petrograd of workmen and soldiers, calling themselves Soviets. These then elected delegates to larger committees, and proposed in this way to establish a government for Russia by electing these committees in all parts of the country. There were now really two governments in Petrograd. Neither of them was as yet assured of support from the country at large, nor was it clear that the Revolution would not be confined to a few large cities. The Soviets in Petrograd promptly refused to accept the platform announced by the Liberals, and for two months active disagreement continued in Petrograd while the organization of Soviets went on in other parts of Russia.

On May 15, a coalition was formed, headed by Prince Lvoff, the result of a compromise between the Liberals and the Soviets. The new government now proposed that all the Allies should sign a peace with the Germans upon the basis of no annexations or indemnities. Inasmuch as this would have left the French and

Belgians in the same danger at the end of the war which had all but destroyed them at its beginning, they could not consider any such terms. This was fatal to the Liberals and during the next month a great shift took place in the parties in Petrograd, for this revolution seems to have taken place chiefly in a single city. At any rate, what happened in Petrograd seems to have settled the issue for the whole of Russia. It became presently clear that the majority of the Soviets in Petrograd were radicals, not moderates, and these larger groups came to be called presently the Bolsheviki, which is a Russian word meaning majority. Although only a very small party when the Revolution first broke out, they gained strength steadily in Petrograd.

RUSSIAN MOB, MAINLY WOMEN, BEARING RED FLAG, ADVANCING ON THE DUMA IN PETROGRAD, MARCH 1917.

In July some hope was held out still of creating a government which should represent more than one Russian party. The Liberals now withdrew and Kerensky, the leader of the Moderate Socialists, became head of the state and admitted into the government a number of radicals, including some of the Bolsheviki. Attempts were made to hold national conferences which should secure the support of all Russia for this government, and Kerensky undertook to restore the discipline of the army. But the Allies refused to recognize him, knowing the extent of the pro-German interests and afraid therefore to recognize a government which might result in putting Russia into German hands. Kerensky seems not to have been pro-German and the result was exactly what the Allies had been most anxious to avoid. The pro-Germans came into control in the person of the most radical of all the Russian parties, the Bolsheviki.

The latter accepted the aid of the Germans, took German money, and possibly had the aid of German soldiers as well, upset the coalition government, and installed themselves in control in Petrograd. The two leaders were Lenine and Trotsky. Neither of these names are their true names and both had been professional agitators before the war. Lenine was about forty-seven years old, had been a student and had been exiled to Siberia for his socialistic ideas; his brother had been executed for them; and he grew up hating the Tsar. When released, he went to Switzerland, where he became a leader of the socialistic agitation. Trotsky lived a long time in New York, where he published a Socialist paper. While it is probable that these men accepted German aid merely to get themselves into power, with the full intention of getting rid of the Germans as soon as they could, the result was entirely favorable to the latter.

The Bolshevists proceeded to negotiate with the Central Powers, and signed, in February, 1918, the treaty of Brest-Litovsk, in which they yielded to the Germans a great deal of territory in western Russia, and perhaps received a promise of German money and support necessary to continue their own authority over Russia. They were an insignificant minority of the Russian people and could hope to control only by reason of the fact that the vast majority were densely ignorant and were scattered over so vast a country that they could not organize effective opposition. Russia had always been governed from Petrograd, and the control of Petrograd continued to carry with it a nominal right to govern Russia. Nevertheless the Bolsheviki must get support. They distributed the land to the peasants, gave the factories to the workmen, abolished all private property, and proposed that every one in Russia should work with his hands. In order to destroy the educated and proprietor class, they began a series of murders and massacres which resulted in the deaths of thousands of people.

Russia, however, is a very large country and many parts of it refused in 1918 to be governed from Petrograd. A separate state called the Ukraine was organized in southern Russia, a separate government was organized for Siberia, and still others in the Caucasus, in Finland, and in Poland. The Germans themselves organized new governments along the Baltic coast in Lithuania. At the time this is written Russia is divided into several states, of which the Bolsheviki control only one, which contains, however, Petrograd, Moscow, and the largest part of the old Russia.

Why the United States Entered the War

On August 4, 1914, the President formally declared the neutrality of the United States in the war which had just broken out, but the war was not many days old before it began to be clear that American sentiment was anything but neutral. For three years event after event only convinced the American people more firmly that the German cause was not ours and that the cause of the Allies was ours. As time went on the number of people who had any doubt of this fact became smaller and smaller, and in 1917 the vast majority of the nation without question was convinced that this was our war, and that we could stay out of it only at a risk to principles we held dear and at grave danger to ourselves. Belgium, France, Great Britain, and Russia had been for nearly three years fighting our war and it was our duty and our privilege to aid them.

Unquestionably the facts instrumental in creating these feelings in the American people had been first and foremost the invasion of Belgium and the German chancellor's declaration that the treaty protecting Belgium had been nothing but a scrap of paper. If such was to be international morality, no promises or agreements would ever after be worth anything. Then the atrocities in France, so horrible that for a time Americans felt them impossible to believe, gained credence and men came to know that the worst was only too clearly true. Not only were the atrocities facts but they were

JOHN BULL FEEDING HIS DEAR LITTLE FRIEND.
Illustration from German prison paper, printed by the German government, distributed to the American prisoners to rouse hatred of England. Copy brought to America by a St. Louis boy and loaned to author.

not chance facts. The cruelty was purposeful, intentional, no mere accident of warfare. The German was consciously a Hun. He meant to destroy his enemy forever while he had the chance. And the babies in arms, the children in the streets were as truly Belgians and Frenchmen to be slaughtered as the men in the armies. The Germans were striving to destroy a nation. Nothing so terrible had been conceived within the memory of man.

The sinking of the *Lusitania* and the execution of Edith Cavell, as well as the murder of Captain Fryatt for the "horrible crime" (to German thinking) of attempting to sink a submarine, convinced even the most obstinate minds in the United States that the German was the enemy of civilization. As time went on the scraps of paper multiplied. To President Wilson's warnings, the Germans replied with promises, which they broke in rapid succession. They agreed to give warning before sinking ships; to make adequate provision for the escape of the passengers and crew; but on the first of February, 1917, they issued a notification that all vessels would be sunk without warning. This was a direct violation of the solemn pledge given by the German government to the United States the year before.

The German intrigues against this country had also increased. The Secret Service seized papers upon German spies in this country which demonstrated an extent of operations contrary to the laws and rights of the United States truly extraordinary. German agents were placing bombs on ships, fomenting a revolution in Ireland from the United States, and organizing a great conspiracy in India, purchasing writers and lecturers, stirring up strikes in American factories, blowing up buildings, all justified by the same morality which sank the *Lusitania*.

The result was a conviction in American minds that the Imperial German Government had repudiated the fundamental principles of law and humanity and could be restrained and made to respect law and right only by being defeated in war. The American people became convinced that Prussian militarism and autocracy were a menace to the nations and civilization of the world and endangered the homes, rights, and natural privileges of men all outside of Germany. The war had become a combat between the democratic nations on the one side and the principles of militarism on the other. Autocracy as developed in Germany was a type of government with which free nations could not live in peace. The German system intended the destruction of all the United States had stood for since the founding of this country. Only by its annihilation could democracy be rendered safe.

Such being the conviction of the American people, the entry of the United States into the war became necessary in the spring of 1917. The Russian Revolution in March completed the German victories in eastern Europe. In 1914 and 1913 Poland had been overrun and the Russian armies beaten. In 1916 the Russian armies had been again destroyed and Rumania laid waste. The political revolution in Russia would now relieve the Germans of all further fear of war in the east and would enable them to throw their entire army against the French, British, and Italians in the west. There was more than a possibility that the Allies would not be able to hold the lines against such an access of strength. The French had borne the greater part of the burden of the war up to this time and still held the major part of the lines in France. The British had suffered great losses in the campaigns of the preceding year, and, with all the magnificent strength which they had still to put into the field, could scarcely offset the numbers the Germans could now bring to bear.

There was no lack of confidence in London and Paris that the Allies could themselves prevent the Germans from winning the war, but they were by no means so confident that they could win it without America's help. And they saw and President Wilson saw that the calamity to civilization would be almost as serious if the Germans were not beaten as if the Germans were to win. The United States must come to the aid of its true friends and allies in Europe before it was too late. The Russian Revolution meant that we could not possibly delay longer. The country was now solidly behind the President, as perhaps it had not been before, and he felt able to take the step with the consciousness that the nation would stand behind him to "the last drop of blood and the last dollar."

The specific causes of the American declaration of war were the facts which stood for this determination. The German order declaring unrestricted submarine warfare from February 1 convinced us finally that the Germans never proposed to keep any of the promises they had made or to respect any American rights. It showed us clearly what we would have to expect if the Germans won. In January, 1917, the State Department made known the Zimmermann Note, in which a responsible German official offered Mexico our southwestern states if she would join Germany and Japan in a war upon us. This was nothing more than confirmation of what President Wilson already knew, but it was a demonstration of the extent to which Germany was willing to go which the nation heretofore had not known. Accordingly the German Ambassador was dismissed and diplomatic relations severed on February 3. When it became clear that the Germans were executing their threat of unrestricted submarine warfare, armed neutrality was recommended by the President on February 26, and on March 12 American merchant vessels were ordered to be armed.

Then came the news of the Russian Revolution and the President saw that the moment for action had come. On April 2, 1917, he appeared before the assembled Congress and urged the recognition of a state of war with Germany. "With a profound sense of the solemn and even tragical character of the step I am taking and of the grave responsibilities which it involves, but in unhesitating obedience to what I deem my constitutional duty, I advise that the Congress declare the recent course of the German Imperial Government to be in fact nothing less than war against the Government and people of the United States; that it formally accept the status of belligerent which has thus been thrust upon it...."

"A steadfast concert for peace can never be maintained except by a partnership of democratic nations. No autocratic Government could be trusted to keep faith within it or to observe its covenants. It must be a league of honor, a partnership of opinion. Intrigue would eat its vitals away; the plottings of inner circles who could plan what they would and render account to no one would be a corruption seated at its very heart. Only free peoples can hold their purpose and their honor steady to a common end and prefer the interests of mankind to any narrow interest of their own..."

"... The world must be made safe for democracy. Its peace must be planted upon the tested foundations of political liberty. We have no selfish ends to serve. We desire no conquest, no dominion. We seek no indemnities for ourselves, no material compensation for the sacrifices we shall freely make. We are but one of the champions of the rights of mankind. We shall be satisfied when those rights have been made as secure as the faith and the freedom of nations can make them."

Congress responded with a declaration of war against Germany on April 6, and one against Austria-Hungary on December 7. The exact reason why the latter declaration of war was delayed is not yet known, but probably because of the expectation that Austria-Hungary might be drawn away from Germany and a separate peace signed with her.

Messines Ridge

South of the city of Ypres in a corner of Belgium which the Allies had held tenaciously, there was a high ridge of ground which projected into the British line and flanked two sections of it. From this the Germans had harassed the British for months. To hold it they had fortified it for a depth of over a mile with a degree of ingenuity and completeness not surpassed during the war. Barbed wire entanglements covered every approach. All sorts and kinds of guns were concealed there. Deep concrete dugouts, many feet underground, had been constructed, able to withstand any amount of pounding by heavy artillery.

It was a position too strong to be carried by assault, the British soon learned, but could not the entire embankment be blown into the air from below, if not from above? It would take time, courage, and skill. Underground tunnels would have to be dug from the British lines long distances to the ridge and under it, but the feat might be successfully performed. For nearly two years several corps of Australian, New Zealand, and British sappers tunneled and dug and finally located nineteen mines containing a million pounds of ammonite.

On June 7, 1917, after two weeks of artillery "preparation" of the position, the mines were exploded with complete success and over the fragments swept an infantry attack directed by Sir Henry Plumer, one of the most successful of the British field generals of the war. In a few minutes the German lines on a front of ten miles

SKETCH FOR 'LONDON GRAPHIC' OF FRENCH CHARGE BEHIND
BARRAGE (SEEN IN FRONT OF TROOPS) IN 1917.
Note slower pace and uneven formation.

were captured. It is more correct to say that the site where they had been was captured, for there were no trenches or dugouts left. The British occupied the spot where the German lines had been. Then followed the storming of Messines Ridge itself, the second German line. The forests, which the Germans had calculated would shelter them, were burned down by streams of blazing oil. Within three hours the second line was carried, and by the end of the day the rear defense line fell, so that the entire salient was wiped out in one of the most gallant actions of the war.

An eyewitness thus described the assault. "All through the night the sky was filled with vivid flashes of bursting shells. From an observation post I watched this bombardment for that moment when it should rise into a mad fury of gun fire, before the troops, lying in those fields, should stumble forward. The full moon had risen, veiled by vapors. The drone of a night-flying aëroplane passed overhead. The sky lighted a little and showed great smudges like ink blots on blue silk cloth, where the British kite balloons rose in clusters to spy out the first news of the coming battle.

"The cocks of Flanders crowed. Out of the dark ridges of Messines, gushed up enormous volumes of scarlet flame from exploding mines, and of earth and smoke, all lighted by flame spilling over into fountains. Fountains of fierce color so that the countryside was illuminated with red light.... The ground trembled and surged violently... Thousands of British soldiers were rocked like that before they scrambled up and went forward to the German lines." As day broke, rockets rose from the latter, distress signals white, red, and green, flung up by the few who still lived in that zone of fire.

To the troops engaged, one of the most extraordinary thrills of this battle was the moving forward of the gun batteries from the positions they had held for two years and a half. When the good news came of the success of the attack, the signal was given, the horses were harnessed to the gun limbers and dashed out at a gallop, past the old screens, up the slopes they had watched so long. And from thousands of hot, dusty throats rose a great cheer,

ITALIAN TRENCH IN MOUTAINS, 1915.

sweeping along the British front, as they watched the gunners go up the ridge, where they unlimbered in new positions and began a new phase of the fighting. As an eyewitness said: "There had been up to that time nothing like it in excitement and sense of victory."

The aviators performed astonishing feats. They attacked not merely German aëroplanes but the German troops. Flying far over the German lines, they swooped down upon groups of men on the march and killed them with machine gun fire from the air; one man thus destroyed a large body of troops preparing a counter-attack. He then cleared out a whole trench full of German soldiers, who scuttled like rabbits for their dugouts. Other aviators swooped down upon the German batteries, killing the crews with machine gun fire. One airman swooped so low he cleared a motor car by only four feet, splashing bullets all round the car as he passed, and barely saved his own machine, as the driver steered the car into a ditch, where it upset.

ITALIAN FIGHTING IN THE ALPS

None of the armies engaged in this war had greater difficulties to meet than the Italians. On practically the entire battle front, they were holding lines in the mountains which produced a type of modern warfare utterly different from that in France. The difficulty there was to see anything; the trouble in Italy was that the enemy saw too much. The trenches of both sides were clearly outlined in the mountain air and the artillery on bright days could pick out the positions with extraordinary accuracy, but the greatest difficulties were those created by travel in the mountains. Everything to be used for attack or defense had to be carried up a mountain side many thousands of feet. Water in particular for the troops in the trenches was a great problem and eventually all the important positions were supplied by water piped up the mountain side and pumped up at regular intervals.

In many instances the trench line ran through districts covered both winter and summer with ice and snow; snowshoes, skiis, sleds were essential for the troops. Imagine a regiment marching on snowshoes or a dispatch bearer with important papers sliding down the mountain on a sled! In some cases a precipice was being held and the troops on top were supplied by means of elevators. A crane was rigged out over the precipice and a car was hauled up and down on a wire by an engine, and in other cases a wire was strung across a chasm or over a river or from one mountain peak to another, and a trolley car running on the wire was used to send men, ammunition, and food across the gap. Funny little railroads were built up the sides of the mountains, running on the cog system.

The amount of preparation often necessary to hold a line in the mountains was extraordinary to contemplate. When the troops got up there, the ground was frozen solid, perhaps several feet. Moreover it had been frozen for years, perhaps for centuries; it had never been anything but frozen; it would never thaw out. They had to blast out a trench as if they were blasting rock. Snow blindness also caused much suffering. Dark glasses or snow glasses were essential for all the men.

On no section of the front was camouflage so necessary, because nowhere could a man walking along a mountain some miles off be seen so clearly. It was necessary for the troops to dress winter and summer so as to be indistinguishable. The trenches had to be covered with white screens in winter and green in summer. The cold was particularly difficult to endure. The men in France suffered from it but the cold in the mountains was intense and the soldiers must stay day and night in open trenches in positions where a fire would advertise their location to the Austrians. The question of warm food in the front line trenches, very essential in so cold a temperature, was a hard problem to solve. The defense was easier perhaps than in France because the enemy was easier to watch and because he had great difficulties to overcome in scrambling up the mountains. But it was not easy to maintain contact with all parts of the line and to keep up the constant watch to prevent surprise.

One picturesque incident in the Julian Alps during the summer of 1917 illustrates this difficult and picturesque warfare. The general staff decided to take some Austrian batteries on top of a precipice forty feet high. It could be reached only by crossing a swift, deep river and must be scaled in full sight of the Austrians and within the range of their guns. The Italians decided to make the attempt at night because, while darkness to them was a great obstacle, it was to their enemy a greater. With extraordinary ingenuity they first put out the *eyes* of the Austrian batteries. They concentrated on the mountains opposite the position to be attacked a row of brilliant searchlights, and, when the moment for the attack came, turned the full glare upon the Austrian position. It literally blinded the gunners. The light was so intense that they could see absolutely nothing of what was going on below them.

It was necessary for the Italian engineers to throw pontoon bridges across the river and that meant noise, which of course would inform the Austrians what was going on. They must therefore *deafen* the Austrian gunners. This was done by a tremendous cannonade creating so loud a roar that the noise of the hammering and pounding could not be heard. Once the eyes of the Austrians had been put out and their ears had been deafened, the Italians threw across the pontoons, the troops rushed over the river, scaled the precipice, and were upon the astonished Austrians before the latter knew what was being attempted. The positions were carried with a rush and at once the guns were turned upon the Austrians. That single feat compelled an Austrian retreat of nearly seven miles, because those guns commanded an entire mountain valley.

Fighting the Submarine

No sooner had the submarine commenced its operations than the necessity of combating it was clear. For a while the greatest attention was given to methods by which merchant ships might escape destruction. Dodging and zigzagging were attempted with some success. Flight at top speed proved to be the most reliable method. Then elaborate camouflage was tried with great success. A ship painted in blue and white squares or in zigzag lines merged in the waves when seen at a distance, and the submarine could not tell which way she was traveling, even when the ship was clearly visible. Camouflage also spoiled the submarine's aim with torpedoes. This difficulty the submarine met by coming to the surface and sinking the ship with gun fire. As the war went on, the Germans developed new types of submarines, huge affairs, carrying heavy rifles, the shells of which were able to riddle a ship.

Then came scouting and patrolling, directed by wireless from the shore and intended to cover certain areas of water most commonly used by merchant ships. In this the United States Navy in the last year of the war played a very active and distinguished part. But it was necessary to do a good deal more than merely to get the merchant ships through. The submarines themselves must be destroyed. The sinking of one such craft might prevent the loss of twenty ships. Vulnerable to destroyers and cruisers on the surface, the submarine had only to submerge and rest for a while on the bottom to elude all pursuit. To meet this method of defense, the depth bomb was invented. A destroyer steered at full speed straight to the spot where the submarine had submerged and as she passed it, rolled over the side or stern something not unlike a large tin ash can which sank rapidly and was timed to explode at a depth of from twenty to two hundred feet below the surface. The explosion was effective throughout a wide area, and, unless the submarine was extremely fortunate, the crew of the destroyer, circling back to review results, would be almost sure to see a dark oily smudge appearing, with fragments of clothes and wood.

Then came the "Q" boats, meaning Queer boats. Their purpose was to lure the submarine to the surface, where it could be destroyed by concealed guns. The "Q" boat pretended to be a

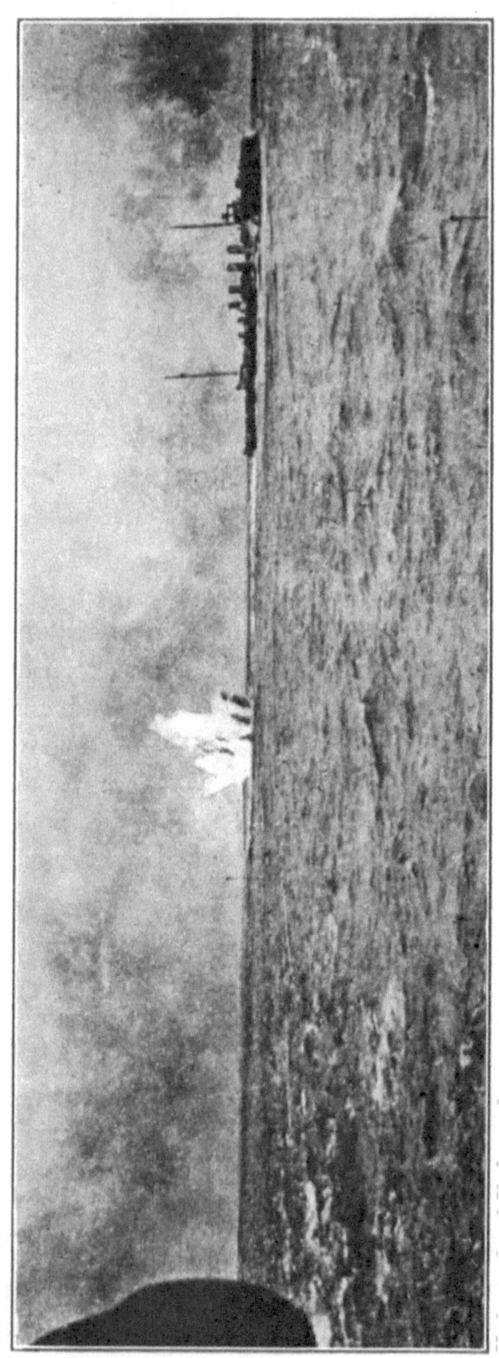

PHOTOGRAPH OF ACTUAL DESTRUCTION OF SUBMARINE BY DEPTH BOMB DROPPED BY U.S. DESTROYER.

helpless merchant craft. Here would come puffing along an old rusty tramp steamer with the crew loafing around on deck and all serene. Suddenly, up pops a submarine which signals with gun fire that the ship is to be abandoned. The crew tear around in a panic. The submarine comes closer and becomes impatient. Suddenly a white flag shoots to the masthead; there is a rattle of chains and a clattering down of steel bulkheads; out pops a great rifle, and in fewer seconds than it takes to tell it the submarine is going down, riddled with shot and swept by machine guns.

Such a drama could not be enacted more than a few times. The submarines became exceedingly wary of all innocent-looking craft. In February, 1917, the Q 5 was chugging along when suddenly her commander saw a torpedo coming toward her. With iron nerve he deflected the course of the ship a trifle and allowed the torpedo to hit aft, blowing a hole forty feet wide in her side. The gun crews were already concealed inside; panic stations were ordered; the camouflage crew were rushing around outside in a well-acted confusion; and the boats were lowered and shoved off. Apparently the ship was abandoned, but inside were the commander and the gun crews waiting for the submarine to come up and show herself.

The chief engineer reported that the ship was sinking fast. The commander ordered him to keep the pumps going until the water put the engine fires out. Meanwhile the submarine was watching the ship through its periscope. Slowly it came to within five yards of the boats, not ten yards from the ship itself, observing, watching, well aware that it was difficult to be hit under the water at that angle, and knowing that it could submerge immediately. Despite the fact that his ship was going down the British commander was forced to wait. It was no use to fire until the submarine came up, but apparently the submarine had no intention of coming up until the ship went down.

At last after many anxious minutes, the submarine rose to the surface, and came slowly toward the ship. Patiently the British officer waited until it was near enough for every gun to bear.

Then up went the white flag, down clattered the bulkheads, and a terrific gun fire poured upon the doomed vessel. The German commander was complacently climbing out of the conning tower; the first shot neatly beheaded him. The crew of the submarine came pouring out of the hatchways and were swept off by the fire of the machine guns as the submarine sank for the last time. Some hours later, assistance summoned by wireless rescued the men in the small boats, and as the Q 5 was still afloat she was successfully towed back for repairs.

In June, 1917, another "Q" boat went through very much the same sort of stage play to get the submarine to appear. The panic party abandoned the ship and for thirty-five minutes the men on board waited and waited, with the water getting higher every minute. Then a long distance off the periscope of the submarine broke the surface and came toward the ship. As it approached, the submarine submerged, passed under the ship, and came up on the other side out of range. Night was coming on; unless the submarine came up presently there would not be enough light to hit her, and the British boat was going down rapidly.

The men in the boats here tried a new game which completely fooled the German commander. They started pulling for the ship again as if to take possession. This convinced him that the ship had really been abandoned and up came the submarine in a hurry. Open came hatches and the angry Germans began pouring from them with machine guns to shoot the "treacherous Englishmen." It began to look as if the British in the small boats were going to be shot by the submarine and by their own men as well, but they pulled like mad through the range of their own fire.

Then suddenly down clattered the steel screens and a broadside of yellow flame leaped over their heads. Half out of the water, the submarine listed as the oil spouted from the rents in her hull. The crew scrambled out of her hatches, held up their hands, and shouted "Kamerad." The British ceased fire and the submarine rushed off at top speed, attempting to escape, and sweeping into the water to die the poor fellows on her deck. Grimly the British guns broke out again and continued fire until not one remnant was left. They rescued a few of the hapless Germans and were themselves presently rescued by destroyers, waiting around over the horizon for the "Q" boat to finish its task.

Zeebrugge and Ostend

There were few exploits in the history of the war more conspicuous in gallantry than the blocking of the harbors of Zeebrugge and
Ostend in the spring of 1918.[4] Both were submarine bases from
which went forth the slinking craft that infested the seas around
Ireland and accounted for the loss of so many ships and the death
of so many brave fellows. If these harbors could be closed, it was
possible that the submarines might find it so difficult to venture
out from Germany itself that their activities would be immensely
restricted. A good many of the deadly craft could probably be
bottled up at Zeebrugge, if not at Ostend, and effectively put
out of the game. So elaborate, however, were the fortifications,
so numerous the searchlights, big guns, little guns, destroyers,
and garrisons, that it was clear that any attempt against that base
would be one of the utmost danger.

At Zeebrugge, there was a canal with wharves on either side
of it and protected from the action of the sea by a long mole or
breakwater. The plan was to fill three old cruisers, the *Intrepid*, the
Iphigenia, and *Thetis*, with concrete, to attach mines to their hulls,
work them into the very neck of the canal, and sink them across
it. Two others similarly prepared were to be sunk in the harbor
of Ostend. An old battleship, the *Vindictive*, aided by ferry boats,
destroyers, smoke boats, motor launches, and indeed a whole swarm

4   This chapter has been placed here so as to avoid breaking the narrative of the
great German offensive in 1918 by inserting it in its chronological place.

of craft, was to attack the great mole guarding the Zeebrugge Canal, create a diversion, and draw the fire of the German guns while the cruisers were working their way into the canal. To render the diversion convincing, blue-jackets and marines were to be landed on the mole and were to attempt to destroy such stores and guns as they could. The small motor launches were to carry off the crews of all these various vessels which were to be sunk and to render aid to any of the other craft which got into difficulties.

It was absolutely essential that all weather conditions should be exactly right. The night must be dark; the sea calm, so that the small craft might operate without too much danger; and above all, the Germans must be surprised. It was on the night of April 24, 1918, that the *Vindictive*, followed by two ferry boats, headed toward the mole, while around her rolled a thick smoke screen created by the small launches plying near by. The wind blew this toward the shore and concealed the ship, and it was not until she was close upon the mole that the wind suddenly changed, whirled away the smoke, and showed the startled Germans what was intended.

"There was a moment immediately afterwards," says the British official account, "when it seemed to those in the ships as if the dim coast and the hidden harbor exploded into light. A star shell soared aloft, then a score of star shells; the wavering beams of the searchlights swung around and settled to a glare. The wildfire of gun flashes leaped against the sky; strings of luminous green beads shot aloft, hung and sank." A tremendous fire from all the batteries upon the shore burst upon the *Vindictive* as she laid her nose against the concrete side of the mole, thirty feet high. She let go an anchor and the two ferry boats, brought for the purpose, began to shove her up against the high side of the mole.

In order to get the sailors and marines on shore, it had been necessary to construct a series of drawbridges which could be lowered from the ship on to the mole, and up which the men must scramble, peppered all the while by German machine guns. The ship rose and fell with the tide more than had been expected. The

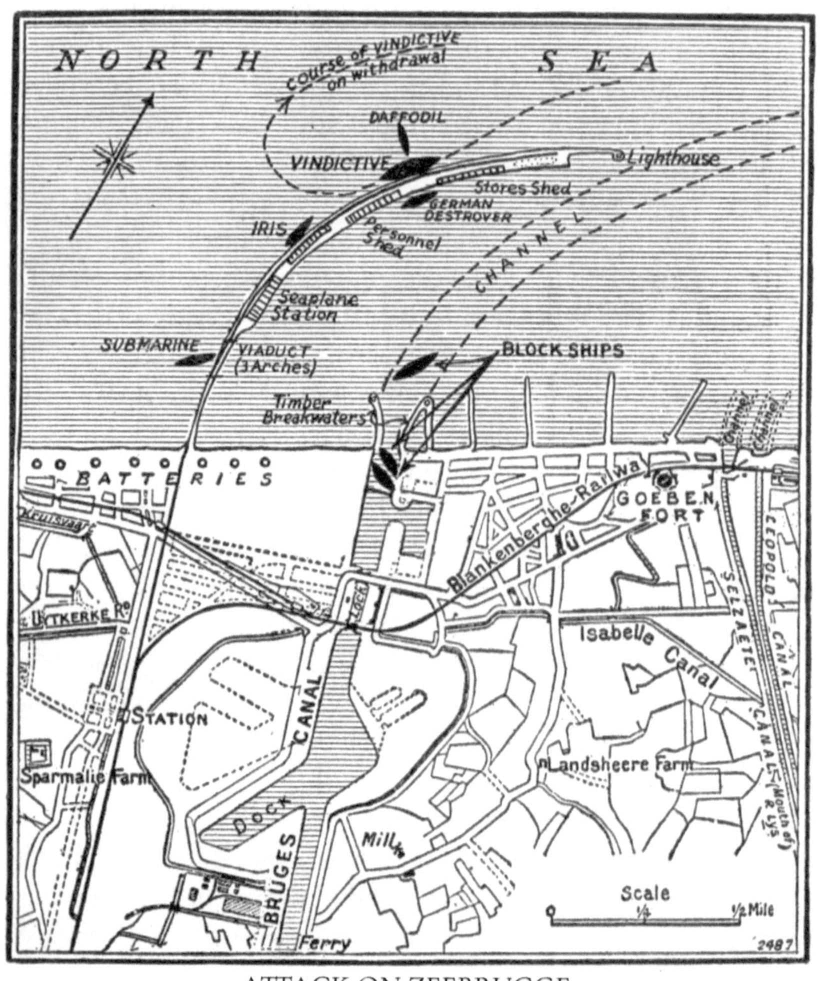

ATTACK ON ZEEBRUGGE.

gun fire was extremely severe and getting off the ship at all turned out to be an extremely hazardous and costly adventure. The men were magnificent, and as soon as possible swarmed on shore. The Germans abandoned the mole without a struggle and contented themselves with sweeping it with machine gun fire. One by one, the great store buildings and sheds burst into flames or crumpled as the dynamite which the British marines set went off.

Meanwhile the three cruisers were making their way into the canal. The first fouled one of the German defense nets and went ashore on a mud flat. The *Intrepid*, smoking like a volcano to conceal her from the Germans, and with all her guns blazing away at the shore, steered straight into the canal, followed by the *Iphigenia*. Her commander placed the nose of the ship on the mud of the western bank, ordered the crew into the motor launches clustering around, and blew up the ship by means of electric switches in the chart room. Four dull bumps told him that the work was complete. The *Iphigenia* was then beached on the other side of the canal, blown up, and dropped exactly across the canal closing it from one side to the other. Her commander missed the motor launch, and was compelled to take refuge in a Corley float, a sort of life boat carrying a chemical which lighted a flare as it touched water. Originally intended to save the man by showing his position to the rescuers, it now picked him out as a target for the Germans and they promptly gave him unremitting attention. He was saved by drifting into a huge cloud of smoke thrown off by one of the cruisers, caught a rope from a passing motor launch, and was towed along for a while before he could be hauled on board.

As his launch cleared the canal and came forth into the open harbor, the water spouting all about them from the German shells, they saw the success of another phase of the expedition. An old submarine laden with explosives had been run into the mole, her crew picked off by the waiting motor launches, and blown up. "A huge roaring spout of flame tore the jetty in half and left a gap of over a hundred feet." It would be some time before the Germans would get out again upon the mole. The *Vindictive*, her work done, now blew her whistle, gathered in such of her men and wounded as she could, was pushed off from the mole by the two ferry boats, and limped out of the harbor, literally riddled with shot and shell. There she was received by destroyers and cruisers who were supporting the operation.

An attempt made that same night on the harbor of Ostend was a failure, but on May 11, the *Vindictive* herself successfully carried out the enterprise. The night promised well; it was nearly windless, the sky a leaden blue and with no moon; the sea was still, enabling the motor craft to cooperate. In the darkness, without a light, the *Vindictive* made her way towards the shore, shrouded with smoke thrown up from the smoke ships. A motor boat preceding her lighted flares on the water to show the way to the harbor

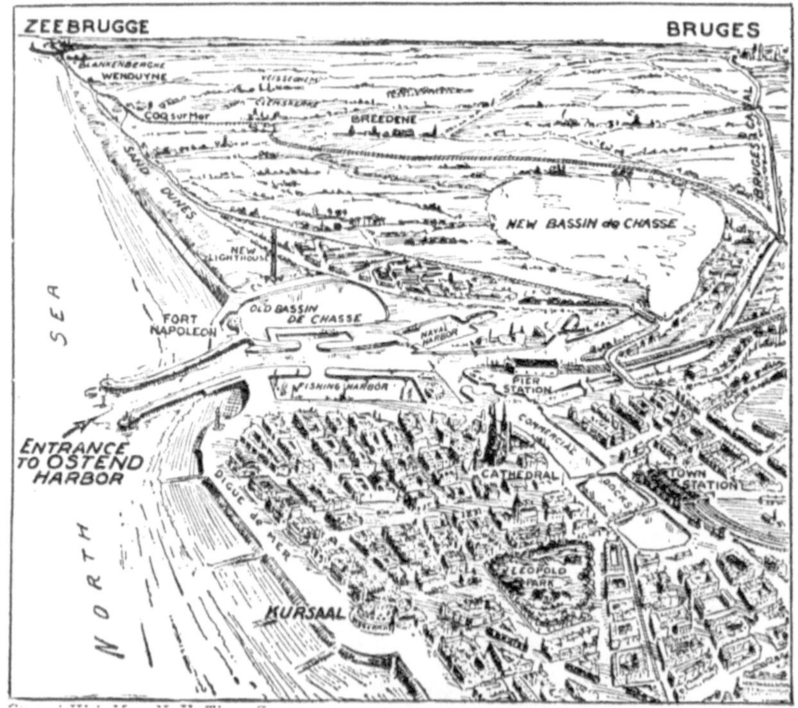

OSTEND HARBOR.

mouth. Fifteen minutes before the ship was due at the entrance, two motor boats dashed in and torpedoed the high wooden piers on either side of the entrance, both vanishing in the roar and leap of flame and debris.

Suddenly there appeared high in the air a flame that sank slowly earthwards, a signal from the fleet of aëroplanes, cruising over the town, ready to drop bombs upon it at the proper moment. The same instant came the shriek of the first shells thrown from the great guns of the British marine artillery, brought up to occupy the German heavy artillery. A tremendous roar from the shore replied as every one of the many guns began action. Star shells shot up, lighting the great smoke plumes; green flares and strings of luminous green balls, which the airmen called "flaming onions," soared up and lost themselves in the clouds. Through all the glare and hail of shell, the *Vindictive* pushed steadily on.

And then came a fog, a real fog, dense, thick, moist! The *Vindictive* lost her way; the motor boats could not see each other; their flames were lost in the fog. Twice the old battleship cruised across the harbor entrance, missing it both times. The third time there came a sudden rift in the mist and she saw the entrance dead ahead. She steamed over the bar and once she was in the German guns poured shells upon her. She was hit every few seconds, her decks and turrets destroyed, her guns put out of action, her officers and men killed and wounded. She laid her battered nose against the eastern pier and tried to swing across the channel, but she was too hard and fast in the mud to be moved. They blew the main charges beneath her, tearing out her bottom plates and sinking her in the channel. Her commander was dead already and many of the officers. Every man alive was taken off in motor launches which immediately ranged alongside. One by one, they made their way through the fog, back to the waiting cruisers and destroyers outside. The deed was done. Ostend harbor would no longer be useful to the Germans.

The Battle of the Tanks

The war had scarcely begun before the deadly effect of machine gun fire was clear to the British and they set about experimenting with some sort of defense for the advancing troops. After a year and a half of experiment they produced the tank, which was first used on September 16, 1916. They had found an American machine created for the purpose of carrying heavy loads over bad roads. It was called a caterpillar tractor, and had no wheels but ran on a sort of endless chain moved by machinery and on which the tractor crawled forward. The tread of the chain was so broad that it could run over all sorts of mud, soft earth, and bad going without getting stuck. This provided the first requisite. The new weapon must not be impeded by ground dug up by shells; it must be able to climb through trenches or over them; it must be able to walk on barbed wire entanglements.

The British now put armor on the car, mounted guns in it, and thus created a land battleship which was impervious to small artillery fire. The purpose was to tramp down the barbed wire entanglements, which hindered the infantry, to hunt down the German machine gun nests, walk right up to them and clean them out. It had been proved that artillery fire could not wipe out the underground dugouts. At Verdun there was under one of the hills a dugout, called the Crown Prince, eight hundred feet long and twelve feet high, in which a whole regiment might take refuge, and from which it could pour out when the defense was needed.

FRENCH TROOPS CHARGING PROTECTED BY
LARGE FRENCH TANK, 1918. NOTE THE MEN
ARE LYING DOWN, NOT RUNNING.

The first time the tanks went into action the Germans were
astonished and the British troops were so delighted that they were
hardly able to stand from laughter and joy. One of the correspondents thus described one of the first engagements. "A tank had
been coming along slowly in a lumbering way, crawling over the
interminable succession of shell craters, lurching over and down
and into and out of old German trenches, nosing heavily into soft
earth, and grunting up again, and sitting poised on broken parapets
as though quite winded by this exercise, and then waddling forward
in the wake of the infantry. It faced the ruins of the château and
stared at them very steadily for quite a long time, as though won-
dering whether it should eat them or crush them. Our men were
hiding behind ridges of shell craters, keeping low from the swish
of the machine gun bullets and imploring the tank to 'get on with
it.' Then it moved forward in a monstrous way, heaving itself on

jerkily like a dragon with indigestion, but very fierce. Fire leaped from its nostrils. The German machine guns splashed its sides with bullets…. But it got on top of the enemy's trench, trudged down the length of it, laying its sand-bags flat and sweeping it with fire."

One tank would march up single-handed to a whole trench full of Germans. It would crawl around until it could rake it and thus force the whole company to surrender. When the infantry came up, it would hand over the prisoners, who stood there holding up their hands, and lollop off in search of new adventures. One tank took a town single-handed, driving the Germans into the cellars, and wandering undisputed up and down the streets. The machine gun bullets rattled on its sides like peas, but to no purpose. Another tank got stuck in the mud and the Germans rushed upon it. "They flung bombs at it, clambered on to its back, and tried to smash it with the butt ends of rifles, jabbed it with bayonets, fired revolvers and rifles at it." When the infantry arrived, between two and three hundred killed and wounded Germans lay on the ground around it. Presently, with a good deal of grunting and grinding, the tank heaved itself up and waddled off to find new foes.

But the tanks were at first not so effective as they were interesting. They were used at the Somme in September, 1916, and in the next year at Arras, Messines Ridge, and elsewhere, but were not really effective until the battle of Cambrai on November 20, 1917. The troops were here led against the Hindenburg Line by some hundreds of tanks on a thirty-two-mile front. The assault penetrated the German defenses to a depth of five miles, but inasmuch as the Hindenburg Line was here about twelve miles wide, they did not go through it. Nevertheless this was the largest single gain the Allies had made during the entire war.

It was a quiet part of the line, as the war went, and the surprise attack was therefore attempted against a relatively thinly held part of the German line. There could be no artillery preparation, for that would merely advertise what was coming. The ground was hard and dry and it was expected that the tanks would themselves be able to crush down the barbed wire, take the trenches, and perform the work usually done by the heavy artillery. Several hundred tanks were secretly, slowly concentrated along the thirty-two miles of front and hidden from the curious aëroplanes in woods and villages.

On November 20, the mists of the morning were extremely heavy, and out of them as day broke came trudging down upon the astonished Germans scores and hundreds of tanks. They trampled the barbed wire entanglements and slaughtered the Germans with a barrage of machine gun fire. Behind came the infantry, cheering, shouting, leaping, and laughing, and overhead was a tremendous barrage fire from the British heavy artillery, meant, now that the surprise was sprung, to crush the trenches immediately ahead of the tanks, to silence the German batteries, and to prevent the bringing up of reënforcements. The surprise was complete and the success astonishing. The Germans were killed or ran or surrendered, and the tanks and infantry rumbled gayly on, as line after line of the strong defenses fell.

Here had been concentrated great bodies of British cavalry. They were to ride round the infantry and tanks, once the formal defenses had been broken through, dash forward into the open country behind, and prevent the bringing up of reënforcements. The tanks and infantry moved slowly; the cavalry was to gallop, occupy as advanced positions as possible, and hold them until the infantry could come up. It was the first time in the war that great bodies of cavalry had been used for anything except scouting and the carrying of messages. The most picturesque element of the old warfare had practically disappeared from this war nor did the cavalry on this occasion accomplish much.

Great as was the success, it was not great enough. The British infantry outran their supplies, artillery, and reënforcements, and, before the position could be consolidated and defended, a fierce German counter-attack retook much of the ground. The technique of gaining ground in a hurry had been established. The technique of holding it had not yet been learned.

With Allenby in Palestine[5]

Few campaigns of the war thrilled the western world to a greater extent than that in Palestine and Asia Minor. Few events caused a deeper satisfaction than the capture of Jerusalem by Allenby in December, 1917. It was certainly not because of the extraordinary importance of the campaigns themselves, nor yet because the military operations displayed greater skill or courage than those in Europe. Remarkable as they were, they certainly cannot be compared with the great movements in France. But the fact was that the western world saw Allenby achieve what the Christian world had failed to win in the Middle Ages, saw him take possession for the first time in nearly eight hundred years of the place in the world most sacred to Christians.

His quiet entry into Jerusalem was the achievement which Richard, the Lion Hearted, Philip Augustus, and a long line of knights and pilgrims had shed their blood in vain to accomplish. The Christian world had believed for centuries that Palestine should not be in the hands of the Infidel and yet in his hands it had remained. Now it was returned once more to Christian possession. He was a crusader, that quiet general in khaki. The imagination of the western world clad him in burnished armor and placed upon his breast the magic cross of the eleventh century. The hopes, aspi-

---

5   For a gripping account of the soldiers who fought under General Allenby in the Middle East, see *The Aussie Crusaders*, available from Living Book Press.

BRITISH CAMP IN PALESTINE.

rations, traditions of the Christian world invested the campaigns in Palestine with a significance which few in history have had.

The British also found deep joy in Allenby's victory because a British force had pushed up the Persian Gulf from India, had invaded Mesopotamia in the first years of the war, and had finally been captured in 1916 by the Turks. The British never accept defeat and they burned to wipe out the stain on their arms before a general victory in Europe should ingloriously overthrow the Turk in Asia Minor.

People too found the military operations in the Near East romantically interesting, not because different things were being done than in France, but because the appearance of warfare was different. Aëroplanes and tanks in the desert, cooperating with Arabs on camels, seemed certainly more romantic than they did in France or Italy. The campaign was of the older type; there were never enough troops on either side to make necessary a trench line. Eventually the one great crowning exploit of the campaign was

BRITISH AUXILIARY TROOPS ADVANCING IN PALESTINE.

that in which the British cavalry in force rode around the Turks and caught them in the rear, while Allenby's infantry attacked them in front. These are the probable reasons for the interest of the public in these campaigns.

The story itself is soon told. On April 29, 1916, General Townshend surrendered at Kut-el-Amara. British forces at once started from India, advanced up the Tigris and Euphrates, and on February 24, 1917, General Maude retook Kut-el-Amara. A campaign was waged then during the summer and autumn, by Allenby from Egypt, on Jerusalem, which fell December 10. In 1918 both British forces, aided by Arabs, pushed steadily on. September 22 was the great victory over the Turks in Syria. On October 1 the British entered Damascus; October 26 Aleppo surrendered, followed on October 31 by the surrender of Turkey, and the war in the Near East came to an end.

BOOK VI

THE WAR IN 1918

The German Plans for the Campaign of 1918

The Germans saw in 1917 that it would be essential for them to win the war in 1918. If they delayed, they would never win it at all, and a failure to win a military decision would be complete disaster. The Americans could not arrive in force in 1918, but in 1919 they would place in the field millions of well-trained men who would decidedly outnumber the Germans and win the war without a doubt. We must never forget the character of the war: it was for the Germans an aggressive war intended to win control of Europe, an object to be attained only by substantial victory.

But in 1918 they considered their object all but assured. Russia had been defeated partly by the German army but principally by the revolution. She was now ready to become a German political and economic colony in which the German secret service could mold things at pleasure. What mattered the loss of colonies in Africa and in the Pacific! The lost German territory had at most a few millions of people, crude and undeveloped, buying little and producing less. Even Mesopotamia was undeveloped and without inhabitants and only time could render it the sort of market adequate to meet the German needs for expansion.

But now at their very door was a colony of one hundred and eighty millions of people, already producing exactly what Germany wished to buy, already buying exactly what Germany was anxious

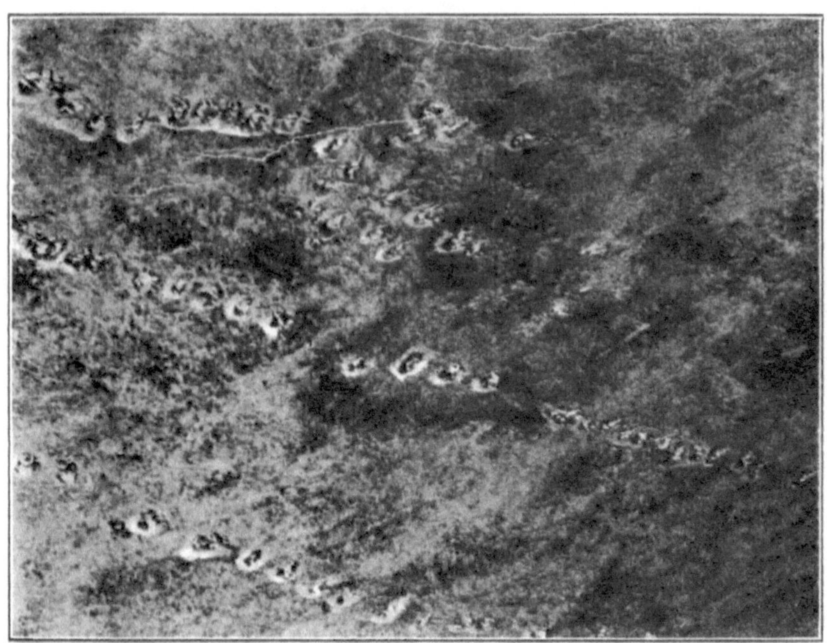

FRENCH AEROPLANE PHOTOGRAPH OF ADVANCE ATTACK
IN THREE WAVES DUG IN TO ESCAPE OBSERVATION.

to sell. It was in their hands already, its resistance overthrown for good. They had only to assure their future possession of it to have in their hands the solution of all serious problems. Nothing stood in the way except the obstinate British and the stubborn French in the west, who were beaten, but declined to admit it. The war itself had created the great Pan-German Confederation. Austria, Hungary, Bulgaria, and Turkey had been so tightly bound to Germany by circumstances that they could never again escape. The miserable peoples, who had hitherto stood out and refused to cooperate, had been trampled on and destroyed during the war while the trampling had been good. Rumania and Serbia had been crushed too flat to offer further opposition. Poland, which stood in Germany's path to her new colony in Russia, had also been weakened and destroyed in a thousand ways. Her people had been slaughtered, her factories demolished, her fields laid waste. There was nothing there the Germans thought to give them future anxiety. So too of Belgium, the natural outlet for German commerce, the new German seacoast on the Channel. The Belgians had been treated as people should be who refused to cooperate with Germany. The mailed fist had smitten them and ground them in the dust. Italy had been defeated and could be punished at any moment for her treachery.

The new empire which was to dominate the world was a fact; it was necessary merely to extort recognition of it from the British and the French. Negotiations and peace offers had been rejected with disdain and with insults. The submarine had tried valiantly to achieve a decision but had not brought England to her knees. A victory in France was essential. Everything must be staked on winning it in 1918. To fail then was to lose the war, for victory thereafter would be impossible; the Americans would see to that.

The means for victory the Germans thought were at hand. The great armies in France could be strengthened and made irresistible by bringing the armies from the east, from the south, from

FRENCH TEMPORARY TRENCHES TO STOP
GERMAN ADVANCE, MARCH, 1918.

Italy. The entire equipment of great guns could now be concentrated upon any part of the French front. There remained only the question of whom to strike and where. The High Command determined to attack the British and destroy them. Their army was newer and less well trained than the French; the Germans thought it less well officered and its general staff less competent. The British had possible reserves of man power, the French had none; if the British were beaten, the French would be compelled to surrender. The latter had borne the brunt of at least two of the three and a half years of war and had carried no inconsiderable share of the remainder. They could not continue the war alone. To beat the British would be to win the war.

Ludendorff decided to throw an overwhelming force against the right wing of the British army at the junction of the British and French armies. He would force his way through the British line, crush the right wing, and separate the British from the French. He would thus reach the Channel, and coop the British

FRENCH COUNTER-ATTACK WITH LIQUID FIRE
DURING GERMAN FIRST OFFENSIVE, MARCH, 1918.

up in a section of France where, with the Germans on two sides of them, they could be beaten and destroyed at leisure. The same movement would flank the whole French line, imperil Paris, if not capture it, and place the French as well between the fire of the German armies in the new position and of those advancing from Metz and Verdun.

Much time was spent upon the method of attack. The Germans had not studied three years of warfare for nothing. They had not failed to advance so many times without speculating on the reasons why. They came to the conclusion that nothing but an overwhelming superiority of artillery and of men could break the trench line and permit "a war of movement." They would plant their cannon as close together as it was possible for them to operate; a great gun every few yards would not be too many. The infantry evolutions necessary for the movement were practiced for weeks behind the lines by the very men who were to carry them out. The offensive was rehearsed like a theatrical performance. As many divisions as could stand without stepping on each other should attack the British lines. As soon as each had struck its blow and succeeded, it should be replaced by fresh divisions, each coming up successively to relieve the others. The same British troops should therefore be compelled to meet wave after wave of attack from fresh German divisions without any opportunity to rest, and the waves should come fast enough to overwhelm the British before aid could come.

These assaults should be delivered at various parts of the British line, bulging it out in several places. This would compel the British to retreat from the sectors in between to avoid being captured, and thus the attacks would throw back the whole line over a front many miles wide. This method was followed throughout the entire battle: a thrust forward here and a thrust forward some distance away; the line between the points then had to be withdrawn, and a general German advance followed.

THE GERMAN OFFENSIVE OF 1918

In accordance with the plans rehearsed for nearly three months, at the very second agreed upon long in advance, the German offensive rolled forward on March 21, 1918. It was directed against the Fifth British Army, commanded by General Gough, and is known as the battle of Amiens. Military critics declare it one of the most remarkable movements in the history of warfare. It was instantly successful although in the end nothing like as much so as the Germans had anticipated. The Fifth British Army, surprised and enormously outnumbered, was broken and driven back. A great gap, thirty miles wide, was opened between the British and French armies. Another gap to the north some eight miles wide was opened between the Fifth British Army and the Third British Army, which occupied the next sector of the line. For some days the entire Allied cause was in extreme peril. There were on the field no proper reserves of troops to fill these holes, and, if the Germans had known exactly their location and size, they would have won the war. But with extreme rapidity, General Fayolles moved a new French army into the gap between the old French line and the retiring British. He weakened the French line itself, but the Germans did not know that.

The gap between the British Fifth and Third Armies was filled by a scratch division eventually commanded by General Carey, who really deserves the credit for its exploits. There were no troops to be had, but American and Canadian engineers, cooks, chauffeurs,

GERMAN OFFENSIVE, MARCH–JUNE, 1918

road workers, anything that walked on two legs, were picked up wherever they could be found, in ones, twos, and tens, armed with the first implements that came to hand, and rushed up to the gap on trucks, on horseback, on mule teams, on foot. Near by they found a machine gun school with plenty of guns and ammunition. Only a few of the men collected had ever handled a machine gun, but those who knew how fell to work in the crowded minutes of a battle on the outcome of which the fortunes of the world were at stake, and taught the rest how to shoot. For two days the detachment held the gap, which was at that time only a couple of miles wide. The commander then collapsed from exhaustion.

At this very instant, in the providential way often told in novels, appeared a dusty automobile; in it was General Carey looking for his troops. He was pressed into service by the scratch division and told the danger. An old South African soldier of the dare-devil type, afraid of nothing and full of resource, he took the situation in hand. For six days with very little eating and less sleeping, these cooks, chauffeurs, and engineers, men who had never maneuvered in their lives, armed merely with what they could pick up, and led by a general who had never seen them before, convinced the Germans that a great force of experienced troops held the position. They attacked here, rushed to a position a mile away, and attacked again. They lost ground constantly, were beaten time and again, but came back for more. They held the gap; the Germans did not get through. They saved the battle, and it will be a source of pride to many that a division of American engineers sent to France for very different work formed the backbone of this scratch army, and that a good many of the rest were American ambulance drivers. Others were Canadians, a people who fought throughout the war with a gallantry unsurpassed by any nation.

One dramatic feature of this tremendous offensive was warfare in the air on a scale never before attempted. Hundreds of Allied and German machines went out to combat in massed formation. They charged each other, laid down barrages of machine gun fire, swooped down upon advancing troops and annihilated them with a hail of bullets. The losses of men and machines were terrific: the latter fell in tens and dozens, some as the result of collisions, some with pilots killed, others in flames. For two days the battle raged as intensely in the air as on the ground. Then the Allied aviators won. Their victory was one of the vital factors slowing down the German drive and was certainly responsible for the German ignorance of the plights of Fayolles' and Carey's divisions.

But the magnitude of the defeat could not be concealed. The Allied line had been broken and patched up again; but it had bent and bulged repeatedly until more ground had been surrendered in a few days than the Allies had won in three years. The Germans were within a few miles of Amiens and well on the road toward the coast. The Allied reserves came up, however, and the German advance itself slowed down. They had outrun their artillery; they outran their supply trains with food and ammunition; flesh and blood could do only so much and at the end of a week the great rush was manifestly over.

Then in the first week of April, fresh German troops delivered the second blow upon the next sector of the British line around Arras. This was now the key to the entire British position. The line had bulged out so far to the south that if Arras should fall and the Third British Army under General Byng should be defeated, the whole line as far as the Channel must swing back. But to the astonishment of the Germans and the extraordinary joy of the Allies, General Byng's army held its ground and yielded nothing of consequence. Back went the Germans to work on the great bulge at Amiens, trying to push through the sides so they might safely advance further in the center.

Now in April came a great change. General Foch was appointed general of all the Allied armies. He was to command the British, the Americans, and the Italians as well as the French. He was to dictate all the moves of the campaign. This unity of command the Allies had hitherto declined to adopt for various reasons not necessary here to explain, but the great crisis compelled some sort of radical change and the appointment of one general seemed the best measure to take.

By direction of President Wilson, General Pershing offered General Foch the services of all American troops in France, to be used wherever and whenever he could. They were to be brigaded with the French and British troops and commanded by French and British generals. It was one of the wisest of the President's decisions and made the American troops at once available in the field. Our private soldiers were ready to fight, but our general staff and our artillery were not sufficiently experienced at that time to have taken the responsibility of a sector of the front at such a crisis. Probably they would have acquitted themselves well, but the risk would have been too great, for the Germans would have at once singled out that sector for a crushing attack, and the last week had shown that the British and French themselves, despite their experience and training, were not able to withstand the German thrusts. Reënforcements also were poured in from England, and arrangements were made at once in the United States to ship over to France as rapidly as possible the new army which had been training during the previous months. This was the great crisis of the war. Ready or not ready, let the men go to France; the work of Carey's scratch division had shown what could be done by intelligent but untrained men.

But the Germans gave the Allies no rest. On April 9 a great drive was begun against the Second British Army in the sector between Ypres and Arras. Having failed to dislodge Byng's army, the Germans proposed to bulge out the line above him and thus compel him to retire, and at the same time put the British army on the coast in such danger that they also would have to flee. The success was again substantial, although not so great as in the attack of March 21. A great hole was opened out and then considerably widened; the British were compelled to retire from ground which they had won during the previous three years at heavy cost in men.

The net results of these attacks was to put the entire British line in the gravest peril.

And now, fortunately for the Allies, the Germans were compelled to pause for a month to organize a new effort. They had expected the first attack to demolish the British army. The moment it failed to do so, the amount of ground it occupied became an embarrassment to the Germans. They must rearrange their forces, rest their troops, and prepare again for a new thrust. They could not take so much time as they had taken before, but they must take more than they could afford, for the Allies also would have that period in which to prepare to meet the assault.

On May 27, the Germans began what is known as the battle for Paris. Down to the south of the great bulge they had made in March, they directed an attack, just west of the great city of Rheims, directly at Paris. Poison gas was used with especial freedom in this attack and a great concentration of troops and artillery. Once more the Allied line yielded. There were now three great bulges in the line. On June 9 the battle was begun along the river Oise to fill in the gap between the first bulge and this third bulge, but it was only partially successful. The Allied reserves had come up; Foch had had time to make his preparations; and the French and Americans threw back the Germans at more than one point.

Again the Germans paused and took time to prepare for the final and much advertised thrust which was this time to win the war. Using the great bulge just created to the west of Rheims, they proposed to move east from its side and also to attack from the north at the same time, thus striking the French and American armies in this sector on two sides at once. The success of either of these attacks would insure the success of the other, and both would mean the loss of Rheims and the withdrawal of that whole section of the line. Verdun would then be isolated and could be assailed from the rear. It might have to surrender and the whole French right wing could then be crumpled up. Or, if the German High Command preferred, Paris would be at their mercy and they could destroy the center of the French army. The British ought then to be assailed with ease.

Whether the Germans were too confident and made less competent preparations than before, because they believed the French army exhausted and demoralized, we do not know, but this supposedly greatest attack was the least successful of all. It was stopped almost at once; after three days it was clearly a failure, and on July 18 Foch delivered an Allied offensive which at once succeeded and which was to continue until the war was won. In March, the Germans had all but won the war; in April again it looked as if they might win it; in June the decision still was within their reach. One month later it became clear to the Allies that the Germans had lost; two months later victory was in sight; in three months victory was at hand. In four months after the Germans had been conceded in London and Paris to have an admirable chance of winning the war, they surrendered. No more extraordinary and rapid change is recorded in history.

The Strategy of Foch

When Foch took command of the Allied armies in April at the moment when things looked all but at their worst, he determined that the one thing essential was to forestall a decision in favor of the Germans. To attempt to hold the ground against such German assaults was to sacrifice hundreds of thousands of men. Neither the French nor the British could afford to pay that price, even assuming that the ground could be held. The fate of France and of the world depended upon the continued existence of the armies, not upon the holding of a particular line. The French could win by keeping out of the Germans' way and by not allowing the Germans to beat them. They must resist enough to slow down the German advance; they must force the Germans to pay the maximum for what they gained; they must retire in good order and give the foe no chance to open a hole in the lines. But they should retreat and retreat rather than attempt to hold the territory at the expense of human life. Even Paris was not worth the risk of defeat. The loss of the Channel ports would hamper operations but could not result in total defeat. Until the French and British armies should be broken, the Germans could not win.

Moreover, the further and the faster the Germans advanced, the greater became the problem of maintaining their armies. They were advancing into a region without railroads, chewed up by years of warfare, where transportation of food and munitions would be difficult in the extreme. So long as they did not break the Allied

BRITISH MIDNIGHT COUNTER-ATTACK DURING GERMAN OFFENSIVE, MARCH 1918.

line, the further they advanced the worse off they would be. Presently they would put themselves in a position from which they would not be able to extricate themselves except at the risk of defeat. To succeed, the German movement must keep on succeeding. The moment it stopped it was in danger.

Besides, Foch seems to have felt that the great object at this time was to maintain the Allied armies intact until the Americans could arrive in force. At all costs, they must not be beaten before that time. This meant defensive warfare, pursued until it became clear that the Germans could not win. But late in June Foch became convinced that the Germans had failed. They had shot their bolt; they had used up their reserves; and he correctly divined the fact that they had thrust into the battle every man they possessed. They had lost hundreds of thousands during these months of fighting and were now tired and weakened.

Foch knew again that a million Americans had come; millions more were on the way, every week adding to the number in France. They were not, to be sure, experienced troops, only a few of them perhaps were of proper caliber to trust in battle. But they were an admirable reserve. The future was assured: the Americans were on the spot and more Yanks were coming—plenty more. It was possible for him now to throw against the Germans the entire strength of the experienced British and French armies, superb troops, trained by the entire experience of the war. The Americans had made victory possible.

He concluded again that the German advanced positions, won during the great offensive, were only lightly held. There was no long series of trench positions to carry; the Germans had not won this territory to hold it, but merely to use it as a temporary base for a further advance. They ought therefore to be easily driven out of it. If the campaign had been one of movement forward, it might as quickly become one of movement backward, and, once started to the rear, the Germans would probably have to continue the retreat until they reached their old permanent lines. It seemed possible to drive them out of their new gains during 1918, without waiting for further aid from the Americans.

BRITISH BATTERY ADVANCING OVER PLANK
ROAD TO STOP GERMAN OFFENSIVE, 1918. A SHELL
HAS JUST EXPLODED BEHIND THE BATTERY.

So much was eminently desirable. Paris was in danger; it was being shelled by a long-range German gun and the German armies were all but within sight of it. The effect of victory upon the French and British people would be extraordinary, and if they were to undergo another winter of war it was particularly necessary. Unless they began to have the hope of victory to offset the fears of the spring, it was possible that the Allied morale would weaken. Then there was the submarine. It had by no means won the war. Ship-building in England and America had begun to tell; more ships indeed were beginning to be launched than the submarine was at that time sinking; but it was not wise to put too much confidence in ship-building. The new devices for beating submarines were also effective, but it was better not to rely too much upon them. If the German could be driven back to his old lines before the Americans arrived in force, it was a result peculiarly desirable to achieve.

On July 18, therefore, Foch launched the first of a series of offensives against the west side of the great bulge which the Germans had made in their third assault along the Marne just west of Rheims. The object was to pierce the western side of this salient and thus to force the Germans to retire from its tip or run the risk of being captured. The movement was from the first a glorious success and in it the American troops played a splendid part. They showed such dash, vigor, and skill that the French were electrified. Indeed, their spirit infused into the war-worn French and British a new courage and hope. As the pressure on the western side of this bulge continued, the Germans frantically resisted. Then the French attacked the eastern side of the salient, and the French and Americans began pushing in its center. The German Crown Prince had his troops fairly scrambling over each other trying to escape. The retreat, however, was admirably conducted and the Germans did escape, but by August 7 they had evacuated the entire salient, surrendered all their gains in their third great offensive, and Paris was again safe.

Then Foch struck at the great salients to the north which the Germans had driven into the Allied line in March and April. Pushing here and then there, availing himself with masterly skill of the weakness of the German position, the great general and his assistants so conducted the campaign that by the middle of September the Germans were back again on the old Hindenburg Line. All the gains of 1918 were lost; victory was no longer possible—and the Germans knew it. It was only now a question of the time when the Allies themselves could win the war. Ludendorff declared after the armistice that he had so informed the High Command and the political authorities and had demanded the acceptance of any terms they could secure. But it looked to the great majority in Allied countries in September, 1918, as if the full strength of the Americans would still be necessary to drive the Germans out of their defensive system.

The First American Offensive—Cantigny

In all probability the American attack upon Cantigny on May 28, 1918, was the first offensive attack conducted by American troops alone. While not in itself a major operation as this war has judged affairs, its immediate success at once altered the opinion of foreign observers of the value of American aid. It probably led the French general staff to intrust to the Americans the far more important positions at Château-Thierry and Belleau Wood. The offensive was conducted and carried out with magnificent dash and verve by the First American Division, comprising sections of the Regular Army.

Cantigny was a sort of observation post for the Germans, jutting out into Allied territory, and gave them a considerable advantage. It was a strong position because of the number of cellars and dugouts around it, and it was joined by a long tunnel to the chateau in the village. The American infantry had carefully rehearsed the attack behind the lines with tanks and finally went forward in three waves. The tanks preceded the troops, who advanced slowly, not on the run, separated from each other by considerable spaces. With the infantry went an attachment of flame-throwers who were to throw bombs into the cellars and dugouts if the Germans refused to come out. Engineers, signal corps men, carrier pigeons, also went with them; in case the wires should be cut, the carrier pigeons should be used. Overhead the artillery fire roared. The French guns also threw over gas bombs on the German batteries to the rear of Cantigny. Immediately preceding the infantry was laid down a rolling barrage behind which walked the troops, not moving faster than fifty yards a minute and then only half that pace. Suddenly a heavy smoke was thrown to blind the eyes of the German observers.

FRENCH OFFICIAL PHOTOGRAPH OF AMERICAN REGULARS LEAVING THE TRENCHES FOR THE ASSAULT ON CANTIGNY. NOTE THE BROKEN FORMATION AND THE SLOW PACE.

The village might have been a volcano in eruption, shooting up clouds of smoke, first white, then brown, then black—a great dull cloud covering all like a pall, eternally writhing and twisting as if Cantigny were trying to escape its fate. The German defenses were completely leveled by the artillery fire; the trenches were smashed so that they looked like a field plowed by a giant harrow; the German artillery was silenced by the gas and smoke.

At 6:45, the zero hour or the minute for the attack, the observers, watching from behind, had their eyes fixed upon a smooth green slope, dotted with trees, across which the American troops must advance. The moment for the attack came and the great smoke cloud rolled itself between the observers and objective. Then came a rift in the smoke and on the green slope were tiny black figures, like ants, walking forward slowly. "We could see two of the three waves and not a single man out of place, following the barrage like veterans," said one of the officers.

The sun had just risen and through streaky clouds the tongues of red flame from the hundreds of guns were momentarily visible to the watchers behind, but the village itself was nothing but a pillar of smoke. Out of it came back in thirty-five minutes the characteristic American message, "We're here! Everything O.K." Further messages came back to the observers in the staff office: "They can see the Boche throwing down his arms in Cantigny—the colonel has twenty prisoners—the right flank is sending back about a hundred—balloon reports grenade fighting west of Cantigny where our men are mopping up the trenches—one tank returning

FRENCH OFFICIAL PHOTOGRAPH OF AMERICAN
REGULARS "MOPPING UP" CANTIGNY.

from Cantigny—our men are seen walking around the city—flame throwers can be seen through the smoke cleaning out the dugouts."

All had gone absolutely as rehearsed, the artillery fire, gas, shells, smoke screen had prevented the German artillery from operating and had driven the Germans into their dugouts. The rolling barrage kept them there until the Americans were upon them. The Americans had not lost their heads, had walked as they should and had not run, and had executed in thirty-five minutes with a precision which no Allied troops could have surpassed an operation of real difficulty. These were men of the Regular Army.

Château-Thierry

The third great German attack had burst through the Allied lines in the battle for Paris and had reached the Marne at Château-Thierry. Paris only thirty-nine miles away, all but within range of German guns! Paris already bombarded by the long-range, monster gun some sixty or seventy miles distant! As one Frenchman expressed it, "We felt in our faces the very breath of the approaching beast."

It had been throughout the German offensive the strategy of Foch to retreat to save men rather than positions, and, as the lines had drawn back nearer and nearer to Paris, the hearts of the Allied world had stood still for fear that Paris itself might fall into German hands. Dauntless as the French were, it seemed at that moment as if their strength was failing. The British had just suffered two months before a crushing defeat; the Italians were as yet in the gravest danger; there was serious question whether the British and French could themselves resist the Hun alone. Were the Americans ready? Although the American regulars at Cantigny had showed superb skill, they were comparatively only a handful. But there were other Americans. The Second Division was composed largely of marines, the land soldiers who go to sea with the navy, and in desperation the marines were rushed to the Château-Thierry sector to help stop a gap, when even French heroism had seemed almost incapable of resistance.

It was a characteristic modern charge, an all-night charge. On motor trucks, cattle cars, dummy railroad trains, across country

AEROPLANE PHOTOGRAPH OF AMERICAN ASSAULT IN THREE WEEKS, 1918. NOTE THE DISTANCE BETWEEN THE WAVES AND THE WIDE SPACING OF THE MEN.

they hurried, crowded together like sardines. With little food and less sleep, they reached the battlefield. They were not posted in the town—the Third Division of Regulars were there; but along the line to the west of the town itself. The French commander advised and even ordered them to retire. The German advance was so strong that it was idle, he thought, to sacrifice life to stop it. But the American commander declined. It was not the tradition of the marines to retreat, he told the French officer; it was their business to attack. They stormed ahead through the middle of an artillery battle, yelling like wild Indians, ardent, young, irresistible. "Don't go there!" shouted the French, "The boches with machine guns are there!" "That's where we want to go!" shouted the Americans. "That's where we have come three thousand miles to go." It is reported that an American officer hurried up to a French officer, commanding troops who were fighting fiercely and almost hopelessly, and in extraordinarily bad French said, "Vous fatigez vous partir—netre job." "You tired—you go back—our job."

Part of the marines went into action on June 2, in a wheat field hereafter to be famous in American annals. Far in the distance they saw the Germans advance across another wheat field in smooth steady columns, with no attempt at concealment. Indeed, the Germans were so far off that they believed themselves out of danger and the French were amazed to see the marines set their sights and open rifle fire on the Germans. The European tradition still was in this war, that the best that could be done was to fire toward the enemy rather than at an individual man. But just as the American farmers in the Cambridge marshes bothered General Howe's men on the ramparts of Boston, and as Morgan's men at Saratoga picked off Burgoyne's officers, so the American marines each picked out his man and killed him. The Germans were literally paralyzed; men were falling on all sides, very obviously killed—and by rifle fire—and at such a distance. The German lines hesitated, stopped, and broke for cover. The advance was checked. A French aviator, soaring overhead, grasped the situation and signaled,

"Bravo." His signal was caught and passed back through the lines to Paris, echoing again and again and spelling courage and hope.

There was also a bridge across the Marne which the Germans were determined to take and which the Americans determined to hold. The Americans had pushed across the river on the north bank some small companies of machine gun men who were to attempt to hold the Germans away from the town and the bridge during the night of May 31. The Germans filtered into the outskirts of the city and occupied positions on the hills which enabled them to direct a galling fire upon the French and Americans holding the north bank of the river. In accordance with orders, after dark on the first of June the French retired to the southern bank. It was now 10:30 P.M. and pitch dark except for the light of the bursting shells and the flame stabs of the machine guns on both sides. Then there came to the Americans out of the black darkness, the ghostly chant of the advancing enemy and they knew the Germans were coming, shoulder to shoulder, singing loudly to keep up their courage. Presently the shuffling and creaking of their boots was heard by the straining ears of the Americans, and then every gun let loose in the darkness. The enemy waves melted away, but on they came again, only to be met by furious gun fire, and to melt away once more.

One American lieutenant with a squad of thirteen men was somehow or other left on the north bank, and, returning as he understood under orders, he approached the main bridge after the Germans arrived and while the grand attack was proceeding. He and his men worked their way down toward the bridge, took refuge under the stone parapets, and watched the Germans rushing forward and getting shot. The lieutenant knew that his own company was on the other side and in a lull of the firing he yelled repeatedly, "Cobey! Cobey!"—the name of his fellow officer. Cobey heard him, and the next time the German wave retired the American guns ceased long enough for the lieutenant and his men to scramble back across the bridge.

The next day, June 2, the Germans continued heavy shelling of the position and then at nine o'clock under cover of darkness they sought to rush the bridge. But fifteen minutes of heavy machine gun fire squelched the attack. The next night the French engineers laid a charge under the bridge and blew it up, and, as the Germans rushed out of the houses to learn what had happened, a flare was thrown over which lit up the whole scene, and the American bullets again found plenty of targets. The German advance was checked. The Americans had held. France was electrified. Help had come.

Belleau-Wood

To the northwest of Château-Thierry, along the edges of the great German drive on Paris, was Belleau Wood, a forest in which the Germans had established nest after nest of machine guns in a jungle of matted underbrush of vines and heavy foliage. They had placed themselves in positions which they did not believe could be captured. But unless they could be driven from Belleau Wood the success of Château-Thierry would be unavailing. There would come another drive and another from this wood protecting the German flank. Once in Allied hands, the Germans would be forced to retreat from Château-Thierry. On June 6, therefore, the marines began a tremendous assault upon the wood and the towns near it. The method was a rush, a halt, and a rush again by four lines of men some distance apart, the men in the rear lines taking the places of those who fell in the front ranks.

"Men fell like flies," wrote an officer from the field; companies dwindled away; but the attack did not falter. The fighting was literally of the sort for which the Americans first became famous in the American Revolution. It was fighting from tree to tree, from bowlder to bowlder. The wood was so thick and so strewn with rocks behind each of which was a German machine gun that it was impossible for the artillery to wipe out all those nests. It could be done only by the bayonet, by a desperate charge, and the marines, bare chested, shouting their battle cry, "E-yah-yip," charged straight into the murderous fight—and won. In more than one case only one man reached the machine gun, but with his bayonet as his only weapon he killed or captured the defenders, swung about the gun and turned it upon the German positions. In some cases, some Westerner accustomed to a six-shooter at close quarters killed half a dozen Germans while they were thinking about getting out their revolvers. Such feats are not uncommon in the United States but were not understood by the Germans or provided for in Kultur.

Day and night the fighting went on without relief, without sleep, often without water. For six days they were without hot food, but still the marines hung on. Their doggedness was extraordinary. Time after time the officers thought the limit had been reached. They saw their men falling asleep under shell fire, saw them fight on after they had been wounded, and until they had dropped unconscious. But the word kept coming that the lines must hold,

GERMAN MACHINE GUN NEST OF CONCRETE
CONCEALED BY TREES AND UNDERBRUSH
FROM AEROPLANE OBSERVATION.

and, if possible, that the lines must attack. So without water, without food, without rest they went forward. Regiments were reduced to the size of companies, companies became platoons, sometimes with no more than a sergeant or a corporal to lead them. After thirteen days of this extraordinary attack, a captured German officer told of a fresh advance of Germany's finest troops who were to be thrown into the struggle.

There was no help coming for the Americans and men who had fought on their nerve alone for days fought on it still, with their backs to trees and bowlders or their sole shelter the ruins of villages. Time after time the officers sent back such messages as this: "Loss heavy; difficult to get runners through; morale excellent but troops about all in; men exhausted." Exhausted, but holding on! And they continued to hold on in spite of all the Germans could do. Day by day their lines slowly advanced and then on June 24 began the final struggle. The artillery barrage literally tore the woods to pieces, but even its intensity could not clear them. With the bayonet it was finally done and on July 6 the marines were relieved and handed over the hard-won position to British troops.

Once more the Americans had proved the extraordinary quality of their work. They had demonstrated themselves the equals of the best French and British troops, the superiors of the Kaiser's crack regiments who had been pitted against them. We know now that some of the finest troops of the German army had been sent against the Americans in order to make it impossible that they should win their first action. The Germans well knew that the moral effect upon the French and British of an American failure might be of real importance to them, but the Americans again proved themselves the better men.

Three American Exploits

In July, 1918, an American division brigaded with the French was fighting along the Marne. A detachment of eleven men under Sergeant J. F. Brown was suddenly caught by a tremendous German artillery fire and had to take shelter. Along came the charging columns of Germans, too numerous to oppose, and the little band of Americans lay quiet and let them go on. Presently along came more Germans, and Brown saw that the German advance had left him and his detachment within the enemy lines. He ordered his men to scatter and take care of themselves as best they could. No idea of surrender ever entered their heads. They would get back to their own lines, each for himself. They proposed to walk straight through the battle, not only through the German lines but through their own fire!

Presently in the woods he met his own captain, also alone. Finding that the German artillery fire was too heavy for them to pass through, they lay down in a thicket and decided to kill as many Germans as possible before they were themselves killed. By them processioned company after company of Germans. Presently they heard behind them two machine guns. Brown had a rifle, the captain had a revolver, so the two of them crept out to attack the German army. They stalked the machine gun as if it was a grizzly bear and attempted to charge it. The captain was killed, but there was by this time only one man left of the machine gun crew and Brown picked him off with his rifle. He now met an American corporal, also alone, and the two of them started after the other German machine gun. With the rifle Brown killed the gun crew. Now, attracted by the shouting, appeared the eleven men of Brown's command, who were also looking for Germans. All of this, mind you, within the German lines, surrounded by thousands of Germans.

Presently these thirteen Americans discovered a trench filled with German soldiers, armed as usual with machine guns and rifles, waiting to repel a counter-attack in case their own troops should be forced to retreat. Brown posted his twelve men around that trench in twelve places; placed himself where he could rake the trench with his own rifle, and, when he gave the signal, they all opened fire. They fired until their guns became too hot to hold and killed they did not know how many Germans. But the major in command of the trench had had enough of it. He believed himself surrounded by a large force, thought, in fact, that he was within the enemy lines, so he put up his hands and yelled "Kamerad." The thirteen Americans disarmed the trench full of Germans; there were more than one hundred of them, although the Americans did not stop then to count them. With Brown and the corporal leading and the other eleven Americans in the rear, these thirteen dough-boys started out to conduct one hundred prisoners back through the German and Allied lines! They met other parties of Germans, who, seeing this advancing column and believing that somehow or other the battle had gone against them, promptly surrendered. The file of prisoners grew, little by little, until it numbered one hundred fifty-five. By some kind of miraculous luck they came to a place where there was a gap in the German advance lines and in the Allied lines as well, and they did get through. Strange as this tale may sound, it has been vouched for on the authority of well-known correspondents.

Another tale of extraordinary self-possession is told of a single American in the fighting at Belleau Wood. Frank Lenert suddenly found himself surrounded by seventy-eight Germans and five officers. He was a German-American and spoke a language which the boches understood. They questioned him with extraordinary eagerness as to the details of the American attack, and he proceeded in genuine American fashion to "string" them, and did it with that largeness and convincing flow of language which so many Americans are able to attain but which seems to be an unknown quantity in Germany. He told them there were eight regiments around them at that minute and that plenty more were coming. There was an American barrage behind the Germans at that time and they believed that the doughboy told the truth. They therefore begged the honor of surrendering.

Anybody but an American would have betrayed himself, but the self-confidence of this private was entirely equal to the occasion. He accepted their surrender with a gravity which completely convinced them that everything he said was true. They threw their arms away, returned his rifle to him, and started to the rear as eighty-three prisoners. This is one of the largest totals of prisoners taken by a single man. His comment and explanation was that it was no wonder the boches believed the lies their own government told them when they swallowed such lies as his. The American practice of telling a long story with a perfectly straight face again and again accounts for the extraordinary tales which come back to us. The American joke was too much for the German mind.

Another extraordinary adventure was that of the Lost Battalion. During the fighting in the Argonne, a battalion of American soldiers worked itself forward during an offensive at the end of September, only to find itself when day dawned with Germans on four sides. The Americans were in possession of a sort of ravine and were entirely able to defend themselves, but it was a question of death or surrender unless help came. They could stay there but they could not get out, and, having of course no food and only a limited supply of ammunition, they could not hold out more than a short time. They declined however to surrender. The American division to which they belonged soon discovered their plight and an attack was made by the French and Americans to release them.

While it failed, it probably saved their lives, because it kept the Germans too busy to attack them.

Three more attempts at relief were made on the next day, all of which failed. Fourteen trips were undertaken by aëroplanes, however, which succeeded in dropping two tons of food and a good deal of ammunition in the ravine. On the third day it became clear that they must be rescued or they would be compelled to surrender. The Germans realized their plight and sent an American prisoner to them with a note. "Americans! you are surrounded on all sides. Surrender in the name of humanity; you will be well treated."

Major Whittlesey did not hesitate a second. "Go to hell," he shouted, and then read the note to those around him. A ringing cheer went up from those exhausted and hungry men, which the Germans heard and understood from their observation posts. But all goes well that ends well, for within a few hours the American division broke through the German cordon and rescued the battalion. Four hundred and sixty-three men had been cooped up in the ravine and had declined to surrender to nobody knows how many Germans.

It was this spirit of the American troops, this do-or-die tenacity, this unwillingness to surrender even before overwhelming odds, that dashed the hopes of the Germans as it raised those of the Allies. It must not be supposed that these exploits here told showed greater, braver, or better qualities than hundreds of others, but a few only could be told in a book like this and these seemed to be not merely remarkable but authentic.

THE CAPTURE OF ST. MIHIEL

The first independent operation of an American army in France as such was undertaken on September 12, 1918, against the famous German position of St. Mihiel. Hitherto the American troops had always fought as part of the British and French armies. They had occupied important posts, won important battles, but always supported by French or British artillery and directed by foreign officers. At the end of August an American army was organized, all parts of which were American. It was under the direct personal command of General Pershing and took over a section of the line east of Verdun.

The importance of this sector was extraordinary: It was directly opposite the great city of Metz, the key to the eastern end of all parts of the German defense system in France. Through it came the great bulk of supplies that went to all parts of the German lines. Through it must come reënforcements. Metz was also the gateway to Germany and the most important part of the defenses of that country itself. For that reason the Germans had fortified this section of the line with extreme thoroughness.

In the first year of the war they had pushed through east of Verdun a sort of elbow in their line at the point of which was the town of St. Mihiel. This elbow or salient faced Verdun on the east and from it an attack was possible which would cut off the city altogether. Verdun was no less important to the French than Metz was to the Germans; it was the pivot of the French line; if it should

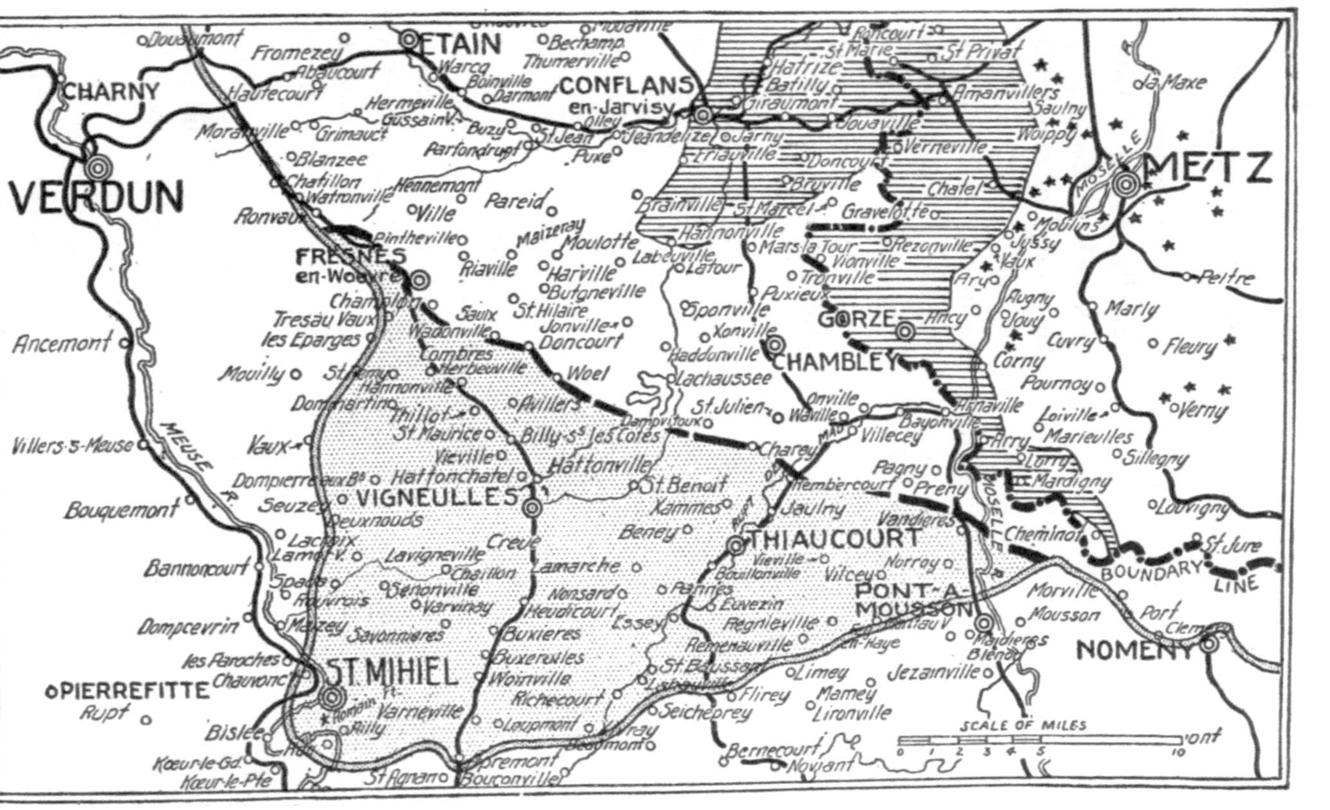

THE ST. MIHIEL SALIENT.

fall, the whole line should have to retire. The French were therefore extremely anxious to wipe out this salient and directed against it immediately a series of great assaults. They failed however to make any impression, and during the four years of war this elbow stuck out from the German line, continually menacing Verdun and making extremely difficult any attack on Metz.

The first American army took over, therefore, a very important problem. It had been, however, for a year or more, what was called a quiet sector, because one on which very little active fighting had taken place for a good many months. The Germans proposed no offensive there. Their great attack against Verdun had failed in 1916 and they were not likely to renew it. From that point of view it was perhaps a less dangerous position for the Americans to take charge of than some other districts.

But the purpose of the Americans was by no means defense. They meant to succeed in a task at which the French had repeatedly failed. Not that they felt themselves braver than the French or better soldiers, but they knew that the methods of warfare had changed in four years and General Pershing believed that St. Mihiel, which had been too strong to be captured by the methods understood earlier in the war, would not be too great a task for the first American army in September, 1918. It was a great task, but not too great. The result would be extraordinary if it should be a success. It was the sort of task which would lend glory to the American army and prove to the French and British that the Americans, all by themselves, were entirely competent to undertake military operations of the first magnitude.

The extent of fortifications around St. Mihiel was unusual. There were, as elsewhere on the German lines, trenches and miles of barbed wire entanglements, but there were few places where the dugouts and underground houses were so deeply constructed and well built as along the sides of this famous salient. The positions were for the most part on the crests of hills, looking down into valleys across which a foe must advance, and steel and concrete houses had been built inside the hills. The greatest fortress of all, a tall peak called Mont Sec, has been described by correspondents as towering into the air like a twenty-story building. From it everything was visible on a clear day for ten miles. The sides of this fortress were steep, covered with woods and ditches. Across them ran trenches and miles of barbed wire entanglements. These were defended by regular underground fortresses or houses located forty or fifty feet within the mountain side; they were comfortably, even luxuriously, furnished, and most of them were built with entrances from both sides of the mountain. On the side away from the Allied lines there were porches, tables at which the German officers used to drink beer, hammocks slung between the trees, and various other devices for making the occupants pass the time pleasantly. Needless to say, fortresses of this kind were impervious to the fire of even the heaviest guns. High explosive shells could not blow the tops off of mountains nor reach fortresses fifty feet underground. The Germans had dug themselves in as early as 1915 and expected to stay there until peace was signed.

To capture such a position by assault, General Pershing realized meant preparations of no ordinary type. One hundred thousand detailed maps were prepared covering the minutest facts of the whole salient. They told where every German position was and just what it was. These maps were corrected continually from the reports of the aviators up to the very morning of the battle. To help the artillery and infantry officers in their work forty thousand photographs were taken.

Then to insure the smooth cooperation of the American forces after they had succeeded in penetrating the first defense, five thousand miles of telephone wires were laid on the borders of the salient before the attack, and to them six thousand telephones were connected the instant the American troops advanced. Behind the troops as they went forward came motor trucks unreeling wires which were to continue this telephone system. Then the signal corps men took the reels of wire on their shoulders and walked with them immediately behind the attacking troops right up to the very firing line. As fast as the troops advanced, the telephone lines came after them, and in the battle-zone during the battle itself there was a telephone system in operation which would have been adequate to handle the business of a city of one hundred thousand people. Ten thousand men were engaged in operating it. Most of the various exchanges, exactly like the exchanges in any American city, were on motor trucks and moved around as the battle changed. The signal corps had thousands of carrier pigeons by which messages could also be sent through should the telephone wires be cut or broken. But the wires held.

Elaborate provisions were made to take care of the wounded, including thirty-five hospital trains, sixteen thousand beds in the battle-zone, and fifty thousand at the base hospital. Happily, only ten per cent of these facilities were needed. This gives some idea of the extent and character of the preparations necessary for a major operation in modern warfare. While these arrangements represented the very acme of military perfection, it must not be supposed that they were superior to or different from the arrangements made by the British and French. We merely showed that we could do it ourselves.

The plan of the attack was simple. General Pershing proposed to push in both sides of this salient or elbow, sticking out of the line, and compel the Germans to evacuate its tip. He was going to push at the base of the triangle on both sides, and, by bending in the lines until his forces met, he would either compel the Germans to run in a hurry and evacuate the strongest part of the district without fighting or he would capture them.

There were four hours of artillery preparation, terrific and intensive, intended to drive the Germans underground and destroy whatever could be destroyed on the surface. Then at five A.M. on September 12, the Americans, assisted by one French corps, advanced. They were preceded by a number of tanks, which could not, however, climb the mountains and were not so useful to them as in some other battles. But, aided by groups of wire cutters, they went through the lines of the German defenses very much as at Cantigny. To their own amazement, they carried everything with a rush and found themselves through the first zone of the German defenses with very small losses and in record-breaking time. The first push had been on the south side of the salient and the second had been on the northern; both had succeeded.

The American army and the world at large were electrified to learn on the following day that the American forces had met and that the salient had been wiped out. Between one hundred fifty and two hundred square miles of territory had been taken from the Germans and many villages had been released from German domination which had been in their hands from the very beginning of the war. Sixteen thousand prisoners, four hundred and forty-three guns, great amounts of material, ammunition, clothes, and food were captured.

The speed of the Americans had been so great that considerable numbers of Germans had been unable to escape from the apex of the triangle. Eventually a good many thousands surrendered. Whole regiments walked out with their officers. In one case the commander, after surrendering, requested that the roll be called in order that he might discover how heavy his losses had been. The whole regiment answered present except one officer and one private, and the commander then suggested that he should march his own command wherever it was wanted. The Americans advancing to the front met the astonishing spectacle of an entire German regiment, marching off the battlefield under its own officers, and guarded only by a half dozen American cavalrymen, lounging in their saddles after the fashion of American cowboys driving a herd of cattle.

The Americans had proved their quality. They had achieved what the French had been most anxious to do for four years. They had relieved Verdun of all apprehension and had ironed out one of the most important creases in the German lines. They had put

Metz within reach of the heavy artillery and were able to shell the most important railroad the Germans had. General Pershing had every reason to be content.

The triumphal entry into St. Mihiel was characteristic of the Americans and French. The American secretary of war, Mr. Baker, with Generals Pershing and Petain, went quietly to the famous little town and walked through its streets, all but unaccompanied, and without ceremony or signs of triumph. But the identity of the distinguished visitors was soon known to the inhabitants. They poured out to receive them, crowded around them, kissing Mr. Baker's hand, weeping. The sudden relief from the galling oppression which they had endured almost unnerved them.

The Final Problem

The problem which Foch had now to meet was extraordinary and difficult. He must carry a defensive system devised by the Germans to prevent the success of any possible assault and which represented the preparations of four years. The German High Command believed that at all costs they must retain the territory of France until peace had been signed. When they came to the peace table they must still hold in their hands northern France and Belgium. Such elaborate defenses must therefore be constructed that it would be impossible to carry them. The British and French for this very reason deemed it essential not to end the war until the Germans had been driven from this very territory, and if possible from the whole country west of the Rhine. Otherwise they must redeem northern France and Belgium at the expense of concessions in Lorraine, in Poland, in the Balkans, or in Italy, which they could not well afford to make. The war also must end in such a way that enough territory could be taken from the Germans to prevent them from ever again making an aggressive assault upon France and Belgium. Foch must therefore win the war in a particular way and in a particular place, and he must overcome the obstacles which the Germans had created during four years to prevent his achieving exactly that end.

On the map are shown the four practically parallel lines of trench defenses which the Germans had constructed between the French border and the battle line. The two anchors of this long

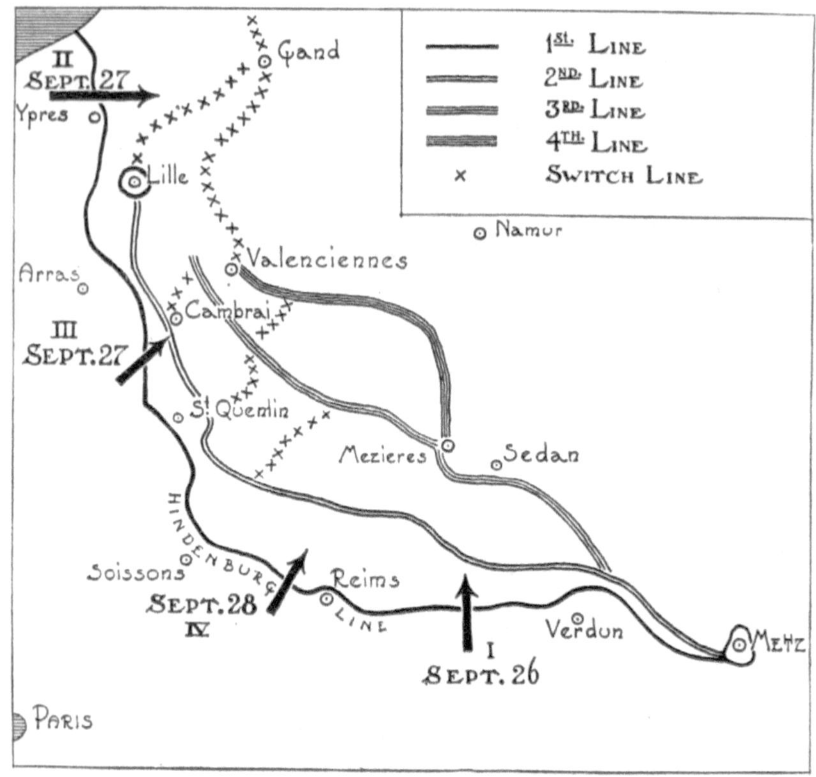

THE FOUR GERMAN DEFENSE LINES AND
FIRST OPERATIONS OF FOCH

line, which stretched from the mountains to the sea something
over six hundred miles long, were Metz, where all four of the lines
ended, and Lille to the north, where three of them terminated. The
loss of Metz would break all four lines, but the Germans regarded
that as unthinkable. The loss of Lille would probably destroy the
first and second lines, but not the third and fourth, which were
devised expressly to meet the emergency of its loss. The whole
system was also constructed so as to provide against disaster by
an Allied success in any particular sector.

The crosses on the map connecting these various trench lines
represent what were called switch lines. They were intended to
divide the territory into compartments or rooms like the water-

tight compartments in a ship. The loss of any one, or perhaps two, of them would not sink the ship. The others would keep it afloat. These switch lines, therefore, were to limit the success of the Allies; when they should carry some portion of the first trench lines, they would still find the Germans prepared to fight them and hold the remaining sections of the first lines.

The first line, called the Hindenburg Line, was strongest of all and was really a zone twelve miles broad at most places and comprised of many trench lines, one behind the other, connected by switch lines of various sorts on just the same principles as the larger system. Elaborate barbed wire entanglements had been created in front of all the trenches. Deep pits had been dug, covered by planks and sod so as to look like solid ground, into which it was hoped tanks would fall. Mines and bombs had been planted

GERMAN DUGOUT ENTRANCE WITH ENTRANCES TO OFFICER'S SHELTERS, HINDENBURG LINE, 1918. THIS SURVIVED THE FINAL ARTILLERY PREPARATION.

which could be exploded as the Allied troops passed. The trenches themselves were of concrete and were believed to be too heavy for the Allied artillery to destroy by any length of "preparation."

Underground at various points were complete houses for hundreds of troops, with dormitories fitted with beds, kitchens, dining rooms, rest rooms, the whole lighted by electricity. In some of these underground houses at least the electric power was provided in characteristic German manner, by a treadmill worked by man power! They compelled prisoners to tramp round on the treadles for hours at a time so that the officers might have light and heat!

The officers' quarters along the Hindenburg Line were underground, safe from shell fire, and so well constructed that they did survive the final attack. When the Allied troops entered them, they found them furnished with brass beds, comfortable chairs and tables, with pictures on the walls, rugs on the floor, and all the appliances of an ordinary house. The Germans meant to live on the Hindenburg Line, if necessary, for years, and they proposed to be comfortable. They proposed also to be safe, and therefore to live underground. The Allied artillery might pound the surface as long as it liked, for as many days and weeks as it chose, but it would not disturb

GERMAN SHELTER FOR LARGE GUN TO CONCEAL IT FROM AEROPLANE OBSERVATION.

the real defenses in the least. This being true, the Germans did not see how the Hindenburg Line could be carried. They had also used the rivers, canals, and marshes of the district with great cleverness to furnish sections of the lines with water barriers which prevented the use of tanks, for the tank is a land battleship and does not swim.

The problem of Foch was great because the Allies had attempted many times in the past years to carry sections of the Hindenburg Line, and, while at an enormous cost of life and effort some small gains had been made, no section of the line itself had been carried. The secondary defenses had always held, and, being twelve miles wide, only an extraordinary drive could pass clear through the zone.

What gave Foch courage and confidence was the new technique of warfare which the Allies had developed. Trench warfare had been at first so new that neither the Germans nor the Allies had understood it. And the history of the war had been during its first years one of experiment with the technique of the new weapons. It had taken the generals time to find out what could not be done; it had taken the troops time to learn how to execute movements which were possible. The German campaign of 1918 made it clear that they had solved the question of breaking through the trenches and fighting through into the open beyond. Foch believed that the Allies had also solved it, and that the Hindenburg Line itself would offer no real obstacle.

The greatest difficulty to meet had been the machine guns concealed in concrete shelters. Human flesh could not stand before machine gun fire, and the artillery, however accurate its aim, had proved itself unable to destroy the kind of shelters that the Germans had constructed. However perfect, therefore, had become the technique of the Allies in other ways, the concrete shelter with its machine guns always prevented the continuation of the advance. It was with this sort of arrangement that the tanks were intended to cope. They were to roll in upon these concrete shelters and clean them out. The first tanks, however, were large, slow, and clumsy. The German aëroplanes were quick, and presently the

FRENCH WHIPPET TANKS CHARGING WITH AMERICAN
TROOPS, 1918. NOTE SLOW PACE OF INFANTRY.

German gunners began to drop high explosives on the tanks, and
the moment the technique of the German large artillery became
capable of destroying the big tanks, their usefulness could be only
partial. Nor could they assault positions protected by water nor
yet operate in mud or in wet weather.

The French therefore invented a new kind of tank, called the
whippet, a small tank holding only two or three men, moving
with great rapidity, and so much lighter than the others that it
could move over rougher and wetter ground. It was nevertheless
sufficiently well armored to withstand machine gun bullets and
swift enough to be far out of the way before large shells came over.
Here was a method of dealing with this final obstacle.

The new Allied attack therefore need not start with a long
artillery bombardment of days or hours, which merely adver-

tised what was coming and when. A brief but intense fire could now accomplish all the destruction possible aboveground at any moment. Poison gas could then be started, if the wind was right, and both would keep the Germans underground. What was called a creeping or rolling barrage would then be laid down by the artillery. The Allied guns would fire all together and drop on a certain line on the German trenches a row of shells that would create a zone of solid fire. This would prevent the Germans from coming out of their dugouts and incidentally destroy the barbed wire entanglements in front of the troops.

Behind the barrage would come the Allied infantry; slowly the barrage would move forward, the Allied gunners lengthening their range; with the troops would be the whippet tanks, which would dash forward and clean out the machine guns as they revealed themselves. Thus line after line of the trenches could be carried. Of course, the utmost accuracy and foresight were necessary for any such movement. The aëroplane work must be perfect, must tell where the Germans were, and show the artillery exactly what to do. The artillery must hit exactly what it aimed at. The troops must move in exactly such a way to exactly such spots. With these methods, Foch felt sure the whole German defense system could be destroyed—and he was right.

At a time when things looked black in the summer of 1918, Foch was asked by a distinguished man whether he really had a plan for winning the war. General Maurice, the British official observer, tells of the great general's reply. Laconic always and sparing of words, he employed only gestures. He struck out with his left arm, then with his right, then more rapidly with the left again, and finally gave a tremendous kick with his right leg. Three rapid blows and a kick—such was indeed his strategy.

Breaking the Hindenburg Line

The attacks delivered by Foch against the Germans toward the end of September presumed a superiority in numbers for the Allies, and depended upon delivering crushing attacks at different parts of the German line, each superior in weight to the force the Germans had. He would also deliver a number of almost simultaneous blows at various portions of the line, considerable distances apart so that the Germans might not be able to meet this strategy with their old device of drawing men from other sections of the line. He must, however, if possible, surprise the foe, and therefore must attack without extensive collections of men and material which the German aviators would see and understand, and also without extensive artillery preparation of the old type, which had practically told the enemy, "I shall strike you here in three or four days."

On September 26, therefore, Foch threw the French and Americans against the Hindenburg Line between Rheims and Verdun. The operation was immediately successful in penetrating the German lines and presently drove through the first zone of defenses to the open beyond. He did not wait for success on this section but the very day after the attack had begun in the south hurled the Belgians and British against the German lines between Ypres and the coast. He meant to strike at the two ends of the line so as to make reënforcement of either part as difficult as possible. Success in the north would outflank the other lines of defense which rested upon Lille.

FRENCH CHARGE IN LIAISON FORMATION: THE FINAL FRENCH MILITARY ACHIEVEMENT.
NOTE HOW SCATTERED THE MEN ARE AND HOW SLOW THEIR MOVEMENTS.

He had already determined that his chief strategy should be to break and turn the German right wing and throw it back through France and Belgium on the German frontier. His object was that which the French and British had constantly held throughout the war. They must so fight it as to expel the Germans from French and Belgian territory. No victory would be worth winning which ended with the Germans on French soil. Foch must therefore aim his drive at the right wing, capture Lille, the terminus of all the German defense lines in France, and bend back the whole system on Metz as a pivot, very much as a door swings open. This is eventually what he did. Having first pushed down near the hinges of the door, he then hammered the lock.

On that same day, September 27, he struck at the middle of the door, reaching out toward Cambrai. On September 28, he launched a French army against the sector just west of Rheims on the battle front already familiar to the French and Americans. The result of these four attacks, delivered with tremendous weight on such widely separated sections, set the whole German line rocking from the mountains to the sea. At either end the first line was completely broken. The Hindenburg Line had fallen at both ends. Being much stronger in the middle, the resistance was longer and further operations became essential.

On October 8 the decisive operations of the war were launched. To the British was given the honor of dealing the crushing blows against the center of the German line. Three armies, elaborately prepared and drilled, were simultaneously thrown against the section of the Hindenburg Line between Cambrai and St. Quenten. Within three days they all drove through the entire twelve-mile zone of the Hindenburg Line itself, cut the second great defense line behind it, and chased across the open territory between the second and third lines, halting at the third line just south of the great city of Valenciennes, which was also the key to the fourth line.

Meanwhile Foch redoubled the activities of the armies at either end of the line. To the north, the British and Belgians, reënforced by the French, broke through the final defenses of the second German line and swung down north of Lille, attacking the switch line which connected that city with Ghent. They therefore threatened the northern end of the entire German defense system, and if they could cut the switch line, they would compel the evacuation of the whole northern end of the line. That should be the final blow.

In the third and fourth weeks of October the Allies began to reap the fruits of the great offensive. The Germans themselves were compelled to abandon without fighting the first sections of all the defense lines. They retired rapidly behind the second switch line which connected Ghent and Valenciennes. Lille was surrendered; Douai, Cambrai, St. Quentin, all of them great positions on the

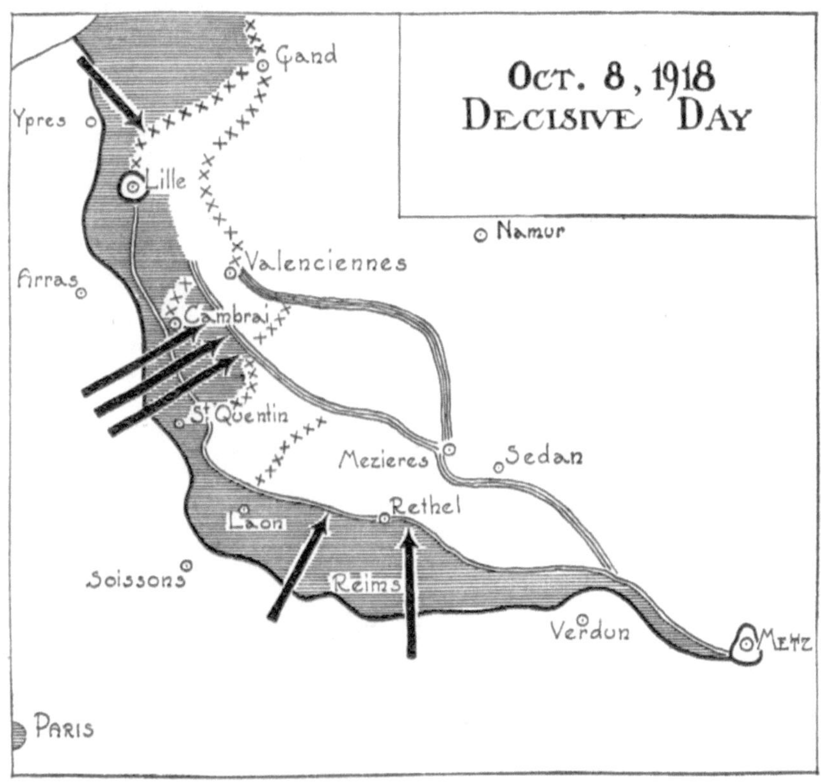

THE ALLIED OFFENSIVE—1918

second line of German defenses, fell without a blow. The entire first section of the switch line from Lille to Ghent was lost. The first of the water-tight compartments between the second and third German lines had also been lost. The Germans now had been driven from all of the territory between the second and third lines north of St. Quentin, though the other water-tight compartments between the second and third lines still held. They were therefore using the fourth line in Belgium, then the third line below Valenciennes, and below St. Quentin the second line.

The last week in October they were forced to evacuate the last water-tight compartment between the second and third lines just east of St. Quentin. In the first week of November Foch struck hard at the third line south of Valenciennes. The British and Canadians on November 2 completed the operation by taking Valenciennes

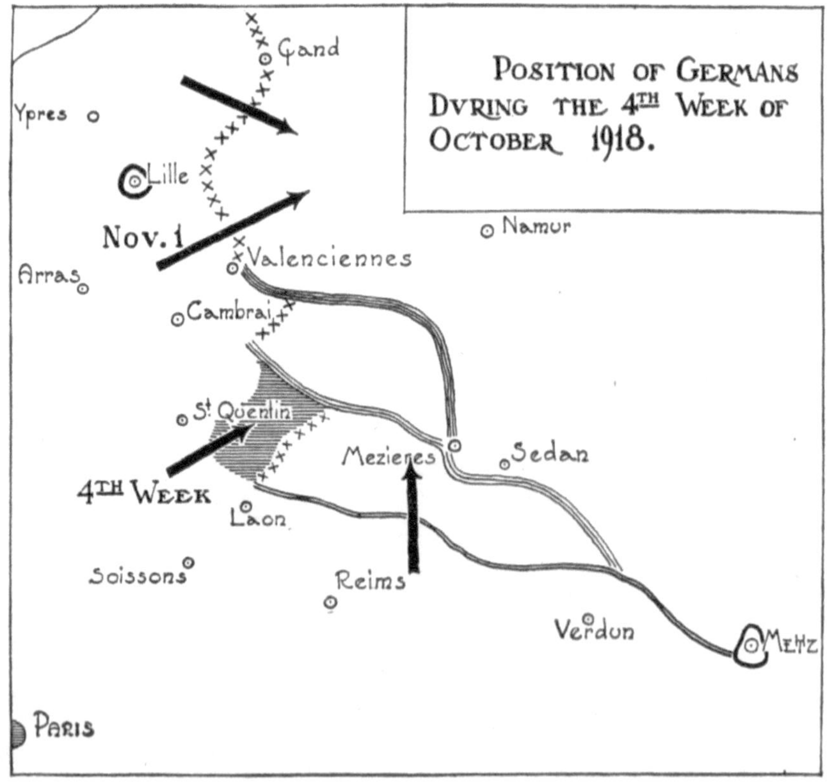

itself, and broke clean through the fourth defense line into the open Belgian fields beyond. At the same time, the Belgians and British were assailing the switch line south of Ghent and the Americans and French were proceeding north of Rheims through the second line of the German defenses upon Sedan. This had been the scene of the defeat of the French army in the Franco-Prussian War in 1870 and its capture was a matter of great satisfaction to the French.

The German lines were now everywhere broken; their armies everywhere in rapid retreat. Ludendorff early in September had counseled the German government to sue for peace, and there was now in the beginning of November no question whatever of the necessity of that measure. Bulgaria had already unconditionally surrendered, thus throwing open the entire rear of the military position of the Central Empires. The Allied armies would be able in the following spring to begin a great campaign against Austria's defenses on the Danube itself. There could be no question of the result. Austria would be crushed beyond recognition. Convinced of this, the Austrians had surrendered. Allenby had succeeded in defeating the Turks in Asia Minor and Palestine and the Turks had also thrown up the sponge. Everywhere Mittel-Europa was crumbling. The great state which the Germans believed already created in the fall of 1917 was dissolving before their eyes.

They well knew that a conclusive final assault upon their rapidly retreating army had been arranged by Foch for November 13 and 14. They therefore made haste to request terms for an armistice in order to save their army from destruction. The war was lost; better a thousand times, they argued, to save what they could. Better to surrender than to be beaten flat.

In considering the question of foregoing the destruction of the German army, the Allied generals were moved by the consideration that while they might refuse to accept the armistice, might prolong the war and destroy the German army, it would undoubtedly cost many hundreds of thousands of lives and much suffering for the Allied peoples themselves. Beaten though it was, the German army was far from demoralized. Driven out of its defense lines of the previous years, it had behind it nevertheless strong natural defenses of mountains and rivers. Behind them, if given to understand that Germany must fight for her very life, that army was capable still of prolonged resistance. The Germans no longer had it in their power to win the war, but if the Allies insisted, they did have it in their power to make the winning of the war infinitely costly to the Allies. Wisely, Foch counseled the granting of the armistice. He would spill no blood that could be saved.

But he would propose to the Germans that which should make impossible a resumption of the war. The terms of the armistice insisted that the Germans surrender the remainder of the territory they had occupied in France and Belgium and as well all of Germany west of the Rhine. They also surrendered the three most important cities and crossings of the Rhine itself—Cologne, Coblenz, and Mainz; a zone sixty miles wide was drawn around each of these cities and beyond it the German troops must retire. The French, British, and American armies were then to occupy the entire district up to the Rhine and the three sixty-mile zones in addition. This placed the Germans at so great a disadvantage that the reopening of the war was unthinkable. They were also to surrender railroad cars, aëroplanes, artillery of all sorts and kinds, ammunition, money, enough of everything essential to the prosecution of the war to foreclose any attempt to begin it again.

The Germans had really no option except to agree or to sell their lives as dearly as possible; they chose to surrender. Messengers came through the French lines by arrangement and were received by General Foch in his private railway train, which had been throughout the campaign his headquarters. When the Germans were admitted, Foch dealt with them as Bismarck had dealt with the French in 1870. He compelled them to address him in French and spoke to them in his own language and not in German, just as Bismarck had compelled the French to speak German in order to humiliate them; there was a poetic justice in this which the world was glad to see. The German emissaries requested an armistice, but Foch compelled them to admit in actual words that they came to beg for one. He then read them in French the terms agreed upon, sternly silenced their protest that the terms were too severe, handed them the paper, and dismissed them. A courier was dispatched with the paper through the lines to the German headquarters at Spa and they were given three days in which to accept or reject the terms. The length of time which the courier would take to go and come made the time the Germans had for deliberation not much more than one day. Before the expiration of the period he returned, the German delegates appeared before Foch, and signified their acceptance of the terms. Thus on November 11, 1918, came to an end the greatest war in history.

The Allied world burst into a delirium of joy. Great crowds surged through the streets of the principal cities in France, England, the United States, Canada, and Australia, shouting, singing, screaming, ringing bells, tooting horns. Everything that made a noise was useful. Not many such demonstrations are recorded in history.

Who Won the War

To the people at present alive there are few questions more interesting than the identity of the victor. It is something all are anxious to ascertain and each of the Allied nations is anxious—and justly so—that its own part should not be forgotten. In a very real sense the Belgians won the war. But for that first gallant struggle at Liege, but for the delay they interposed in the German program at the very outset, the French would have been overwhelmed, and, as the Germans calculated, the war would have been brought to an end before it could have been begun.

Unquestionably the French army won the war. Not so much by reason of the battle of the Marne or of any particular engagement, but because of what the French army was. The Germans were entirely right: so perfect a machine as their own army must infallibly win against armies hurriedly put together after the war began. The war was saved for the Allies by the French army—an excellent, competent force, all but as well drilled as the Germans, which bore the brunt of the conflict throughout. In the first year the French were compelled to take the entire weight of the German assault, for the British army, great as its assistance was at the first critical moment, was too small to assume the real weight of the battle. The French artillery possessed a gun, the famous 75's, which was superior to anything the Germans had. It was a light field gun, throwing a good sized shell and capable of being fired at an astonishing rate of speed and with extraordinary accuracy.

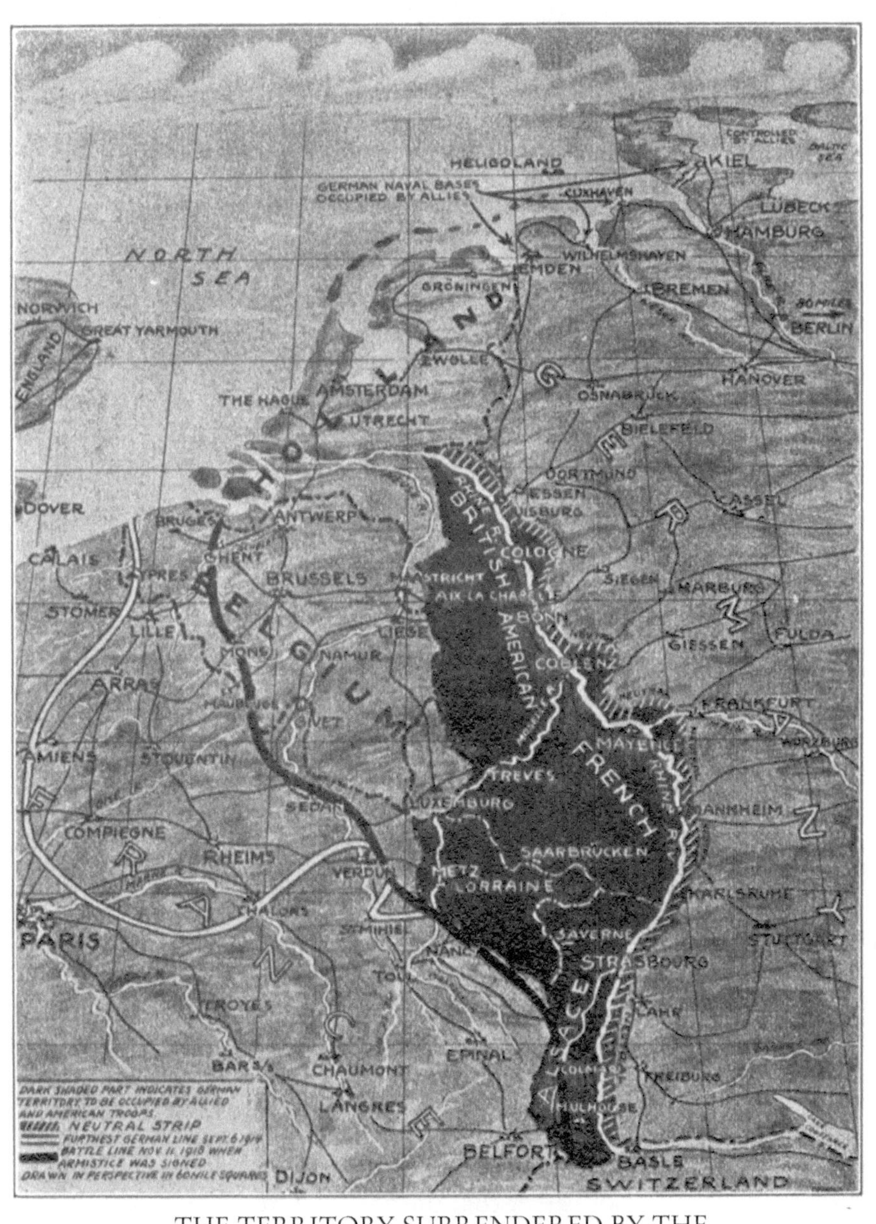

THE TERRITORY SURRENDERED BY THE
GERMANS AT THE ARMISTICE.

The 75's alone checked the German army in the first invasion of France and won the battle of the Marne.

In a very real sense of the word the French general staff won the war. It was from the outset the brains of the Allied army. Without any disparagement to the gallant British, Italian, and American officers, the great military minds on the Allied side were those of the French. They alone had had years of experience, training, and study; they knew best the field of battle, as well they might; it was their own country; they had thought more carefully about methods of defense and attack. The great generals were, therefore, Joffre, Foch, and Petain, a trio who will stand out in history above all other names on the Allied side. But behind them, making possible the final victory, stand dozens of Frenchmen, whose names are not so well known, but whose cooperation in the French general staff furnished the real nucleus of the organization that won the war.

On the other hand, it must not be forgotten that without the work of the British fleet the war would have been lost at the outset. It was essential that Great Britain should manufacture for France. In the first rush of the German invasion the French had lost the greater part of their coal mines, most of their iron mines, and their most important industrial section. With these had been lost thousands of hands who would have performed great services for France. Keeping the British factories at work overtime meant raw materials, merchant vessels must bring them, and the fleet must protect them. The British army had to be transported to France and supplied and maintained there. Germany again must be thoroughly blockaded; if she could have attained access to the markets of the world, the war might have gone on indefinitely or have resulted in an Allied defeat. The British navy coped successfully with the submarine, with mines, and all the other deadly instruments which the Germans thought would of themselves win the war.

Then we must not forget that the loyalty of the British Empire at the very outset of the war was all-important to victory. The Germans had supposed that the British self-governing colonies would desert the moment war broke out, but as one man they rose to the crisis and gave their all for the Empire. Canada indeed contributed, if anything, a larger proportion of men and suffered more from casualties even than France. Australia, New Zealand, and South Africa were close seconds. From all poured to the mother country men and supplies indispensable to the conduct of the war.

The Russians also won the war. If they had not moved in August, 1914, had not sent regiments into the battle with nothing but sticks in their hands and stopped the German advance with great piles of bodies, the Germans might still have overwhelmed the French and British and have won the war in the west at the beginning. It has seemed to most students that the Russian campaign in Poland in August and September, 1914, gave Joffre his opportunity at the battle of the Marne. The Germans were compelled to send enough men east to give the French a chance to fight with a prospect of real success. Again in 1915 and in 1916 the Russians hurled themselves against the Germans in offensives which seemed impossible of success in order to lessen the pressure on the French and British in France. The services of the Russian army to victory must not be forgotten.

Then there will be few to deny that the arrival of the British millions in 1915 and 1916 was a decisive event for victory. Without such extensive and tireless support as the British army gave, the French must have been overwhelmed. The whole German calculation, indeed, had been based not merely on the assumption that the Russians would be slow and incompetent but that the British would be unable to create an army of any real value before the French were exhausted. We cannot conceive of the war without the British army any more than we can think of it without the great British factories, munition works, coal mines, and fleets. The Allied offensives of the first three years were in large measure made possible by the arrival of the British and many of the important movements in the last year of the war were executed by them.

Italy's entry in 1915 was by no means without its contribution to the final result. Had Italy joined the Central Empires and assailed France in the rear of the trench line or had compelled France to send enough soldiers south to meet another foe, the war would have lasted few months indeed. The mere fact that Italy stood neutral in a sense made victory possible. When she entered the war, she completed the blockade of the Central Empires and stopped the smuggling which must otherwise have gone on through Italy as through Holland and Denmark. The Italians again really compelled the Germans and Austrians to keep hundreds of thousands of men in the Alps who might otherwise have been winning battles in France or Poland. The final campaign of the Italians against

THE REARRANGEMENT OF EUROPE TO WHICH
THE ALLIES PLEDGED THEMSELVES.

the Austrians in the fall of 1918 contributed to the rapidity and finality of the downfall of the Central Empires.

But without the United States victory would still have been lost. The war could not have been finished without us. The mere knowledge that the Yanks were coming infused in 1917 new courage into the exhausted French and stubborn British. They had begun to fear that although the Germans could not beat them they might not themselves be able to beat the Germans. From the outset in a proper sense the United States had been a participant in the war. From the outset, the Allies could not have gotten on without us. From the first weeks of the war our factories were working overtime making ammunition, clothing, shoes, and a thousand things indispensable to the maintenance of the French and British armies. Our farms were producing wheat, meat, cotton, and sugar, without which the British and French people must have starved. In a very real sense of the word the United States fed the Allied armies. The work of the American Red Cross and of the various other American organizations for the assistance of France was from the outset essential to the continuing of the war. Beyond question the American Relief fed Belgium and northern France while in the hands of the Germans and saved the population from extinction. Few historians will be so shortsighted as many people in the United States to-day who seem to feel that we did nothing of consequence toward the winning of the war until 1917. We were in the war from the outset and without us the war would not have lasted until 1917. Wars to-day are fought by nations and not by governments. Though we were technically neutral as a government, the American nation was working night and day for the Allies from the very beginning. There were here and there some exceptions, men and women, disloyal to the country, who did their best for the Central Empires; but they were an inconspicuous minority.

Then in 1917 the United States entered the war and from that moment the end seemed no longer a question of doubt. The Allies had but to hold out through 1917 and perhaps 1918, and the American millions in 1919 would crush the Germans out of existence. It was as certain as the multiplication table and as sure as the rising of the sun. From that knowledge came a morale and a courage which were great factors in the war in 1917. When the war ended there were some two million American soldiers in France, a vast number of civilians supporting the army, and the entire American fleet was in European waters doing yeoman service against the submarine. American troops fought in nearly all the divisions of the Allied armies in the final offensives from July to November, 1918. An official American army was in the field and carried out with great success and gallantry the capture of the salient at St. Mihiel.

Nevertheless, it must be admitted that the French and British dealt the German his final death blow. Only a portion of the American troops in France took part in the actual fighting and they formed only a relatively minor clement in the entire Allied forces. The coming of the Americans did enable Foch to throw against the Germans without reserve all the trained French and British troops he had. But for the Americans he must have retained large numbers of experienced men as a final reserve in case his battle plan should miscarry. The mere presence of the Americans, despite the fact that they did not fight, was an all-important factor in the final battle. Without us it could not have been fought. The whole scheme would have been too risky to have been attempted. In as true a sense as in any other of these cases, the United States won the war.

Yet it ought to be clear that the winning of the war was a complex operation, involving the assistance and cooperation of several nations, all of which played essential parts in the war as it took place. We cannot omit Belgium at the outset nor America at the end; but for the French and the British the war would have ended before the Americans arrived. The Russians, the Canadians, the Italians, and the Australians all too played their part. If any had to be left out, it would be difficult to know what the result would have been. All were indispensable to the final victory.

Chronological Tables

Certain variations in the dates assigned events are to be found and have not yet been authoritatively settled. They are not however in most instances of substantial importance. These lists follow the Statesman's Year Book for European events and the list published by the Committee on Public Information for those relating to the united States.

1914

June 28.	Murder of Archduke Francis Ferdinand at Serajevo.
July 23.	Austro-Hungarian ultimatum to Serbia.
July 28.	Austria-Hungary declares war on Serbia.
July 31.	German ultimatums to Russia and France.
Aug. 1.	Germany declares war on Russia and invades Luxemburg.
Aug. 2.	German ultimatum to Belgium, demanding a free passage for her troops across Belgium.
Aug. 3.	Germany declares war on France.
Aug. 4.	Germans enter Belgium.
Aug. 4.	Great Britain declares war on Germany.
Aug. 4.	President Wilson proclaims neutrality of United States.
Aug. 6.	Austria-Hungary declares war on Russia.
Aug. 7.	Liége occupied.
Aug. 10.	France and Great Britain declare war on Austria-Hungary.
Aug. 16.	British expeditionary force landed in France.
Aug. 18.	Russia invades East Prussia.
Aug. 20.	Brussels entered by Germans.

Aug. 21-23. Battle of Mons-Charleroi. Dogged retreat of French and
British in the face of the German invasion.
Aug. 23.   Japan declares war on Germany.
Aug. 23.   Kiaochow in China bombarded by Japanese.
Aug. 24.   Fall of Namur.
Aug. 25.   Fall and destruction of Louvain.
Aug. 25-Dec. 15.   Russians overrun Galicia. Lemberg taken
(Sept. 2); Przemysl besieged (Sept. 16 to Oct. 15, and again
after Nov. 12). Dec. 4. Russians 3 ½ miles from Cracow.
Aug. 26.   Allies conquer Togo, in Africa.
Aug. 26-31.   Russians defeated in battle of Tannenberg.
Aug. 28.   British naval victory off Helgoland Bight, in North Sea.
Sept. 5.   Great Britain, France, and Russia sign a treaty not to
make peace separately.
Sept. 6-10. First battle of the Marne.
Sept. 7.   Extreme point of German advance.
Sept. 7.   Germans take Maubeuge, in northern France.
Sept. 11.   Australians take German New Guinea, and other Ger-
man Pacific island possessions.
Sept. 12-17.   Battle of the Aisne.
Sept. 16.   Russians driven from East Prussia.
Sept. 22.   Three British armored cruisers sunk by a submarine.
Sept. 27.   Successful invasion of German Southwest Africa. by
General Botha.
Oct. 9.   Germans occupy Antwerp, the chief port of Belgium.
Oct. 13.   Belgian government retires to Havre, which remains its
seat during the war.
Oct. 16-28.   Battle of the Ysre. Belgians and French halt Ger-
man advance.
Oct. 17-Nov. 15.   Battle of Flanders, near Ypres, saving Chan-
nel ports.
Oct. 20-27.   German armies driven back in Poland.
Oct. 28-Dec. 5. De Wet's rebellion in British South Africa.
Nov. 1.   German naval victory off the coast of Chile.

Nov. 3-5.   Russia, France, and Great Britain declare war on Turkey.
Nov. 7.   Kiaochow captured by the Japanese and British.
Nov. 10-Dec. 14.   Austrian invasion of Serbia.
Nov. 10.   German cruiser Enulen destroyed in Indian Ocean.
Nov. 21.   Basra, on Persian Gulf, occupied by British.
Dec. 8.   British naval victory off the Falkland Islands.
Dec. 16.   German warships bombard towns on east coast of
             England.
Dec. 17.   Egypt proclaimed a British protectorate, under a sultan.
Dec. 24.   First German air raid on England.

1915

Jan. 1-Feb. 15.   Russians attempt to cross the Carpathians.
Jan. 24.   Naval skirmish off Dogger Bank, in North Sea.
Jan. 25Feb. 12.   Russians again invade East Prussia, but are defeated
             in the battle of the Masurian Lakes.
Jan. 28.   American merchantman William P. Frye sunk by Ger-
             man cruiser.
Feb. 4.   Germany's proclamation of "war zone" around the Brit-
             ish Isles after Feb. 18.
Feb. 10.   United States note holding German government to a
             "strict accountability" for destruction of American lives
             or vessels.
Feb. 19.   Anglo-French squadron bombards Dardanelles forts.
Mar. 1.   Announcement of British blockade of Germany.
Mar. 10.   British capture Neuve Chapelle, in northern France.
Mar. 17.   Russians capture Przemysl, in Galicia.
Apr. 17—May 17.   Battle of Ypres. First use of poison gas.
Apr. 25.   Allied troops land on the Gallipoli peninsula.
Apr. 30.   Germans invade the Baltic provinces of Russia.
May 1.   American steamship *Gulflight* sunk by German subma-
             rine; two Americans lost.
May 2.   Battle of the Dunajec. Russians defeated by the Germans
             and Austrians and forced to retire from the Carpathians.

May 7.   British liner Lusilania sunk by German submarine (1134 lives lost, 114 being Americans).

May 9-June.   Battle of Artois, or Festubert (in France, north of Arras). Small gains by the Allies.

May 13.   American note protests against submarine policy culminating in the sinking of the husitania. Other notes June 9, July 21; German replies, May 28, July 8, Sept. 1.

May 23.   Italy declares war on Austria-Hungary.

May 25.   American steamship Nebraskan attacked by submarine.

June 3.   Przemysl retaken by Germans and Austrians.

June 9.   Monfalcone occupied by Italians.

June 22.   The Austro-Germans recapture Lemberg, in Galicia.

July 2.   Naval action between Russians and Germans in the Baltic.

July 15.   Conquest of German Southwest. Africa completed.

July 14—Sept. 18.   German conquest of Russian Poland; capture of Warsaw (Aug. 4), Kovno (Aug. 17), Brest-Litovsk (Aug. 25), Vilna (Sept. 18).

Aug. 19.   British liner Arable sunk by submarines (44 victims, 2 Americans).

Aug. 21.   Italy declares war on Turkey.

Sept. 1.   The German ambassador, von Bernstorff, gives assurance that German submarines will sink no more liners without warning.

Sept. 8.   United States demands recall of Austro-Hungarian ambassador, Dr. Dumba.

Sept. 25-Oct.   French offensive in Champagne fails to break through German lines.

Sept. 27.   Small British progress at Loos, near Lens.

Oct. 4.   Russian ultimatum to Bulgaria.

Oct. 5.   Allied forces land at Saloniki at the invitation of the Greek government.

Oct. 5.   German government regrets and disavows sinking of *Arabic* and is prepared to pay indemnities.

Oct. 6—Dec. 2. Austro-German-Bulgarian conquest of Serbia; fall
of Bel-grade (Oct. 9), Nish (Nov. 1), Monastir (Dec. 2).

Oct. 13.	Germans execute the English nurse, Edith Cavell, for
aiding Belgians to escape from Belgium.

Oct. 14.	Bulgaria declares war on Serbia.

Oct. 15—19.	Great Britain, France, Russia, and Italy declare war
against Bulgaria.

Nov. 10—Apr.	Russian forces advance into Persia as a result of
pro-German activities there.

Dec. 1.	British under General Townshend retreat from near
Bagdad to Kut-el-Amara.

Dec. 3.	United States government demands recall of Captain
Boy-Ed and Captain von Papen, attaches of the German
embassy.

Dec. 6.	Germans capture Ipek, in Montenegro.

Dec. 15.	Sir Douglas Haig succeeds Sir John French in command
of the British army in France.

Dec. 19.	British forces withdraw from parts of Gallipoli peninsula.

1916

Jan. 8.	Evacuation of Gallipoli completed by the British.

Jan. 13.	Fall of Cettinje, capital of Montenegro.

Feb. 10.	Germany notifies neutral powers that armed merchant
ships will be treated as warships and will be sunk without warning.

Feb. 15.	Secretary Lansing states that by international law com-
mercial vessels have right to carry arms in self-defense.

1917

June 7.	British blow up Messines Ridge, south of Ypres, and
capture 7500 German prisoners.

June 10.	Italian offensive in Trentino.

June 12.	King Constantine of Greece forced to abdicate.

June 17.	Portuguese troops on west front.

June 26.	First American troops reach France.

June 29.   Greece enters war against Germany and her allies.
             Allenby takes command in Palestine.
July 1.   Russian army led in person by Kerensky, the minister of
             war, begins an offensive in Galicia, ending in disastrous
             retreat (July 19-Aug. 3).
July 20.   Kerensky succeeds Prince Lvoff as premier of Russia.
July 31-Nov. 6. Battle of Flanders (Passchendaele Ridge); British
             successes.
Aug. 15.   Peace proposals of Pope Benedict published (dated Aug.
             1). United States replies Aug. 27; Germany and Austria,
             Sept. 21.
Aug. 15.   Canadians capture Hill 70, dominating Lens.
Aug. 19-24.   New Italian drive on the Isonzo front.
Aug. 20-24.   French attacks at Verdun recapture high ground
             lost in 1916.
Sept. 4.   Riga captured by Germans.
Sept. 8.   Luxburg dispatches ("Spurlos versenkt") published by
             United States.
Sept. 15.   Russia proclaimed a republic.
Oct. 17.   Russians defeated in a naval engagement in the Gulf of
             Riga.
Oct. 26.   Brazil declares war on Germany.
Oct. 24-Dec.   Great German-Austrian invasion of Italy.
Oct. 27.   Fall of Cividale;
Oct. 28.   fall of Gorizia;
Oct. 29.   fall of Udine;
Oct. 31.   Italians reach the Tagliamento in the retreat;
Nov. 4.   British troops reach Italy;
Nov. 9.   Italian line withdrawn to the Piave and there established.
Nov 2.   Germans retreat from the Chemin des Dames, in France.
Nov 3.   First class of Americans with German soldiers.
Nov 4.   British troops reach Italy.
Nov 7.   Overthrow of Kerensky and provisional government of
             Russia by the Bolsheviki.

Nov 9.   Italians on the Piave.

Nov 9.   British capture Gaza.

Nov 9.   Versailles Supreme War Council established.

Nov. 13.   Clemenceau succeeds Rihot as French premier.

Nov. 20-Dec. 13.   Battle of Cambrai.

Nov.29.   First plenary session of the Interallied Conference in
           Paris. Sixteen nations represented. Colonel P. NI. House,
           chairman of American delegation.

Dec. 3.   Conquest of German East Africa completed.

Dec. 6.   United States destroyer *Jacob Jones* sunk by submarine,
           with loss of over 60 American men.

Dec. 6.   Rumania agrees to armistice with Germany.

Dec. 7.   United States declares war on Austria-Hungary.

Dec. 9.   Jerusalem captured by British.

Dec. 22.   Peace negotiations opened at Brest-Litovsk between
           Bolshevik government and Central Powers.

Dec. 28.   President Wilson takes over the control of railroads.

1918

Jan. 8.   President Wilson sets forth peace program of the United
           States.

Jan. 18.   Russian Constituent Assembly meets in Petrograd.

Jan. 19.   The Bolsheviki dissolve the Russian Assembly.

Jan. 28.   Revolution begins in Finland; fighting between "White
           Guards" and "Red Guards."

Jan. 28-29. Big German air raid on London.

Jan. 30.   German air raid on Paris.

Feb. 1.   Germany and Austria-Hungary recognize the Ukrainian
           Republic.

Feb. 3.   American troops officially announced to be on the
           Lorraine front near Toul.

Feb. 5.   British transport *Tuscan* in with 2179 American troops
           on board torpedoed and sunk; 211 American soldiers
           lost.

Feb. 9.   Ukrainia makes peace with Germany.

Feb. 10.   The Bolsheviki order demobilization of the Russian
             army. Formal announcement that Russia was no longer
             a participant in the war.

Feb. 14.   Bolo Pasha condemned for treason against France;
             executed Apr. 16.

Feb. 17.   Cossack General Kaledines commits suicide. Collapse
             of Cossack revolt against the Bolsheviki.

Feb. 18-Mar. 3. Russo-German armistice declared at an end by
             Germany; war resumed. Germans occupy Dvinsk, Minsk,
             and other cities.

Feb. 21.   German troops land in Finland.

Feb. 21.   British capture Jericho.

Feb. 23.   Turkish troops drive back the Russians in the northeast
             (Trebizond taken Feb. 26, Erzermn Mar. 14).

Mar. 2.   German and Ukrainian troops defeat the Bolsheviki
             near Kief in Ukrainian.

Mar. 3.   Bolsheviki sign peace treaty with Germany at Brest-
             Litovsk. Ratified by Soviet Congress at Moscow, Mar.
             15.

Mar. 7.   Finland and Germany sign a treaty of peace.

Mar. 10.   Announcement that American troops are occupying
             trenches at four different points on French soil.

Mar. 11.   Great German air raid on Paris, by more than fifty
             planes.

Mar. 13.   German troops occupy Odessa on Black Sea.

Mar. 21–Apr. 1. First German drive of the year, on 50-mile front,
             extending to Montdidier.

Apr. 5.   British and Japanese armies landed at Vladivostok.

Apr. 9–18.   Second German drive, on a 30-mile front between Ypres
             and Arras.

Apr. 14.   Foch commander in chief.

May 6.   Rumania signs peace treaty with the Central Powers.

May 7.   Nicaragua declares war on Germany and her allies.

May 9-10.   British naval force attempts to block Ostend harbor.

May 14.   Caucasus proclaims itself an independent state; but the
            Turks overrun the southern part, and take Baku Sept.
            19.
May 24.   Costa Rica declares war on the Central Powers.
May 25–June.   German submarines appear off American coast
            and sink 19 coast-wise vessels, including Porto Rican
            liner *Carolina*, with loss of 16 lives.
May 27–June 1. Third German drive, capturing the Chemin des
            Dames and reaching the Marne River east of Chilteau-
            Thierry. American marines and French in Chilteau-
            Thierry sector.
May 28.   American forces near Montdidier capture village of
            Cantigny and hold it against numerous counter-attacks.
May 31.   United States transport *President Lincoln*, sunk by U-boat
            while on her way to the United States; 23 lives lost.
June 9–16. Fourth German drive, on 20-mile front east of Mont-
            didier, makes only small gains.
June 10.   Italian naval forces sink one Austrian dreadnought and
            damage another in the Adriatic.
June 11.   American marines take 8011 prisoners in Bellew Wood.
June 14.   Turkish troops occupy Tabriz, Persia.
June 15.   Official announcement that there are 800,000 American
            troops in France.
June 15-July 6. Austrian offensive against Italy fails with heavy
            losses.
June 21.   Official statement that American forces hold 39 miles
            of French front in six sectors.
July 10.   Italians and French take Herat in Albania.
July 13.   Czecho-Slovak troops occupy Irkutsk in Siberia.
July 15-18. Anglo-American forces occupy strategic positions on
            the Murman Coast in northwestern Russia.
July 15-18. Fifth German drive extends three miles south of the
            Marne, but east of Rheims makes no gain.
July 16.   Ex-Tsar Nicholas executed by Bolshevik.

July 18-Aug. 4. Second battle of the Marne, beginning with Foch's counter, offensive between Soissons and Château-Thierry. French and Americans drive the Germans back from the Marne nearly to the Aisne.

July 27. American troops arrive on the Italian front.

July 31. President Wilson takes over telegraph and telephone systems.

Aug. 2. Allies occupy Archangel in northern Russia.

Aug. 8-Sept. Allies attack successfully near Montdidier, and continue the drive until the Germans are back at the Hindenburg Line giving up practically all the ground they had gained this year.

Aug. 15. American troops land in eastern Siberia.

Sept. 3. The United States recognizes the Czecho-Slovak government.

Sept. 12-13. Americans take the St. Mihiel salient near Metz.

Sept.15. Allied army under General D'Esperey begins campaign against Bulgarians.

Sept. 16. President Wilson receives an Austrian proposal for a peace conference, and refuses it.

Sept. 22. Great victory of British and Arabs over Turks in Palestine.

Sept. 26. Americans begin a drive in the Meuse valley.

Sept. 30. Bulgaria withdraws from the war.

Oct. 1. St. Quentin (on the Hindenburg Line) taken by the French.

Oct 1. Damascus captured by the British.

Oct 3. King Ferdinand of Bulgaria abdicates.

Oct 3. Lens taken by the British.

Oct 4. Germany asks President Wilson for an armistice and peace negotiations; other notes Oct. 12, 20, etc. similar notes from Austria-Hungary Oct. 7, and from Turkey Oct. 12. Wilson replies Oct. 8, 14, 18, 23.

Oct 7. Beirut taken by a French fleet.

Oct 8.   Cambrai taken by the British.
Oct 13.   Laon taken by the French.
Oct 17   Ostend taken by the Belgians.
Oct 17   Lille taken by the British.
Oct. 24-Nov. 4. Allied forces (chiefly Italians) under General Diaz
                win a great victory on the Italian front.
Oct. 26.   Aleppo taken by the British.
Oct. 31.   Turkey surrenders.
Nov. 1.   Serbian troops enter Belgrade after regaining nearly all
                of Serbia.
Nov. 3.   Trieste and Trent occupied by Italian forces.
Nov. 4.   Surrender of Austria-Hungary.
Nov. 5.   President Wilson notifies Germany that General Foch
                has been authorized by the United States and the Allies
                to communicate the terms of an armistice.
Nov. 6.   Mutiny of German sailors at Kiel; followed by mutinies,
                revolts, and revolutions at other German cities.
Nov. 7.   Americans take Sedan.
Nov. 9.   British take Maubeuge.
Nov. 9.   Abdication of the German emperor William II and the
                crown prince; they flee to Holland Nov. 10.
Nov. 11.   Armistice signed.